THE TRUTH MACHINES

Using case studies and the results of extensive fieldwork, this book considers the nature of state power and legal violence in liberal democracies by focusing on the interaction between law, science, and policing in India. The postcolonial Indian police have often been accused of using torture in both routine and exceptional criminal cases, but they, and forensic psychologists, have claimed that lie detectors, brain scans, and narcoanalysis (the use of "truth serum," Sodium Pentothal) represent a paradigm shift away from physical torture; most state high courts in India have upheld this rationale.

The Truth Machines examines the emergence and use of these three scientific techniques to analyze two primary themes. First, the book questions whether existing theoretical frameworks for understanding state power and legal violence are adequate to explain constant innovations of the state. Second, it explores the workings of law, science, and policing in the everyday context to generate a theory of state power and legal violence, challenging the monolithic frameworks about this relationship, based on a study of both state and non-state actors.

Jinee Lokaneeta argues that the attempt to replace physical torture with truth machines in India fails because it relies on a confessional paradigm that is contiguous with torture. Her work also provides insights into a police institution that is founded and refounded in its everyday interactions between state and non-state actors. Theorizing a concept of Contingent State, this book demonstrates the disaggregated, and decentered nature of state power and legal violence, creating possible sites of critique and intervention.

Jinee Lokaneeta is a professor in political science and international relations at Drew University in Madison, New Jersey.

Law, Meaning, and Violence

The scope of Law, Meaning, and Violence is defined by the wide-ranging scholarly debates signaled by each of the words in the title. Those debates have taken place among and between lawyers, anthropologists, political theorists, sociologists, and historians, as well as literary and cultural critics. This series is intended to recognize the importance of such ongoing conversations about law, meaning, and violence as well as to encourage and further them.

Series Editors: Martha Minow, Harvard Law School
Austin Sarat, Amherst College

RECENT TITLES IN THE SERIES

The Truth Machines: Policing, Violence, and Scientific Interrogations in India
   by Jinee Lokaneeta

Keeping Hold of Justice: Encounters between Law and Colonialism
   by Jennifer Balint, Julie Evans, Mark McMillan, and Nesam McMillan

The Jurisprudence of Emergency: Colonialism and the Rule of Law
(with new Foreword and Preface)
   by Nasser Hussain

Archiving Sovereignty: Law, History, Violence
   by Stewart Motha

The Holocaust, Corporations, and the Law: Unfinished Business
   by Leora Bilsky

Curating Community: Museums, Constitutionalism, and the Taming of the Political,
   by Stacy Douglas

Refining Child Pornography Law: Crime, Language, and Social Consequences,
   edited by Carissa Byrne Hessick

The First Global Prosecutor: Promise and Constraints,
   edited by Martha Minow, C. Cora True-Frost, and Alex Whiting

Hybrid Justice: The Extraordinary Chambers in the Courts of Cambodia,
   by John D. Ciorciari and Anne Heindel

The Justice of Mercy, by Linda Ross Meyer

Dying Inside: The HIV/AIDS Ward at Limestone Prison,
   by Benjamin Fleury-Steiner with Carla Crowder

Sacred Violence: Torture, Terror, and Sovereignty, by Paul W. Kahn

Punishment and Political Order, by Keally McBride

Lives of Lawyers Revisited: Transformation and Resilience in the Organizations of Practice,
   by Michael J. Kelly

Among the Lowest of the Dead: The Culture of Capital Punishment,
   by David Von Drehle

Punishing Schools: Fear and Citizenship in American Public Education,
   by William Lyons and Julie Drew

Suing the Gun Industry: A Battle at the Crossroads of Gun Control and Mass Torts,
   edited by Timothy D. Lytton

Transformative Justice: Israeli Identity on Trial, by Leora Bilsky

The Truth Machines
POLICING, VIOLENCE, AND SCIENTIFIC INTERROGATIONS IN INDIA

Jinee Lokaneeta

University of Michigan Press
Ann Arbor

Copyright © 2020 by Jinee Lokaneeta
All rights reserved

This book may not be reproduced, in whole or in part, including illustrations, in any form (beyond that copying permitted by Sections 107 and 108 of the U.S. Copyright Law and except by reviewers for the public press), without written permission from the publisher.

Published in the United States of America by the University of Michigan Press
Manufactured in the United States of America
Printed on acid-free paper

A CIP catalog record for this book is available from the British Library.
Library of Congress Cataloging-in-Publication data has been applied for.

First published March 2020

Library of Congress Cataloging-in-Publication Data

Names: Lokaneeta, Jinee, author.
Title: The truth machines : policing, violence, and scientific interrogations in India / Jinee Lokaneeta.
Description: Ann Arbor : University of Michigan Press, [2020] | Series: Law, meaning, and violence | Includes bibliographical references and index.
Identifiers: LCCN 2019047666 (print) | LCCN 2019047667 (ebook) | ISBN 9780472074396 (hardcover) | ISBN 9780472054398 (paperback) | ISBN 9780472126477 (ebook)
Subjects: LCSH: Police—India. | Police questioning—India. | Lie detectors and detection—India. | Forensic sciences—India. | Torture—Goverment policy—India. | Violence—Government policy—India.
Classification: LCC HV8247.L65 2020 (print) | LCC HV8247 (ebook) | DDC 363.25/40954—dc23
LC record available at https://lccn.loc.gov/2019047666
LC ebook record available at https://lccn.loc.gov/2019047667

CONTENTS

Acknowledgments	vii
Chapter 1. Introduction	1
Chapter 2. Police as a Site of State Power: Custody Practices and Policing Logics	20
Chapter 3. Transnational Borrowings, Scientific Contestations, and Cultural Productions	48
Chapter 4. The State Forensic Architecture: Forensic Psychologists and the Art of Scientific Interrogations	78
Chapter 5. Courts and Legal Discourses: The (Flawed) Art of Government	113
Chapter 6. Scaffold of the Rule of Law: Terror Suspects and the Experience of Violence	136
Chapter 7. Conclusion	162
Notes	167
Bibliography	225
Index	241

Digital materials related to this title can be found on the Fulcrum platform via the following citable URL: https://doi.org/10.3998/mpub.9729771.

ACKNOWLEDGMENTS

Threads to this book emerged from disparate moments. A chance conversation with the late legal scholar Nasser Hussain in Berkeley and his excitement at a time when most were mystified with my project gave me the confidence to proceed; he is sorely missed.

The wonderful Dr. Ramanadham memorial lecture by Dr. Amar Jesani on narcoanalysis and my consequent conversations and collaborations with him were crucial in reminding me about the role of semi-state actors in understanding state violence.

Despite skepticism about access and whether short visits were adequate to gain insights into the techniques, conducting field research was an exciting aspect of the project. Pratiksha Baxi's constant urge to visit the field and Nivedita Menon's report of a comment by a retired director general of police (DGP) that "narcoanalysis was introduced to replace physical torture" ensured that I was hooked into an in-depth study.

In the absence of much funding, the generosity of friends and family allowed me to visit five Indian cities for interviews. In Ahmedabad the camaraderie of Hiren Bhai and Niyati Ben sustained me in 2013. I enjoyed their hospitality and witnessed some of the amazing work they and Saroop Ben do. Prita Jha created moments of conversations and became a friend in the city.

It is hard to think of my Hyderabad trip without mentioning Kalpana Kannabiran and Kavita Datla. Kalpana invited me to participate in a meaningful conference on violence studies, allowing me to spend some time with scholars who I most respect; she also reconnected me to the Andhra civil liberties world. Meeting Haragopal and Vanamala, visiting Balagopal's house and spending some time with Vasantha, and an amazing dinner conversation with Vasanth Kannabiran were reminders of the inspiring world that I am fortunate to be touched by.

Hyderabad is memorable for the time spent with my dear friend Kavita Datla, who in her usual generosity shared her home with me (as her parents stayed elsewhere and her aunt sent Kavita and me amazing food). She went to the archives as I conducted interviews, and evenings were just debriefing and hanging out. It is still hard to believe that Kavita is no longer around. There are sentences in the book that she brilliantly added, and in moments of doubt I recalled her calm insistence on the value of this work. I miss her deeply.

My Hyderabadi friend Biju Mathew put me in touch with his friends—activists, journalists, and lawyers—and most of all the space: Lamakaan. I also thank Ali Mir and Satish Kolluri for connecting me to the city.

In Mumbai my cousins Siddharth and Sanjita Mohanty took great care of me as I traveled through the expanse. Anand Teltumbde and Amar Jesani put me in touch with key persons, reconnecting with Rithambara Hebbar and Mohua Bannerjee (at the Tata Institute of Social Sciences) was a pleasure. Also in Mumbai I began an invaluable friendship with Srimati Basu, whose humor, brilliance, and shared love for food and popular culture has pushed this project in more ways than she can imagine. She patiently read, heard presentations, and gently pushed me to bring it all together.

Being a visiting scholar at Azim Premji University in Bangalore allowed me to enjoy the city and enabled my interviews, thanks to Sudhir Krishnaswamy. I am thankful to Shalini Anant for contacts at the National Institute of Medical Health and Neuro Sciences (NIMHANS).

In Delhi I thank Rebecca John for her willingness to converse despite her busy schedule. Nivedita Menon, Aditya Nigam, Anupama Roy, and Ujjwal Singh have always taken keen interest in my work and remain critically engaged friends. Uma and Anand Chakravarti and Upendra Baxi have inspired me through their lifelong work and continued conversations. Discussions with Vrinda Grover, V. Geetha and Shalini Gera have laced my understanding of state violence.

Writing groups initiated by my dear friend Paula Chakravartty and with Kavita Datla (in New York City, followed by happy hours) were important moments in the manuscript writing. Panels on policing, rule of law, and forensics helped shape this project, and I thank all the discussants and co-panelists, especially Nick Cheesman, Frank Cody, Jennifer Culbert, Leonard Feldman, Deana Heath, Santana Khanikar, James Martel, Vasuki Nesiah, Paul Passavant, Jothie Rajah, Guillermina Seri, Mitra Sharafi, and Mayur Suresh for their willingness to read, engage, and hang out. Renee Cramer's friendship and Consortium of Undergraduate Law and Justice Programs camaraderie developed in Law and Society gatherings. Conversations with Akhil Gupta in Hyderabad and through his work are crucial to this book.

My mentors Susan Burgess, Judith Grant, Mary Hawkesworth, Tim Kaufman-Osborn, Austin Sarat, and Marita Sturken continue to provide me with support. A special thanks to Austin Sarat for his continued excitement for my research and to James Martel and Lisa Hajjar for their consistent encouragement.

My colleagues at Drew University have always been a source of encouragement. I thank Carlos Yordan, Phil Mundo, Hans Morsink, Wendy Kolmar, Jason Jordan, Pat McGuinn, Tim Carter, and Catherine Keyser. Lydia Feldman always makes Smith House a welcome space. Dean/Provost Deb Liebowitz has been extremely supportive in more ways than I can mention. Most of all, I thank my students for their continued interest in the seminar on torture and the students in the policing class who forced me to explain the relationship between state, policing, and science in a comparative context. Thanks as well to Carolina Caicedo and Naeem Khan for their research assistance. Drew's research grants and American Political Science Association's small research grant enabled key travel. An earlier version of chapter 5 appeared as "Creating a Flawed Art of Government: Legal Discourses on Lie Detectors, Brain Scanning, and Narcoanalysis in India." *Law, Culture and the Humanities*, November 2014. DOI:10.1177/1743872114559881

I am eternally grateful to those who opened their lives to me during the course of these interviews, including those I end up critiquing in the book, and while I learned a lot from all of my interviewees, a special mention has to be made of the inspiring lawyers and activists I met in Hyderabad, Mumbai, Delhi, Bangalore, and Ahmedabad. Vikash Narain Rai personally put me in touch with contacts wherever I traveled, and I am always thankful for his insights.

A special thanks to Debra Osnowitz for wonderfully chiseling the arguments in the book, Prabhjot Sachdev for the engaged transcriptions, Parijat Desai for editing support, and Elizabeth Demers and Danielle Coty at the University of Michigan Press for their enthusiasm and support.

Four scholars read this manuscript in entirety, and I am overwhelmed by their generosity. I thank Keally McBride for her extremely insightful comments as a fellow political theorist; dear friend Bhavani Raman for pushing me always to connect to history in meaningful ways; Pratiksha Baxi for giving language to crucial ideas sprinkled throughout this work as always (and for her lifelong friendship that sustains me through life's unpredictable turns); and Ritty Lukose, whose friendship and ability to find meanings and connections in different parts of the manuscript has crucially helped shape its final form.

My life in NYC and elsewhere is richer due to the warmth of my dear friends Puneet Bhasin, Shakti Jaising, Sangeeta Kamath, Chirag Mittal, Stephanie Nawyn, Vasuki Nesiah, Rupal Oza, Prachi Patankar, Ashok Prasad, Sekhar Ramakrishnan, Ash Rao, Svati Shah, Aradhana Sharma, Jayeeta Sharma, Prachee Sinha, Sue Susman, Zoya Vallari, and Ramaa Vasudevan. Maliha Safri is a force of nature, as she inspires me to live life and enjoy the city to the fullest even as Drew, academics, and political concerns define our lives together. My sessions with grad school friend Sangha Padhy at the Columbia University library (thanks to the New York Public Library's MaRLI program) and our cookouts keep me grounded and calmer. Sushi dinners and rich conversations with Karuna Mantena have punctuated the book writing process, for which I am grateful. Priyanka Srivastava and Deepankar Basu have made Amherst a welcome getaway destination filled with political conversations, food, and friendship. Dipti Khera has made NYC a much more exciting place with her insights on the art world and her friendship. Ruchi Chaturvedi manages to intersect my political and intellectual NYC life all the way from Capetown. Francoise Briegel's intellect, confidence, and friendship are precious.

Friends and family in India are the life-sustaining force as always, and distances have mattered less across time and space. They have the ability to make our trips special through food, conversations, and enduring friendships: Janaki Abraham inspires through her ability to follow any path she chooses—personally and professionally—and I am lucky to be her longtime friend; Kishore Jha's friendship through the ups and downs in life have moved me; Amit Bhattacharya and Amiti Sen help me understand the pulse of Delhi and ply me with incredible food each time; Shahana Bhattacharya's balance of teaching, involvement in the People's Union for Democratic Rights, and intellectual work amazes me. Only she would make time for bird-watching on a rainy morning to follow through on a promise. Our Delhi trips are also made richer by the company of Archana Agarwal, Hilal Ahmed, Keval Arora, G. Arunima, Madhulika Bannerjee, Saumyajit Bhattacharya, Anuj Bhuwania, Arudra Burra, Subhash Gatade, N. Jacob, Mona Mishra, Ritu Mishra, Siddharth Narrain, Nazima Parveen, Anjali Sinha, Yogender, and Madhvi Zutzhi. My old Kirori mal college gang of Tarun Bhartiya, Alok Dash, Manas Das, and Avinash Jha keeps me going.

Family in Dilli, Orissa, and Bihar shower their affection each time I visit. I thank my cousins Biswajit Mohanty and Babita Varma for their support. Kalyani and Itishree make each Orissa visit memorable. Rabi Mousa and Sudha Mousi, Gour Badabapa (who sadly passed away recently) and Bulbul Badabou, and Mark Juergensmeyer and Sucheng Chan remain a constant source of inspiration. Bihar trips are full of joy and relaxation, especially thanks to the warm efforts of the awesome women of the family—Pramila, Dharamshila, and Ratnamanjari—and remind me of my late mother-in-law, Chandrakali Devi. My father-in-law R. N. Mishra's pride in my academic life is a constant source of support, and nieces/nephews Neha, Abha, Rahul, Kunal, Shalini, Madhu, Saloni, and Animesh (and their families) make me happy.

My brother, Berkeley, and sister-in-law, Brinda, unflinchingly support me in all my endeavors. Adya makes me proud as a feminist and aspiring actor. And Raeva never ceases to amaze with her talent and determination.

My parents, Manoranjan Mohanty and Bidyut Mohanty, are forever inspiring and constantly amazing everyone by their ability to be intellectuals, fun companions, and being meaningfully engaged in society. I can only thank them for their continued support in all my ventures in life. Sangay Mishra is difficult to thank, but alongside his willingness to read through my numerous drafts, his patience, determination, indulgence, love, and companionship make me tick.

Chapter 1

INTRODUCTION

In May 2008 fourteen-year-old Aarushi and forty-five-year-old Hemraj, a domestic worker, were murdered at their home in a suburb of Delhi, India. Aarushi's parents, Rajesh and Nupur Talwar, were charged for the double murder. In 2013 they were convicted by the fast-track Central Bureau of Investigation (CBI) court, despite lack of clear evidence.[1] By 2016 a public campaign had emerged challenging the verdict and demanding a retrial.[2] In an attempt to exonerate the parents, the campaign emphasized the results of narcoanalysis (use of drugs for interrogation) on Hemraj's friends, and in 2017 the Allahabad High Court overturned the verdict.[3] The *Aarushi* case represents the hold of narcoanalysis in both popular imagination and state practice.[4]

The Indian police began using narcoanalysis along with brain scanning and lie detectors in the early 2000s. Despite a lack of scientific grounding, these forensic techniques gained prominence in India as police and forensic psychologists claimed success.[5] Lie detectors (or polygraphs) record physiological changes in the body while a person answers questions. Brain fingerprinting (BFP) and brain electrical oscillation signature (BEOS) tests use an electroencephalogram (EEG) to indicate whether a person has participated in a crime or has experiential knowledge of it. Narcoanalysis, or truth serum, refers to injecting a suspect with Sodium Pentothal to extract information. Expert claims for all three methods promise access to legally actionable truth. I therefore term these three techniques "truth machines."

The police in postcolonial India have often been accused of using torture or third-degree interrogation in both routine and exceptional criminal cases and have been deemed responsible for hundreds of custodial deaths each year.[6] In a context where torture is the norm, both the police and forensic psychologists have claimed that lie detectors, brain scans, and narcoanalysis represent a paradigm shift away from the more physical third degree. In the mid-2000s most state high courts in India upheld this rationale. Though employed in only a fraction of criminal investigations, these techniques have been used in thousands of cases over the years. Nonetheless, the leak of narcoanalysis videos to the media, together with criticism by human rights activists, generated widespread condemnation, and in 2010 the Indian Supreme Court disallowed the involuntary use of truth machines as well as evidence obtained from them.[7] Lacking a Supreme Court ban, however, the police continue to request and use these three techniques and other emerging ones.

Internationally, states use DNA testing and other forensic techniques in an effort to apply science to criminal justice. Yet psychological techniques such as lie detectors, brain scanning, and narcoanalysis have largely been deemed unreliable.[8] In contrast, the Indian state has persistently focused on truth machines even as other forensic techniques, such as DNA, remain underused. In December 2017, in response to a report of custodial deaths in Maharashtra, the director general of police sent an internal circular requesting police to use forensic science. According to news reports, "Elaborating on the scientific methods, the circular suggests that the police opt for lie detector, polygraph, brain mapping and narco analysis tests."[9] In January 2019 the Delhi High Court expressed surprise that the forensic science laboratory (FSL) in New Delhi, the capital of India, lacked a narcoanalysis machine, thus requiring suspects to be taken to the Gujarat FSL, and asked that a test machine be operational in Delhi within three months.[10]

I focus on the three truth machines to examine the workings of the Indian state and its police as a site of state power. I place my work within recent debates in political theory on policing and the state that draw upon ethnographic data and comparative critical analysis. Based on interviews with police, lawyers, forensic psychologists, and human rights activists in five Indian cities, along with analysis of textual and visual materials, this book explores two primary themes. First, I consider whether existing theoretical frameworks for understanding state power and legal violence are adequate to explain innovation in everyday police practices. Second, in the workings of law, science, and everyday policing, I theorize state power and legal violence with a study of both state and semi-state actors.[11] Given untrammeled opportunities for torture, why do liberal states attempt to create a state forensic architecture by making lie detectors, brain scans, and narcoanalysis prominent elements of policing?[12]

Two frameworks explain the relationship between state power and legal violence in liberal democracies. The first is Max Weber's rational bureaucracy framework, which assumes a state monopoly over violence.[13] The second is the notion of exception, associated with Giorgio Agamben, which explains state violence in conflict areas and crisis situations.[14] In India, where state violence is hyper-visible, theorists either assume that violence is so dominant that it need not be analyzed or argue that law is violence.[15] Interactions among law, science, and policing, however, reveal the police as an institution founded and refounded in everyday interactions with non-state actors. Relying on a confessional paradigm, the state attempts to replace physical torture with truth machines that lack scientific validity. The relationship of the police to violence is thus complex.

In contrast to a more monolithic conception of the state and its supposed monopoly over violence, I find the police and state power contingent. Attention to truth machines reveals the texture of violence experienced by certain sections of the population, even under the rule of law. A focus on truth machines also exposes state power as decentered thereby creating sites of critique and possible intervention. I therefore theorize a contingent state reflected in the use of legal violence and exhibition of power. Here the term "contingent" connotes fissures in the state's ability to always monopolize violence successfully.

The notion of a contingent state points to a more disaggregated state and police, which might limit legal violence even as the state attempts to remain unitary. Indeed, the negotiation between the unitary and contingent state is visible in everyday practice and affects people's experience of the state and policing. In India, truth machines represent a technical solution for the ills of the criminal justice system. In a liberal democracy more generally, these techniques also offer insights into efforts to resolve the tension between law and excess violence and thereby provide implications for other democracies.

POLICING, CRIMINAL JUSTICE, AND THE HUMAN RIGHTS MOVEMENT

The Indian criminal justice system is notorious for its backlog of cases. In 2018 former chief justice of India Dipak Misra and new chief justice Ranjan Gogoi mentioned 33 million cases, with 27.8 million in the lower courts.[16] About 60 percent were more than two years old, and 30 percent more than five years old. Misra noted the implication: "[A] large number of undertrials languish in jails across the country as they don't get bail and many even spend more than their sentence had they been convicted."[17] The backlog may be linked to the courts, but it places an additional load on the police and the prison system. Consequently, the police experience pressure to resolve cases at their own level.

The Indian police are charged with crime control, investigations as well as law and order.[18] Policing in India is subject to Article 246 of the Indian Constitution, and, in general, each Indian state can set its own rules for police recruitment and governance. Despite states' autonomy to organize their policing, however, police bodies in India remain modeled on the Police Act of 1861, promulgated by the British, so the upper ranks of state forces come from the central government.[19] Once recruited through the Indian Police Service examinations, new members of the police force are sent to the states and placed under the charge of the state governments.

In 2014 the Indian police had just over 1.7 million agents. For a population of 1.22 billion, this number means 1 police officer for every 708 people.[20] The backlog of cases and the proportionally low numbers of police in India are important for understanding Indian policing, but so too are reports of police violence and a general lack of confidence in the police. Human rights groups have noted high levels of distrust in the Indian police. For example, in a 2005 survey, 87 percent of respondents said the police were corrupt, and 75 percent reported poor-quality service.[21] Police violence takes the form of torture, illegal detention, extrajudicial killings, deaths in police and judicial custody, and police participation in communal conflicts.[22]

Reports of the National Human Rights Commission (NHRC) compiled by the Asian Centre for Human Rights (ACHR) indicated that between 2001 and 2011, 1,504 people died in police custody (about 150 per year) and 12,727 people died in judicial custody (1,414 per year).[23] The number of custodial deaths has since increased to 5 per day. As the ACHR reported, 1,674 custodial deaths occurred between April 2017 and February 2018, including 1,530 deaths in judicial custody and 144 deaths in police custody.[24] No data are readily available on incidents of torture, although some queries in Parliament have led to an acknowledgment of 855 individuals tortured from 2010 to 2011, which greatly underestimates the incidences mentioned in reports.

In parts of the northeast and in Kashmir, extraordinary laws such as the Armed Forces Special Powers Act make torture, illegal detentions, and extrajudicial executions easier.[25] The Indian Supreme Court has been considering an aggregate case involving 1,528 cases of encounters/extrajudicial killings in Manipur between 1979 and May 2012. Media reports documented 1,000 encounters in 2017, in which about 32 people were killed in Uttar Pradesh.[26] Torture is pervasive in routine criminal investigations, in terrorism cases, and in conflict areas.[27] But as human rights reports note, custodial violence disproportionately affects the poor and socially vulnerable, including migrants, *dalits*, women, tribal members, LGBTQ communities, and religious minorities (notably Muslims and Christians).[28] Of course, routine torture can affect anyone.

The prevalence of torture and custodial violence is not a recent phenomenon, either in its occurrence or in its reporting by officials and human rights organizations. Nonetheless, continued reporting of such pervasive violence, together with international recognition, has required the Indian state to address it. As then attorney general Mukul Rohtagi told the world during the United Nations Universal Periodic Review process in 2017, "The concept of torture is completely alien to our culture and it has no place in the governance of the nation."[29] Denial thus becomes one response to high levels of documented violence.

Custodial violence has been most directly challenged by a thriving civil liberties and democratic rights movement, alongside active intervention of national and international nongovernmental agencies (NGOs). The civil liberties and democratic rights movement in India can be traced back to the post-Emergency period, which began after the Indian Emergency of 1975–1977,[30] when an acknowledgment of the need to strengthen undermined democratic institutions followed the emergency. Crucial in raising awareness of human rights were many newly formed groups in the 1970s and 1980s: the People's Union for Civil Liberties, the People's Union for Democratic Rights (PUDR), the Association of Protection of Democratic Rights, the Committee for the Protection of Democratic Rights, and the Andhra Pradesh Civil Liberties Committee. Also contributing to the visibility of human rights were reports of international human rights groups such as Amnesty International.

The Indian state responded by passing the Human Rights Act of 1993, leading to the formation of the National Human Rights Commission, a quasi–state monitoring body. Custodial deaths became a major focus of the NHRC. In 1997

India also signed the United Nations Convention against Torture and Cruel, Inhuman, and Degrading Treatment (although it remained unratified). In the 1990s the Indian Supreme Court contributed to human rights with attention to custody in two landmark cases, the *Nilabati Behera* case and the *D. K. Basu* case. These two cases focused on compensation for custodial death and a process for ensuring accountability and safeguards against illegal detention and torture. Their precedents, however, have been inadequately followed.[31]

Scholars have pointed to the implications of violence for the Indian state and for democracy more generally. The 2017 *Journal of Democracy* published a special issue on India's democracy at seventy, noting, "At 70, the Republic of India remains a paradox. It is the globe's biggest democracy, and one of the developing world's oldest. It has a competent senior judiciary and a working federal system. Yet it does only a middling job at enforcing public integrity and the rule of law."[32] As political scientist Sumit Ganguly in "The Troublesome Security State" says, "Even as India rightly celebrates a nearly unbroken record of democratic rule stretching over seven decades, its citizens—and still more crucially its political leaders—need to take stock of their country's failure to safeguard certain vital features of the liberal-democratic order."[33] Custodial violence constitutes a part of this failure.

In this context of human rights scrutiny and pressures on the Indian state, truth machines emerged in the 1990s and 2000s as a way to adopt scientific methods to combat torture and physical, third-degree interrogation. Given internal and external demands to protect human rights, the Indian state and its police encouraged methods of investigation that resolved the challenges of the criminal justice system while minimizing levels of custodial violence. Hence truth machines, I argue, can provide insight into the workings of a contingent state that is neither a Weberian bureaucracy nor an exceptional exercise of state power.

METHOD OF THIS STUDY

I documented my observations in field notes, which provided a chronicle for developing my analysis. Among my field notes is this segment:

> I entered the room and the young men were a little embarrassed. I came back too early from my lunch because there wasn't much to eat at the canteen, and

I was anxious to get on with my interviews. They had just opened their tiffin boxes with rice, *daal* (lentils), *roti* (tortilla) and *sabzi* (vegetable), and they insisted that I share the food and were quite amused at my refusal to eat white rice. The lunch shifted the mood completely. The interaction was no longer based on just the director's command. There was an eagerness to share their work and acknowledge challenges of research. They also offered to demonstrate the voice analyzer on me.[34] I had often thought about whether I ever wanted to experience the techniques. A journalist, Vicky Nanjappa, had persuaded a psychiatrist to apply the narco test to him.[35] In two other labs, they insisted on showing me how the lie detector worked including a demonstration on a pregnant woman, which is usually not recommended. I didn't want to be subjected to any of the other techniques, but the voice analyzer seemed harmless. They asked me several questions, and the person monitoring the graph seemed dissatisfied with the answers and urged the questioners to probe further. I answered questions about why I went to the U.S., why I work on this subject, and what is my research. A report required each moment to be individually analyzed and would take hours. I declined to wait for the actual results, but they informed me that I was genuinely disturbed while talking about my first book on torture. My own voice recording remains in one of the research labs that I study, even as I recorded the test alongside. But most of all, the experience represented an access that I had to the interviewees alongside my ambivalent relationship to the forensic psychologists that I met and the truth machines that I studied.

In addition to my observations in the field, I analyzed cases, reports, and documents related to narcoanalysis, brain scanning, and lie detectors. I also conducted sixty-six interviews with lawyers, police officials, forensic psychologists, medical professionals, and human rights activists on the use of these techniques in the Indian criminal justice system. To investigate this phenomenon, I traveled to three Indian cities: Gandhinagar, Gujarat; Mumbai, Maharashtra; and Bangalore, Karnataka. I also visited New Delhi and Hyderabad, two major cities where lie detectors have been used in criminal investigations. I conducted most of the interviews in 2013 and 2014. I returned to Delhi in 2015 and to Gujarat in 2016 for follow-up interviews. In each city, I visited the FSLs where truth machines were used. I also analyzed videos of narcoanalysis, available in the media or shared with me, to determine whether videos affected the outcomes of trials and helped legitimize the use of truth machines.

Even though my analysis focuses primarily on India, I consider comparable experiences in the United States. This book is thus a continuation from my first book, *Transnational Torture*, where I emphasized the need to study the theoretical implications of state power and legal violence across democracies in both the West and the non-West. The U.S. was also a reference point during my fieldwork, as a number of the activists and lawyers I met in India expressed amazement at my access to the FSLs and the willingness of police and forensic psychologists to share their experiences. They generally attributed my ease of entry to my location as a researcher in the United States.

I did make a large number of contacts in India thanks to one retired DGP who was willing to make calls and definitely enabled my access to police officers and forensic psychologists. Other contacts, however, seemed to emerge from my emails as a U.S.-based professor with an ambiguous name that didn't obviously reveal my origins.[36] More important, however, the United States was a constant reference in my interviews, just as U.S. jurisprudence often appears in Indian judgments. As I argue in chapter 3, the origins of the lie detector, brain fingerprinting, and narcoanalysis in the United States had much to do with their emergence in India. My interviewees often said that in "your U.S." this happens or these techniques are used.

Focusing on these three scientific techniques, my interviews investigated the ways state and semi-state actors interact with each other, their perceptions about the functioning of truth machines, and their use of violence during interrogations.[37] Analyzing these scientific techniques reveals the state's constitutive powers and connections to violence. As Akhil Gupta notes, "An ethnographic focus, perhaps more than any other approach makes evident that the materiality and solidity of the state dissolve under scrutiny."[38] Fieldwork is not the only source of data for this research, but an ethnographic sensibility informs the interviews and textual analysis.[39]

THE STATE: THEORETICAL AND METHODOLOGICAL FRAMINGS

Political science is often considered synonymous with the study of state. In contrast to a more reified and unitary notion of the state that has largely dominated the discipline (and also rationalized its rejection), anthropologists Aradhana Sharma and Akhil Gupta argue for studying the state's cultural constitution—

that is, how the state is formed.[40] This framing focuses attention on the state's everyday practices as well as how people experience state processes and officials in their lives. Sharma and Gupta point to the mundane activities that form the basis of interaction between the state and its citizens and the representation of practices that collectively produce and reproduce the state. As Gupta explains in his essay "Blurred Boundaries," "Studying the state ethnographically involves both the analysis of the everyday practices of local bureaucracies and the discursive construction of the state in public culture."[41] Ethnographic methods can thus inform political theorists seeking to conceptualize the state.

In an era of globalization, theorists like Wendy Brown have articulated a story of the nation-state's decline.[42] In contrast, according to Veena Das and Deborah Poole, the story of decline that dominates much of political theory assumes a Weberian "rationalized administrative form of political organization."[43] Instead, they argue, features considered the basis of the state's claim to legitimacy—namely, territorial boundaries and a monopoly on violence—were always threatened at the margins, which could range from being excluded from state practices to writing rendered illegible, all with an assumed impact on "bodies, law and discipline."[44] Margins point to spaces, practices, and regulations "where the state is constantly refounding its modes of order and lawmaking."[45] State and law are thus formed in everyday interactions. As Das writes:

> I do not regard law as a sign of the sovereignty of the state or as an institution through which disciplinary regimes are put into place. Rather, I approach the law here as a sign of a distant but overwhelming power brought into the framework of everyday life by the representation and performance of its rules in modes of rumor, gossip, mockery, and mimetic representation and also as a resource for seeking certain rights, although a resource whose use is fraught with uncertainty and danger.[46]

Within political theory, Timothy Mitchell's concept of state as "structural effect" represented a similar move. Mitchell notes two primary ways that the state had been studied in the American social sciences in the post–World War II period. First, the concept of state was considered too narrow and ideological and was therefore abandoned, causing a turn to systems theory.[47] Second, in the 1970s, when the state was brought back in, it was conceptualized as autonomous from society, and the focus was on the subjective intentions of rule making, decision making, and policy making.⁴⁸ Instead, Mitchell suggests, distinguishing between state and society constitutes an act that generates power.⁴⁹

Law, for instance, often appears as an external code applied in society. For Mitchell, the state (and law) "is represented and reproduced in visible everyday forms, such as the language of legal practice, the architecture of public buildings, the wearing of military uniforms, or the marking out and policing of frontiers."⁵⁰ Representations of the state become crucial in state reports and in the production and circulation of state discourses. And, representations affect people's interpretations of the state. A distinction emerges, however, between the observations of Akhil Gupta and Timothy Mitchell that "the state" is reconstituted and Das and Poole's suggestion that the state collapses at its borders. As Mitchell explains, "The task of a critique of the state is not just to reject such metaphysics, but to explain how it has been possible to produce this practical yet ghostlike effect. What is it about modern society, as a particular form of social and economic order, that has made possible the apparent autonomy of the state as a freestanding entity?"⁵¹

Rather than assume, a priori, a Weberian notion of the state, I follow this scholarship to analyze how the state is constantly formed in everyday interactions and cultural representations.⁵² I am interested in exploring the processes through which, under certain conditions, the state is constituted as unitary or, as Mitchell suggests, as a structural effect. This study thus focuses on the state in its "disaggregated, decentered, multilayered, pluri centered and fluid nature,"⁵³ while recognizing the ways in which discourse continually attempts to render the state autonomous and abstract. As Gupta remarks, "A disaggregated view of the state makes it possible to open up the black box of *unintended outcomes* by showing how they are systematically produced by the friction between agendas, bureaus, levels, and spaces that make up the state."⁵⁴ Nayanika Mathur also notes the importance of studying state actors occupying the lower echelons of the Indian bureaucracy, who make laws legible in an everyday sense:⁵⁵ "And the primary means through which this occurs is by the production, circulation, reading, and filing of the correct documents—through the assembling of what I study as the paper state."⁵⁶ Earlier scholarship primarily considers sites where the state is represented by bureaucracies and legal systems.⁵⁷ I focus here on policing, which is defined by its proximity to violence. The state in the Weberian sense may claim a monopoly over legitimate violence, but the police then become the everyday manifestation of state violence. As a site of state power, policing is characterized by its close relationship to violence, especially in interrogations. Here I apply ethnographic methods for studying bureaucratic practices to an analysis of police violence and the postcolonial discourses of science and modernity.

Law, State, and Violence

Scholarship on the Indian state has seldom focused on the relationship among state, law, and violence. Sudipta Kaviraj has famously written, "There is no end in sight of Indian society's strange enchantment with the modern state."[58] Here he refers to the popular conception of the state among the marginalized, which leads them to plead with the state to resolve their grievances: "What is significant in a narrative of the state is that disadvantaged groups who often volubly declare their disillusionment with the Indian nation—its offer of common citizenship—and are bitterly resentful of all incumbent or potential governments, still need something like a strangely disembodied idea of the state to articulate their grievances in the modern social world."[59]

In his essay for the *Oxford Companion to Politics in India*, Partha Chatterjee provides an overview of Indian scholarship on the state.[60] Between 1947 and 1967, he notes, the field was dominated by the modernization narrative and the congress system in consensus making, in line with the Nehruvian model of development; in contrast, Marxists pointed to the state's class character. From the 1970s, 1980s, and beyond, the class character had to be understood more carefully, with landed elites, the bureaucratic class, and corporations on one hand and interest groups, regional parties, and pressure groups on the other.[61]

Chatterjee's focus, however, is mostly on the 1990s and 2000s, when the state withdrew from social welfare in the wake of liberalization and the responses of private actors, including NGOs and those with corporate and noncorporate capital.[62] During this period, state institutions remained the focus of elites demanding formal rights (civil society) and the site of negotiation for the marginalized (political society), even as the latter always requires illegal and exceptional state acts. Therefore, Chatterjee notes, even as forms of interaction with the state changed, to subvert the role of "democratic majorities," the state remained a major actor: "While the reforms since the 1990s have undoubtedly led to the withdrawal of the state from many sectors in which it was previously the dominant or even the sole player, the importance of the state as the chief regulator, facilitator, arbiter, and even allocator of resources for society as a whole has by no means diminished."[63]

For both Chatterjee and Kaviraj, the police emerge only as agents of repression. For Kaviraj, the popular conception of the state is "not the army and the police, the coercive apparatuses, which are dreaded and hated by large parts of the population for being violent and venal."[64] For Chatterjee, who mentions the Indian Police Service as a part of the civil service, the army is the continuity between the colonial and the postcolonial state. Surprisingly, however, the police as an institution of state power receive only an occasional mention, even though negotiation of political society occurs with the police more than any other site of state power. As Chatterjee explains, "Those in political society make their claims on government, and in turn are governed, not within the framework of stable constitutionally defined rights and laws, but rather through temporary, contextual, and unstable arrangements arrived at through direct political negotiations."[65] Thus, for both of these scholars, questions of law, state, violence, and policing as institution and practice are subsumed in a story of the police as a repressive state institution.[66]

Scholars such as K. G. Kannabiran, K. Balagopal, and Ujjwal K. Singh have highlighted state, law, and violence in India.[67] These scholars, also activists for civil liberties and democratic rights, have focused primarily on state violence resulting from a continuation of colonial laws, antiterror legislation, and orientations that undermine people's rights and are often upheld by the courts. This scholarship, discussed in chapter 5, contributes greatly to our understanding of state violence. Yet, I argue, these scholars ignore state innovations and negotiations that have established specific techniques of policing.[68]

Rather than state institutions like the police and their development, the emphasis of much scholarship has been on extraordinary laws and conflict areas.[69] However, police innovation suggests particular motivations for replacement of physical techniques of interrogation with psychological, scientifically informed methods thereby inviting focus. The question is whether police practices are a response to the pressure of democratic norms, as Darius Rejali suggests in other contexts, or whether new techniques stem from a combination of motivations.[70] Studying the everyday practices of police, lawyers, and forensic scientists can yield insights into the nature of state power and legal violence.

Policing Studies in the Contemporary Moment

A segment of my field notes describes my negotiations with the police:

> Police officers loved to regale the stories of their lives, and that mostly led to a cascade of interviews. But one officer recognized my desire to obtain docu-

ments and invited me to follow up. After much coordination, he invited me to his house. I tried requesting him to meet elsewhere, but he just wouldn't budge. It was at that moment that I felt unsure about the interview. This was not a known officer but one I had met through another contact in an unfamiliar city, and even as I made sure that someone accompanied me to the house, which turned out be just a visit to a family home, it revealed my own outlook toward the police. Stories of custodial deaths, torture and encounters abound [in] the civil liberties and democratic rights circle as well as the mainstream narrative of the police, but the strange relationship between me and my interviewees was nonetheless significant. As I chatted with the family[,] partaking the feast they offered, answering questions about my life in the U.S. and giving advice to their daughter who was interested in studying in the U.S., I was reminded of the contrast between my interaction with them and those of a suspect/accused. But most of all, it was a reminder of the failure of political theorists in adequately theorizing the police in terms of their everyday practices and work, through the interactions that makes our theorist-beings uncomfortable.

At this moment in political theory, political science, and scholarship on India, police violence has become the focus of analysis. As Jeffrey C. Isaac noted in his introduction to a 2015 issue devoted to U.S. policing in *Perspectives on Politics*, "It is now clear that a truly general, comparative, and nonparochial political science must account for the fact that the topics of policing, police brutality, incarceration, and repression more generally are not limited to authoritarian regimes."[71] Keally McBride reiterates this point in her review essay in the same journal: "Policing is one of the most frequent ways that the physical movement of people is regulated and the authority of the state is made visible; hence, it is one of the most important institutions of democracy and citizenship in our country [U.S.] that has been largely ignored by political scientists."[72]

A plethora of literature on policing is emerging in the United States, building on earlier scholarship that explored the police in comparative contexts. Within political science, we broadly see three sets of work. One is linked to critical carceral studies. A number of scholars focus on the rights and experiences of African Americans and others in prisons, often with calls for prison abolition.[73] A second set addresses excessive force leading to killings of unarmed African Americans with police impunity.[74] A third focuses on a critique of the criminal justice system in the United States more generally and this has led to more intentional interest in comparative case studies.[75] Scholars rarely restrict themselves to political science or political theory; nonetheless, their work constitutes a moment of reckoning within the discipline regarding questions of policing and violence.

In the scholarship on India, four types of literature provide a solid foundation for the study of everyday police practices: testimonial narratives, large-scale empirical work, volumes on impunity, and scholarship on contemporary policing.[76] Testimonial narratives have come from those directly affected by state violence. Among them are *Framed as a Terrorist* by Mohammad Aamir Khan, *Colours of the Cage* by Arun Ferreira, *Begunah Qaidi* (in Urdu and Hindi) by Abdul Wahid Shaikh, and *Do You Remember Kunan Poshpora?* by Essar Batul and four others.[77] While fact-finding reports by human rights, democratic rights, and civil liberties groups have painstakingly captured such experiences, the proliferation of media outlets and the narrative style of individual stories can have a particularly powerful impact. Testimonial narratives reveal the everyday experience of prisons, police custody, illegal detentions, torture rooms, interrogation techniques, and the steps in the investigations process. Together, they help to erode a monolithic conception of the state and police as rationalized bureaucracies or sources of exceptional acts. Indeed, testimonial narratives expose and highlight challenges to the scaffold of the rule of law, which I theorize in chapter 6.

Empirical studies document institutional practices at particular sites of state violence, such as torture or the death penalty. Although this literature remains comparatively limited, examples include a 2016 report from the National Law University of Delhi on conditions for those on death row and a report, in the same year, that I coauthored with Amar Jesani on torture prevention initiatives between 1989 and 2014.[78] Human rights groups initiated this work, but more systematic and longitudinal studies continue to build upon existing literature, bridging the arenas of policy, academia, and human rights.

Another type of literature emerging from the intersection of movements, academia, and human rights is scholarship on gender, violence, and the Indian state. For decades, feminist groups and scholars have theorized the relationship between violence and the state,[79] focusing not only on state violence in custody but on violence perpetuated by the state's failure in ensuring women's rights. When voices of women from the margins, who face the state's everyday violence, bring such violence to the fore feminists have grappled with the question centrally. Groups such as Women against Sexual Violence and State Repression have highlighted this issue, and feminist publishers like Zubaan have published volumes on impunity.[80]

Conceptualized as "perhaps the first study ever to attempt an empirical enquiry of impunity," *Landscapes of Fear* systematically created frameworks of analysis through detailed case studies from different regions in India, including the Northeast and Kashmir. A second volume, *Fault Lines of History*, explicitly focuses on sexual violence and the role of the state.[81] As the editors of the first volume, Navasharan Singh and Patrick Hoenig, explain, "Impunity, understood as a systematic exemption from punishment and a denial of redress, works as a double betrayal of our sense of justice: a violation has occurred and, what is more, it has not been rectified."[82] These volumes not only present data empirically but also help theorize aspects of state violence. Impunity and sexual impunity thus emerge as distinct categories of analysis.[83]

Three ethnographies on policing in India were published between 2016 and 2018. Beatrice Jauregui's *Provisional Authority* helps us understand the ways the empowered police can be situationally disempowered; Rachel Wahl's *Just Violence* seeks to explain police motivations for using torture; and Santana Khanikar's *State, Violence, and Legitimacy in India* explains the reasons people turn to the police or the army to intervene in their grievances, even when they face state violence.[84] Focusing on the postcolonial police as a state institution, these books emphasize the words and practices of the police as important phenomena. State violence is, then, part of that analysis.

These four categories of literature on Indian policing, together with the recent focus in political science on the police and excessive force, pave the way for, I suggest, conceptualizing state violence studies,(SVS) in which the state's violence can neither be ignored through a focus on bureaucratic functioning nor assumed as inherent or exceptional. The result has important methodological and analytical implications. Here I emphasize the significance of everyday acts of policing to theorize how the state can exert a monopoly over sovereign acts of violence within the folds of the law and yet, at times, also fail to do so. As my analysis explains, the state thus reveals its contingencies that have significant consequences for those interacting with the state and police.

WHAT TRUTH MACHINES REVEAL ABOUT THE STATE AND POLICING

In *Truth Machines*, I question two dominant frameworks defining the relationship between state power and legal violence. One is the Weberian conception of the bureaucratic rational state that holds a monopoly on legitimate violence. Of course, the state monopoly over violence is never entirely successful. As Charles Tilly notes, it is only an aspiration: "Back to Machiavelli and Hobbes, nevertheless, political observers have recognized that, whatever else they do, governments organize and, *wherever possible*, monopolize violence."[85] The conceptualization of the state holding a monopoly over violence, however, precludes much discussion about the limits of state violence, which is presumably contained, legitimate, and rationalized.

In *Economy and Society*, Weber elaborates the characteristics of modern bureaucracy, among them written documents, special expertise, and impersonal, dehumanized officials. Bureaucratic organization, he explains, emphasizes "precision, speed, unambiguity, knowledge of the files, continuity, discretion, unity, strict subordination, reduction of friction and of material and personal costs," making it technically superior to other forms of organization.[86] Similarly, Weber notes that as bureaucracies develop, "the more it is 'dehumanized,' the more completely it succeeds in eliminating from official business love, hatred, and all purely personal, irrational, and emotional elements which escape calculation."[87] Weber concedes that a bureaucracy can dominate and is not necessarily a mechanism for substantive justice, but his work has promoted a fantasy of the rational, bureaucratic state, giving credence to the assumption that just as rules govern everything, they also govern violence. As Weber says, "The authority to give commands . . . is strictly delimited by rules concerning the coercive means, physical, sacerdotal."[88] The relationship between state power and legal violence in everyday bureaucratic functioning, then, becomes less focused.

In contrast to Weber, Giorgio Agamben's framing of a sovereign exceptional act explains violence operating with impunity over bare life. As Agamben elaborates in his sequel to *Homo Sacer*, *State of Exception*, detainees imprisoned by the United States at Guantánamo Bay represent bare life in a state of exception and in turn represent the new norm of governing in democracies: "In the detainee at Guantanamo, bare life reaches its maximum indeterminacy."[89] Akhil Gupta points out that Agamben's emphasis on a binary between sovereign state and bare life in a state of exception assumes a very centralized notion of sovereignty and a "unified state apparatus."[90] The police, as agents of state power embodying this violence, would then also be constructed as a unified entity, and the colonial continuities of laws and attitudes in postcolonial India would become manifestations of sovereign exceptions. Neither the police nor the violence they enact are the focus. In contrast, as I discuss in chapter 2, drawing on new police science, the police convey both repressive and pastoral aspects.[91] And as chapter 6 explains, even with the exception of terrorism, the police need to create a scaffold of the rule of law.

This book, therefore, points to both the disaggregation of state power, even in its use of violence and the state's attempt to claim a unitary, rationality-based identity. The Weberian notion of a rational bureaucratic state looms large, even as power and the law are reconstituted by state actors who constantly recreate autonomy and a monopoly over legitimate violence. Attention to everyday practices, disaggregated and contingent, thus helps to erode the fantasy of the police as both a centralized bureaucracy and sovereign agents in the state of exception. What we observe instead is a contingent state that manages its own violence by incorporating disparate efforts, like truth machines, to perform its unifying role in a modern, scientific postcolonial society.

Both internal and external pressures led the police to be interested in techniques that could replace state violence. From the 1990s and 2000s the police gradually came to use a combination of lie detectors, brain scans, and narcoanalysis to replace custodial violence. These techniques emerged from contingent circumstances and involved a range of actors and motivations in dialogue: the innovative forensic psychologist, the ambitious scientist with market-driven research goals, and the police official with a "modernizing" zeal. As institutionalized mechanisms for monitoring human rights emerged in the 1990s and 2000s, the disparate efforts of these actors converged in overarching state initiatives to systematize a state forensic architecture that encompassed the police, material conditions, and forensic psychologists.

The truth machines themselves involved new sites of interrogation in forensic laboratories, and new actors, including forensic psychologists, operating together with the police and judiciary. The police impetus to use these techniques varied from the need to delay cases, to a belief in the machines' humaneness, to avoidance of custodial death. Forensic psychologists presented themselves as practitioners of therapeutic arts who used science in custodial situations and were thus distinct from the police. In effect, I argue, with these techniques, forensic science laboratories created new spaces for police work as well as distance from custodial torture. Nonetheless, the overemphasis on confession, the ongoing use of physical torture with laboratory-based medical techniques, the nexus between the police and forensic psychologists, and the insistence on truth machines despite their rejection by the scientific community makes efforts by the Indian state suspect.

Analytically, however, a focus on truth machines allows us to access the anxieties of policing reflected in reform initiatives, the pragmatics of torture in custody, and the state's flawed attempt at an art of government based on a rational regime. New forensics by the Indian police therefore demand new theories of state violence that attend to how the state reinvents and recalibrates its techniques, reordering spaces for critique and intervention. Even if truth machines reflect no perceptible shifts in replacing physical torture, their functioning points us to the interstices that can generate shifts and cracks in state power and offer possibilities for limiting legal violence. The notion of a contingent state thus helps us capture everyday practices as the state seeks to become unitary and to manage its violence.

In chapter 2 I draw on interviews and official reports to focus on the significance of studying the police (state actors) and forensic psychologists (semi-state actors). The relationship of the Indian police to violence is visible in investigations, and the postcolonial desire to modernize institutions is evident in police interviews and reform efforts. Rather than techniques at the margins of FSLs, I argue, truth machines fit India's developmentalist approach to modernization, based on science and expertise. However, these techniques of investigation operated not to replace torture and third-degree interrogation but to prevent the custodial deaths that the police ultimately fear, thus creating a role for police that is both pastoral and repressive.

In chapter 3 I focus on the social and cultural history of narcoanalysis, brain tests, and lie detectors. To consider the cultural production of truth, I trace the origins of these methods primarily in the United States, together with the development of one of the brain tests that originated in India. Truth machines appear to apply science to replace torture, I argue, yet like torture, they posit a body that can betray the conscious will and reveal the truth. The validity of their results, therefore, depends less on science and more on their construction in law, culture, and society.

In chapter 4 I elaborate the state forensic architecture as it emerged from the efforts of forensic psychologists using truth machines, and I explain the significance of forensic psychologists as cyborgs. Ultimately, forensic psychologists reinforce the structure of Indian policing, which has long emphasized violence and confession. The state forensic architecture thus reflects the convergence of contingency, materiality, and expertise, which fit a modernizing discourse marked by uncritical claims of the police and the postcolonial state.

In chapter 5 I focus on the legal discourses of the Supreme Court of India and the high courts (the highest courts at the state or provincial level in India). I document a raging debate between human rights critics and state officials defending the use of truth machines. Even as the courts defended these scientific investigative techniques as a way to replace torture, I argue, the edifice they sanctioned allows for flawed government in a peculiarly postcolonial manner.

In chapter 6 I examine debates on the rule of law with a focus on the experiences of terror suspects in two prominent cases, the *Mecca Masjid* case in Hyderabad and the Mumbai blasts case. The rule of law, I theorize, represents a scaffold that relies on procedures to mask violence. The scaffold, in turn, depends as much on doctors and magistrates as on the police to perform the work of interrogation. Only when this scaffolding is identified can the underlying violence be revealed and contained and a substantive resistance mounted.

In conclusion, I note the importance of the contingent state—a disaggregated conception of the state—with possible sites of critique and limits on legal violence.

Chapter 2

POLICE AS A SITE OF STATE POWER

Custody Practices and Policing Logics

> The policeman, as the most visible symbol of the authority of the State, must act as a responsible public official. He must realise that, to the common citizens, his response or reaction represents the Government's attitude.
>
> —GORE COMMITTEE REPORT[1]

> Are you asking me about the scientific narcoanalysis or the unscientific one?
>
> —BANGALORE POLICE OFFICER[2]

Police officers, as state actors, and forensic psychologists, as semi-state actors, are significant for understanding the state.[3] The Indian police, who are expected to be responsible state officials, play a prominent role in the exercise of state authority. As the most visible site of state power, the police, in their everyday operations, reveal the emergence and application of investigative techniques. Here, through a study of truth machines, I consider the role of the police in violence applied during investigations of suspects in custody.[4] Truth machines comprise three investigative techniques: lie detectors, brain scans, and narcoanalysis. The study of these methods reveal the everyday logics of policing and challenge the more unitary, Weberian conception of the police.

Scholarship on policing has predominantly attributed a more ideological role for the police. In this ideological framing, police have an a priori function, and the "rule of law" in a postcolonial, constitutional framework either enables or fails to restrain police violence. This framing is indeed crucial for understanding aspects of policing, but I focus here on everyday police practices. To access these practices, I draw on reports of police reform and on interviews with police officials and forensic psychologists. Theoretically, my focus on truth machines both provides access to the pragmatic logic of third-degree interrogation and complicates any predetermined, ideological understanding of policing.

Scholarship on policing needs to acknowledge the contestations between the ideological role of policing and its structural contingencies in India. The emergence of truth machines, however unsuccessful their application, is a symptom of this ongoing contestation. Rather than techniques at the margins of forensic science labs, I argue, truth machines fit India's developmentalist approach to modernization, based on science and experts. However, these techniques of investigation operate not to replace torture and third-degree interrogation but to prevent the custodial deaths that the police ultimately fear. As the Indian police deploy truth machines, everyday practices reveal a constantly negotiated balance between repressive and pastoral roles in policing. Police practice (and the state) is thus in continuous formation. Structural contingencies may mediate the relationship of the police to violence in intended or unintended ways, potentially limiting the use of violence and determining sites of accountability.

POLICING, SCIENCE, AND LAW: THE EVERYDAY OPERATIONS OF GOVERNMENT

A major feature of the Weberian, rational bureaucratic state is its monopoly over legitimate violence. As Max Weber famously explained, "Legal coercion by violence is the monopoly of the state."[5] In everyday practice, of course, the police, though not the only state institution, are closely associated with violence and are, for most people, "the most visible symbol of the authority of the State."[6] A common assumption, however, is that the police, like other bureaucratic institutions, are restrained by a set of rules. In his famous essay on bureaucracy, Weber considers rules a major function of modern officialdom: "The authority to give the commands required for the discharge of these duties is distributed in a stable way and is strictly delimited by rules concerning the coercive means."[7]

Scholars often uncritically embrace this formulation. As Guillermina Seri elaborates, "Together with a dismissal of the governing aspects of police, political scientists tend to treat both the police and bureaucratic state apparatuses as politically neutral and as at least normatively subjected to the law. Yet it is through these governing processes delivered through these apparatuses that exclusion thrives."[8] This assumption of a neutrally functioning bureaucracy can allow the state to attribute excessive violence to such conditions as inadequate training and can obscure the violence accommodated in the process of governing.[9]

A focus on everyday police practice thus becomes essential for revealing the underlying processes of policing. Insights from the new police science invite us to think about the "actual operation of government" and the "everyday participants in the institutions of state government."[10] Mark Neocleous further distinguishes between the new and old police science by explaining that the former is much more critical in its approach to understanding the "mechanisms through which police powers operate" as opposed to a way to improve how the police work.[11] A significant theoretical insight from the new police science is that policing is multifaceted. The police have a role not only in punishment for acts already committed but also in prevention, as, for example, in public health or zoning.[12]

As Markus D. Dubber and Mariana Valverde write, "Police works as a sort of temporal-hinge word, allowing the governance of the past to be articulated with the governance of the future."[13] Valverde further notes that, for Foucault, police power constitutes an important part of the state framework as "practices of power-knowledge" and the state represent the "coagulations of practices."[14] The new police science thus points to how state practices and techniques in the everyday operations of government become significant, meriting critical study. The police, then, become an important site where state power is formed and state violence realized.

Drawing from the new police science and from a critique of the Weberian conception of the police as a bureaucracy, I analyze the use of truth machines, which promised to replace physical torture during investigations. A Weberian conception of the bureaucratic state posits a unified, state-sanctioned police institution with intentionally created rules of investigation. As my interviews revealed, however, the everyday practices of policing are much more contingent, and the adoption of truth machines represents less a well-thought-out strategy than a set of varying conditions that render these techniques pragmatically chosen tactics.

These techniques for investigation appear to have been innovations of individual forensic psychologists (discussed in chapters 3 and 4), which grew in popularity during the 2000s. According to one police official, the public eventually came to say, "*Arre wo jooth bola to usse narcoanalysis dal re*" (if he lies, just subject him to narcoanalysis), although "previously the public was never knowing, what is narcoanalysis, what is lie detector, and all.... And even public awareness was so much, even if a criminal does something, the police used to start telling like, we'll subject them for narcoanalysis, ... and they will tell all the truth."[15]

One forensic psychologist described a case in a rural area in which the police had been unable to solve a crime.[16] Angry crowds surrounded the policeman, and in order to extricate him, the police claimed to be subjecting the suspect to narcoanalysis or some other scientific test. The promise of narcoanalysis appeared to calm the crowd, indicating that its legitimacy was greater, presumably, than torture or persistent interrogation. Rather than a well-considered plan, therefore, the police response to the crowd led to the use of naracoanalysis. Here the police rendered narcoanalysis instrumental, even spectacular, and so represented themselves as ethical agents who were eager to solve the crime without resorting to physical torture.[17] Of course, as chapter 4 elaborates, the state also consolidates opportunities, from the emergence of truth machines to their accommodation, to project itself as a rational regime (or what Timothy Mitchell would term a "structural effect"[18]).

Nonetheless, police practice remains contingent, with unstable meanings associated with "practices of power knowledge." This contingency is evident in my conversation with a retired police officer who had thirty-five years of service, a man from Coorg (a former princely state of India). The men of Coorg, classified as a warrior community, often join either the military or the police.[19] During his college days, this officer had been selected for the Indian military academy but had failed to complete his degree because of an incident in which an officer had mistakenly picked up a student who then died in lockup, possibly because of torture. In response, the retired officer, a student leader, had led a *dharna* (protest) and, as a result, was barred from finishing his education and joining the military. Later, he studied law and learned about India's Code of Criminal Procedure (CrPC), which he called the police's *bhagwad gita* (a Hindu religious text). Reading the criminal code, he explained, had led him not to practice law but to join the police, possibly because he had understood the death in lockup as a misuse of law rather than its accommodation of violence.

The retired officer described joining the police after the Emergency in India (1975–1977), when fundamental rights were suspended. With torture and heavy-handedness, the police at the time evoked much fear, resulting in many protests and, eventually, the fall of the Congress Party government, which had held power since Indian independence. As the officer explained, "When I and others joined the police department, there was no narcoanalysis, or such things were unheard of; only third degree and torturing the criminals was the method that was being used, which is not legal."[20] Like many officers, however, he understood the pressure to gain quick answers from suspects and saw torture and third-degree interrogation as means for gaining suspects' cooperation in serious crimes. He had thus come to consider violence necessary and no longer blamed the police for the custodial death. Gradually, he went on to say, "narcoanalysis came; human rights came; we had to use very patient methods, very slow detection. Breakthrough took some time."[21]

For this retired officer, therefore, narcoanalysis was linked to the emergence of human rights, in direct contrast to the views of activists who deem it a form of psychological torture because of its impact on body and mind.[22] Indeed, as former detainee and now activist Arun Ferreira describes, police officers have concealed torture in order to avoid visible marks, ostensibly in response to the human rights regime. "Such concealment, however, did not appeal to all the officers," Ferreira recalled. "Many of the officers spoke nostalgically of the good old days before the spread of awareness of human rights and prisoner rights.... The courts are to blame. In the late 1970s and the early 1980s, the Supreme Court held that even prisoners have human rights. And now we have these numerous Human Rights Commissions ever-willing to raise their voice."[23]

The retired officer's discussion of narcoanalysis emerged in the context of a criminal case that involved a couple from England who were visiting Bangalore. The woman had been raped, and, in a separate incident, her boyfriend had been killed. In the rape case, the woman had used a penknife to stab the driver of a three-wheeler auto when he failed to respond to her questions about the destination. The police officer checked the area clinics and found a man with the suspect's unusual name, Kadrappa, which led to his arrest, but was disappointed when the state investigation unit (known then as the Corps of Detectives, or COD) took over the case. The COD, which supposedly avoids third-degree interrogation, did eventually return the suspect, but the officer's superior asked him also to refrain from using it. The unavailability of third-degree tactics thus required improvisation.

The retired officer went on to tell me a narcoanalysis-related narrative. At the police station, after inquiring whether a suspect drank liquor, the officer had mixed beer with some brandy, which caused the suspect to become so excited after drinking that he provided all the information asked of him. The effects of alcohol, the officer explained, made this intervention equivalent to narcoanalysis and illustrated that neither third-degree interrogation nor scientifically sanctioned narcoanalysis was necessary. The entire episode was also videographed without the suspect's knowledge, and with the confession then legally inadmissible, the officer had pointed to other evidence, including a flower that the rape victim had seen embossed on the three-wheeler and the nurse's confirmation of the suspect's identity. Together, he explained, these pieces of evidence were *pucca* (solid).

When asked whether a reduction in scientifically sanctioned narcoanalysis would return the police to older methods, this officer and his colleagues thought it would. As one officer explained decision making during interrogation, "But other methods are definitely there, like giving him a biryani (special rice dish) if he likes biryani or giving him some alcohol . . . giving him alcohol just to befriend him, just to make him more, you know, avoid or remove his inhibitions. Those kinds of methods, I think, have been used."[24]

Describing interaction between police and suspect, yet another officer claimed that the police were almost at the mercy of the accused, fulfilling their demands for alcohol, ganja (marijuana), or cocaine until they seemed satiated, especially at night. Only then would the police start the questioning.[25]

These processes, of course, undermine the state's claim to scientifically sanctioned narcoanalysis. Indeed, one police officer actually asked whether I was inquiring about scientific or unscientific narcoanalysis. He insisted that even before the scientific use of narcoanalysis by doctors in hospitals, police had requested local doctors to administer drugs like pethidine, a pain medication, or Actifed, a decongestant made of chlorpheniramine and phenylephrine, to make suspects "semiconscious." One suspect had "started telling some sort of things," the officer related, and he continued:

> We tell him, these are the things that you have done, that this is the thing being reported against you, and you did so many things here, and recently there was a case also here on that road somewhere, like Tannery Road, and wherein your name is coming now, and you are a good person. Like that we just, narrat[e] the stories and other things. We'll also tell him; you tell; nothing will happen. God is there. And in that *semiconscious [condition] he starts telling so many things.*[26]

In these instances, police apply practices that both challenge bureaucratic, rule-based policing and reveal it as arbitrary. As techniques emerge, are used, and contrast with other tools, the police, acting ethically, can try to render the science of narcoanalysis instrumental or spectacular, or they can interpret and invent creative techniques that fit the culture of policing, even if these are not formally medicalized.[27]

Critical scholarship and human rights advocacy often suggest that the state and police develop new forms of violence that appear humane and controlled because they are sanitized through language.[28] Such an argument has been applied to more humane forms of execution (as Austin Sarat notes regarding the United States) or to non-scarring methods of torture, such as sleep deprivation or stress positions, rather than whips and razors (as Darius Rejali traces more generally).[29] Human rights scholars have argued that in India truth machines represent a shift from physical to more psychological methods of torture.[30] In contrast, a state-centered narrative points to the very contingent nature of this shift or, more accurately, to the coexistence of several methods. The pressure to perform efficiently leads the police to rely on forensic psychologists, many of whom reiterated to me that the police came to them only in cases with no specific evidence, a need to screen a number of people, or no other way to proceed.[31] Sometimes, they noted, the police would petition for these tests merely to buy time in a case.

Weber identifies rules and precision—the lack of ambiguity—as instruments that make bureaucracies technically superior to other forms of organization.[32] The dominant, Weberian conception of state institutions—in this case the police—is thus a functional, rational bureaucracy. My interviews with police, however, reveal arbitrariness and contingency determining the use of truth machines in interrogation. As Laleh Khalili notes, the more state officials tried to classify detainees in Iraq and Afghanistan as lawful or unlawful combatants or as high-value detainees, the more arbitrary the classifications and related behavior became.[33]

Scholars such as Akhil Gupta have pointed to contingency in the functioning of state officials in other kinds of bureaucracies, where the relationship between contingency and discretionary power is particularly significant.[34] As Guillermina Seri notes in her study of the Argentine police, "Discretion is a core trait of police power."[35] Discretion, I argue, characterizes the actions of individual police officers. Police discretion allows officials to use power at the micro level. Contingency, in contrast, is much more structural and counters the notion of unified, rule-based policing. Contingent conditions, moreover, enable the incorporation, exclusion, or modification of certain practices.

Here the relationship to science determines the contingent action. As my interviews reveal, the arsenal available to the police is often wide ranging, from physical torture and unscientific techniques (in police stations), to scientific techniques (in labs and hospitals), to petitions to delay investigation. This range reflects complexity and variability. Discretion is thus a function of structural contingencies in this site of state power. While official truth machines in labs and hospitals invite legal scrutiny, unofficial techniques remain available to the police, to be used at their discretion. As state narratives, my interviews document the workings of police power in investigations, whether through indeterminate rules or through arbitrary definitions of scientific means. The rational bureaucratic regime, ostensibly based on a monopoly over legitimate violence, is therefore constantly reconstituted in everyday police practices that mediate the relationship of the police to violence.

RELATIONSHIP OF THE POLICE TO VIOLENCE

The structural contingencies that led to the emergence of truth machines for interrogation not only reveal the ongoing tension between the police and the use of violence but also inform theories of policing and the state. Here I consider police violence ideologically, as a state function related to welfare or, in India, related to colonial continuity. I focus on the contestation between the ideological roles and the structural contingencies of the police. In the contestations between the two, I argue, lies the constantly negotiated police relationship to violence.

These negotiations have implications for those subjected to policing. Ultimately, an ideological analysis of the relationship of the police to violence may undermine the consequences, intended or unintended, of structural contingencies for people's lives.

Understanding the Police and Violence

In his collection of lectures titled *Security, Territory, and Population*, Michel Foucault draws from a number of eighteenth-century theorists of policing to note that the police are central to the art of government. Certain tasks, he posits, ensure the population's well-being through detailed regulations: "It is this connection between strengthening and increasing the powers of the state, making good use of the forces of the state, and procuring the happiness of its subjects, that is specific to the police."[36] Mariana Valverde notes that although Foucault does not state this point explicitly, one can identify in his analysis a "police objective of maximizing order, prosperity and efficiency and that exercise much coercion in the name of general welfare or public interest."[37] Foucaldian frameworks thus invite us to study both the repressive and the pastoral aspects of police work.

How, then, do the pastoral and repressive functions of policing coexist? How might the police's pastoral function mediate repression and the contingencies of repressive power? A prominent framework for theorizing policing and the use of violence asserts an ideological, predetermined role for the police. This view is evident in the Marxist conception of the police as a part of the coercive state apparatus or, in Althusserian terms, part of the Repressive State Apparatus representing certain class interests.[38] In contrast, Markus Dirk Dubber attempts to define the source of police power historically, emerging from the householder's control of household members for their own welfare, which he traces from the ancient Greeks to contemporary contexts in the United States.[39] The source of police power here is not law and justice but the household hierarchy.

As Dubber points out, police measures have often been upheld in courts, and the police have avoided constitutional scrutiny because their limits are difficult to demarcate. The ideological role of policing thus stems from a conception of household welfare in the United States that escapes legal scrutiny. Attributing their actions to a higher purpose, this analogy suggests, allows the police to adopt their own version of welfare. As scholars have pointed out, police often attribute their violent actions to their commitment to order, justice, public good, and efficiency. As Julia Eckert eloquently explains regarding extrajudicial executions or encounters, "It is (also) a vision of the purity of 'disinterested' violence, violence that only serves the *production of order*. An autonomous police would be a pure police."[40] Jyoti Belur similarly elaborates: "Interviews with police officers and 'claimsmakers' revealed a discourse of denial that existed: accounts that enabled officers to explain to their audiences why *encounters were justified and inevitable* in the effort to fight crime."[41]

Rachel Wahl, too, situates justification for torture in punishing "terrorists" and "hardened criminals" within an inefficient criminal justice system.[42] In *Just*

Violence she argues that the police are not inherently acting in bad faith or arbitrarily using violence but are instead seeking to ensure security and justice in a corrupt society.[43] Emphasizing the moral duty of the police, Beatrice Jauregui similarly challenges an overemphasis on foundational or essentially coercive violence: "The moral duty of police is structured by cosmic forces and relations to fight and use whatever means necessary to reinstate good order in the face of imminent (and immanent) evil. Perpetration and subjection to violence is an inescapable part of this moral duty."[44] In India such rationales appear in the context of torture, police encounters, and extrajudicial executions. In the United States they are found in Fourth Amendment search-and-seizure cases. As Leonard Feldman explains, the sovereign exception, which shields the police from liability, fails to explain the continued use of necessity arguments in these cases. Rather, they represent "discretionary power oriented towards a vague but nevertheless significant notion of the *public good* and hedged in (imperfectly) by legal constraints."[45] The result is an attempt to explain police violence and coercive action as necessary for justice, order, public good, and efficiency, thereby providing a pretext for the police to act, sometimes within the law and at other times by "correcting" the failures of law in a corrupt, inefficient system.

In scholarship on Indian policing, a dominant framework has also viewed the police as a colonial institution and its repression as a continuation of colonial practice in a postcolonial context.[46] Indeed, the major statute governing the Indian police is still the Police Act of 1861, a British colonial creation.[47] As many scholars have pointed out, the administrative and legal structure that the British used to govern India remained in place after independence, in 1947. This continuity is reflected in the organization of the police.[48] Central to their functioning after independence was the need for surveillance, coercion, and control. As Upendra Baxi notes, "The Indian police is basically a colonial police, both in its organization and operations: it's basically a repressive force."[49]

Literature that emerges from police officials themselves also focuses on colonial continuities and consequent challenges to reforms. For instance, K. S. Subramanian, a former Indian Police Services officer, writes that around 80 percent of police time actually goes toward dealing with actual or potential incidents of violence and much less toward crime prevention and investigation.[50] Hence, Subramanian notes that continuity from the Indian Penal Code (1860) requires the police to prioritize public order and crimes against the state and only secondarily to address crime prevention and investigation. Notably, in one of my interviews, a retired police officer pointed out that police reform has often been led by police officers:

> It came from the colonial hangover, that's right. That is the legacy. We didn't dismantle anything. When we became free, we have not dismantled anything. We have accepted everything which was there. So we continued in that way, and later on, I have a feeling that, it suited the, the politicians in India, because you'll never find any drive or any initiative from [the] political side for police reform. You find this initiative coming from policemen or coming from media or coming from people but from political class, I've never heard anybody talking about, in terms of, police reforms, which is very strange.[51]

Kalpana Kannabiran draws upon a range of scholars to explain the police role from the colonial to postcolonial period. The Indian police, she explains, have consolidated the interests of the propertied classes (per David Arnold) and maintained the governing elites (per Upendra Baxi) partly because of colonial-era laws (per K. G. Kannabiran) that emphasize "law breaker character" (per Madhava Menon).[52] Furthermore, police power in India has historically targeted the poor, women, LGBTQ communities, minorities (particularly Muslims), scheduled tribes, scheduled castes (that is, dalits), and political dissenters. This focus has strengthened the role of police in maintaining hierarchy and social order.[53]

The two dominant frameworks for understanding policing in India are thus its higher purpose in promoting justice and public order and the colonial continuities maintained by political elites. Both frameworks explain important motivations for police violence and choice of targets, but they are distinct.[54] Emphasizing colonial continuities frames police as primarily repressive. Emphasizing the general welfare focuses on the police claim of a broader popular interest, however unevenly. These frameworks do indicate important elements of the relationship of the police to violence. Yet, I argue, in both frameworks, external factors are identified as motivations for the police to protect a status quo, directly or indirectly and to rationalize their violence.

In contrast, a focus on internal debates regarding police reform after Indian independence indicates tension in the relationship of policing to violence, especially during investigations. A focus on reform also helps to explain the emergence and application of truth machines, as well as the structural contingencies in third-degree interrogations. In analyzing discussions of reform and in my interviews with police, I heard accounts that highlight internal reasons for the persistence of torture, contextualize the use of truth machines, and explain the relationship between the pastoral and repressive roles of the police.

THE INDIAN POLICE AND DEMAND FOR REFORM

The embrace of truth machines dates from the 1990s and 2000s.[55] Both the police and other state officials appeared to view these techniques—especially brain scanning and narcoanalysis, together with lie detectors—as legitimate because they promised to deal with the intractable issue of police violence in India. Since Indian independence in 1947, the formal process of police reform in India offers the most visible image of the police desire to be a rational, bureaucratic decision-making body that follows rules and uses modern and scientific methods to safeguard welfare and justice. Indeed, as the *Gore Committee Report on Police Training* noted in 1971, a police officer is to act as a "responsible public official."[56] This report was crucial to state reform, especially in moving police practice toward science and postcolonial modernization.

Gore Committee Report: Science and the Police in a Postcolonial Society

The Gore Committee was established in 1971 to conduct a comprehensive review of training programs at all rungs of the police and to suggest improvements. The committee concluded that the training, especially at the noncentral level, was "in a state of general neglect."[57] The report presents two noteworthy points. First, it identifies the police as central in the transformation of India to a more equal and just society, and, second, it promotes science and modernization in police training. The report notes that training is meant to ensure "knowledge, skills and attitudes required to understand and meet the demands of their [police] new role in a country committed to the establishment of a secular, socialist, democratic society."[58]

To this end, the report also notes a need for a change in orientation, from a colonial force with loyalty to an alien power to a postcolonial force "conscious[ly] divorce[d] from past traditions."[59] As the report continues, "The police have now to be more than ever conscious of their role in safe guarding and fostering the processes of socio-economic growth and development and ensuring social justice."[60] These goals required the police to actively uphold the rights of the socially and economically disadvantaged.[61] More than a force for law and order, the police were thus charged with administering the social justice and development agenda of the Indian state.

Training was to be central to this transformation to a more modern, scientifically informed police force. In explaining one of the training objectives, the report notes, "The techniwque [sic] of administration has moved beyond the pruely [sic] pragmatic one of trial and error into a scientific discipline and apractice [sic] with an organised, ever increasing body of knowledge which has its roots in science and technology and in the remarkable progress in the field of behavioural sciences."[62] A separate chapter of the report is devoted to the role of science and technology in police training and the need for proactive investment and inclusion in Five-Year Plans.[63] "Modern means of communication, electronics, electronic data processing, *forensic science and medicine*, new weaponry, systems analysis etc., have started playing a major role in giving new dimensions to police work in the advanced countries."[64] These, the report concludes, need to be emulated by developing countries.

A retired senior police officer reflected, in an interview, on the continued resonance of this approach: "Wherever the democracy has come, they have gone for these scientific methods, and they have gone in a big way. We are also going there."[65] The Weberian "ideal type" of a rational, formal system of administration becomes most visible here. "'Equality before the law,'" Weber says, "and the demand for legal guarantees against the arbitrary exercise of power demand formal and rational 'objectivity,' unlike the personal discretion flowing from the 'grace of the old patrimonial domination.'"[66] The transition from colonial to postcolonial policing seemed to require such a rational approach. As Srirupa Roy notes more generally about early postcolonial India, science and scientific development became the primary "need" of nation building.[67]

The implication of a science-based approach for police investigation appears in the report's chapter on training sub-inspectors, the officials most responsible for this role. The report specifically cites the need to trust science, scientific aids, and forensic science: "Much of the criticism against the police can be overcome if investigations are conducted quickly, systematically, thoroughly and along scientific lines."[68] More explicitly, the report states, "The increasing consciousness among the people of their legal rights, the *old, rough and ready methods* can no longer be used in investigations and enquiries. A sub-Inspector now has to be very well informed in the techniques of scientific investigation."[69]

The report makes no mention of torture or third-degree interrogation, despite these practices having been a major source of concern in the colonial period. Indeed, the 1855 Madras Commission report resulted in comprehensive changes to the Indian legal codes.[70] But the mention of "the old, rough and ready methods" clearly indicates the pervasive use of third-degree interrogations. The Gore Committee thus prominently advocates scientific innovations to reorient the police and establish a professional bureaucracy to promote social justice in a democratic society: "In the Indian context, the training programmes must aim at providing a professional leadership in administration[,] which can help achieve the speedy transformation of an economically backward society into a secular, modern, technologically advanced society characterised by equal opportunity and social justice."[71]

In creating a training model for the police, the Gore Committee appears to have exhibited a blanket endorsement of science and modern professionalism as the solution to India's policing problems. Such an orientation, I suggest, contributes over time to the embrace of truth machines, which appear to be scientific methods because they are conducted by forensic psychologists based in laboratories, despite their dubious relationship to science. Although these techniques are not the only scientific methods the committee recommended, their uncritical embrace of science and modernization opened the way for a range of claims to scientific expertise and innovation and for the police to occasionally innovate creatively, with or without science.

National Police Commission Reports: A Desire for Reform

In 1977 the Janata government established the National Police Commission (NPC) to consider police restructuring.[72] This effort directly followed the Indian Emergency declared by then prime minister Indira Gandhi between 1975 and 1977 and marked the end of the one-party dominance that had prevailed since independence. The Emergency period had led to the suspension of fundamental rights, enabling widespread deaths, torture, detention, and atrocities on an unprecedented scale throughout the criminal justice system. Political activists and dissenters who opposed the ruling Congress Party were specially targeted, and the police were centrally involved.

The Shah Commission inquired into the emergency that was proclaimed by citing that "the Security of India is threatened by internal disturbances."[73] In contrast to the Gore Committee's optimism about the positive role for the police, the Shah Commission both revealed police violence and exposed political pressures that challenged effective policing. Contradictions between the two reports plagued reform efforts. Discussions of reform revealed two demands: one for police freedom from political control and institutional constraints, including inadequate resources, and the other for police accountability, with practices that would obviate third-degree interrogations. The first demand, however, more often dominated.[74]

The NPC published a total of eight reports between 1979 and 1981 suggesting a complete overhaul of the police system. By the time the final report was released, however, government control had returned to the Congress Party under Indira Gandhi, whose government specifically repudiated the Shah Commission report, quoted in the NPC reports, and denied that excesses had been committed during the emergency.[75] With the new government, police reform remained unaddressed, with no major effort, despite other influential reports. Only in 2006, when the Supreme Court took up the question in the *Prakash Singh* case, did police reform again receive prominent attention.[76]

Acknowledging the close relationship between the use of third-degree interrogation and postarrest investigations, the NPC's fourth report addressed the question of torture and the third degree.[77] The report emphasizes that interrogation "is a difficult and delicate exercise for any police officer and calls for enormous patience and considerable understanding of human psychology."[78] The report notes the need for a suspect or witness to undertake a mental journey from "an initial position of total reluctance" to "full disclosure of facts as known to him and thereby feel resolved of the conflicts in his mind."[79] Such a process suggested a continuing emphasis on pressure and confessions, which called for experts, both state and semi-state actors, who could apply their knowledge.

Both the Gore Committee report and the NPC report thus emphasize the need for expertise, at times the police and at other times forensic scientists, to effect Weberian bureaucratic control of policing. One of the NPC's strongest denunciations was the use of physical force:

> The use of force against an individual in their custody in his loneliness and helplessness is a grossly unlawful and most degrading and despicable practice that requires to be condemned in the strongest of terms, and we do so. Nothing is so

dehumanising as the conduct of police in practising [sic] torture of any kind on a person in their custody.[80]

The report went on to make a range of recommendations to ensure protections against third-degree interrogations, including further training, surprise visits by senior officials (despite claiming elsewhere that some of them approve of such techniques), and incentives for using "clean and honest methods" of investigation. The NPC also encouraged judicial magistrates to inquire into grievous hurt and judicial deaths and to ensure detainees access to medical care and opportunities to complain about ill treatment.[81]

Of course, some actors charged with safeguarding against torture, among them magistrates and doctors, might ultimately contribute to a scaffolding of the rule of law, especially in terrorism cases (see chapter 6). Yet rather than deny the use of torture, the NPC report acknowledged the pervasiveness of the third degree and torture in investigations. The report also reiterated the urgent need for police reform, suggesting, among other things, the need for training experts in less physical means of interrogation. The NPC thus recognized the inevitability of coercion and the likelihood of psychological pressure to achieve results and addressing the challenges of interrogation.

Malimath and Beyond

The most relevant police reform initiative connecting science and modernization to the question of third-degree interrogation arose with the Malimath Committee (2003), established to provide a comprehensive review of the entire criminal justice system. The committee revisited fundamental principles of criminal justice—"presumption of innocence and right to silence of the accused, burden of proof on the Prosecution, and the right to fair trial"[82]—and suggested changes to both constitutional provisions and the three main statutes that govern criminal justice: Code of Criminal Procedure (1973), the Indian Penal Code (1860), and the Indian Evidence Act (1872). As the committee reported, the two main problems with the criminal justice system were "huge pendency of criminal cases and the inordinate delay in disposal of criminal cases on the one hand and the very low rate of conviction in cases involving serious crimes on the other."[83] Inefficiency and failure to provide justice are thus deemed indicators of a deeper malaise: the inability to protect life and liberty, as guaranteed in the Indian Constitution, Article 21.[84]

Recommendations of the Malimath Committee were wide ranging. The committee favored trials that were more inquisitorial than adversarial, with judges playing a more important role in the "quest for truth." The committee's report also proposed that a suspect asserting a right to silence could lead to a conviction based on an adverse assumption of guilt, despite the constitutionally mandated right to silence under Article 20 (3). The report further advocated a change in the standard of proof, from the strict "beyond a reasonable doubt" to the "court's conviction that it is true," a mid-level standard.[85]

A number of scholars rightly criticized the committee's recommendations for their transformation of principles enshrined in the criminal justice system. As Upendra Baxi explains, the report was highly undemocratic in advocating the bypassing of a number of safeguards, such as the right against self-incrimination and due process, measures consistent with post-9/11 efforts to dilute safeguards worldwide.[86] Two aspects of the Malimath report are relevant to police violence: the relationship between truth and torture and the emphasis on scientific investigations, including the use of lie detectors. The Malimath Committee prominently emphasized the pursuit of truth in criminal investigations, taking its inspiration from continental-European legal systems as well as the Indian philosophical tradition of *Satyameva Jayate* (truth alone succeeds). The committee even invoked Gandhi's idea of *Satyagraha* (pursuit of truth).

This overemphasis on truth, I suggest, provides important insights into the difficult relationship between the criminal justice system and questions of violence and torture. For instance, in the section dedicated to increasing the role of courts in determining truth, the report cites a case of custodial death concerning an "innocent illiterate poor citizen of Delhi in Police custody,"[87] in which the Supreme Court recognized the deliberate attempt by fellow police officers to cover up evidence of guilt and ordered another inquiry.[88] The report almost preempts critiques, arguing that not increasing the role of the judge in ensuring truth (and accountability) is to ignore the violence faced by marginalized sections of society, which only a judge can address.

The report's discussion of the right to silence, inevitably linked to torture, appears most directly in the context of investigations: "The aim of the investigation and, in fact, the entire Criminal Justice System is to search for truth. To achieve this objective, the investigating officers must be properly trained and supervised and necessary scientific and logistical support should be made available to them."[89] The report acknowledges that the police, in their desire to get to the truth, "often resort to short cut methods and exhibit negative traits of police sub-culture, namely, rudeness, use of third degree methods, defensiveness in face of criticism, lack of innovativeness[,] etc."[90] Challenging the police to innovate, the committee also notes structural problems with police investigations, citing inadequate staff, political interference, lack of training and facilities, and merging of law-and-order and investigative functions.

The committee turned to forensic science to improve investigative processes, recommending involvement by forensic science teams from the very inception of an investigation, despite an acknowledged shortage of laboratories. Here, the committee relied on the recommendations of the National Seminar on Forensic Science: Its Use and Application in Investigation and Prosecution, held in Hyderabad on July 27, 2002. These recommendations ranged from closer collaboration between police and forensic science laboratories; to more forensic facilities at the district level, including equipment and personnel; to training for forensic scientists, better storage of evidence, and use of electronic gadgets.[91]

The committee's last recommendation, however, is of special significance: "A polygraph machine for lie detector test[s] should be provided in each district."[92] Together with fingerprinting, the use of lie detectors appears to be the only technique mentioned prominently, although the list includes forensic DNA, forensic explosives (analysis), and computer forensics. More important, extralegal methods of interrogation are mentioned only in relation to the lie detector: "The regular use [of lie detectors] will obviate the need for extra legal methods of interrogation."[93] The committee thus seemed to embrace the proposition that torture or third-degree interrogation should be replaced by techniques that extract truth from the body and mind of the accused. This recommendation coincided with broader plans for using truth machines and employing experts distinct from the police (see chapter 4).

Prominent police reform efforts from 1971 to 2003, therefore, suggest three major themes. First, rough methods and third-degree interrogation have always been a part of the discussion. As the Supreme Court noted in 2006, in the *Prakash Singh* case, "non-enforcement and discriminatory application" of the law and lack of accountability for "torture, unauthorized detentions, harassment[,] etc." were considered prominent areas of intervention.[94] Not only elected leaders and the judiciary but also the police had to deal with their own use of torture and third-degree interrogation. The second theme is a general understanding that scientific methods of investigation are the path forward in policing, as in other spheres of the postcolonial state, economy, and society. The third theme is the emphasis on scientific experts in the criminal justice system, which became a condition for the emergence of particular techniques.

POLICING LOGICS: THE PROCESS OF ACCESSING TRUTH

How do police explain their reliance on violence in investigations? While discussions of police reform revealed tension between the use of violence and recommended scientific expertise as a way forward, these efforts offered few explanations for police practices in custody. Attention to the application of scientific techniques, however, offers insights about custodial investigations that are otherwise shrouded in secrecy. In everyday practice we can identify the structural contingencies that inform policing and the pragmatic logic that guides the use of truth machines in interrogations.

These scientific techniques emerged in the 1990s and 2000s amid both narratives of torture and the state's denial.[95] Indeed, custodial torture became an issue only if it had led to custodial death or visible injury. Otherwise, torture was discussed in general terms in police reports and judicial cases.[96] In the National Crimes Research Bureau (NCRB) reports, all custodial deaths were explained away and attributed to "illness/natural deaths, suicides, accidents, escapes from custody, fights, accidents and journey for investigation and treatment."[97] Although a few cases were acknowledged elsewhere in the reports, torture did not appear on the list of explanations. A notable change to the NCRB table in 2015 included injuries sustained from physical assault, but the numbers remained low: nine in 2014 and six in 2015,[98] and state officials continued to claim that torture is alien to Indian culture.[99]

Debates about truth machines in policing could, in this context, break the silence on torture and third-degree interrogation, as these techniques were introduced, ostensibly, to replace them. State officials did explicitly make such claims. Therefore, in my interviews about truth machines, I found both police officials and forensic psychologists willing, even eager, to discuss custodial interrogations and expand on the pragmatic logic of the third degree. Notably, however, my attempts to interview the same people about torture prevention (for another project) were met with resistance and unwillingness to share contacts, perhaps because even as a "public secret" torture raised questions of legitimacy and liability.[100] As Michael Taussig explains, public secrecy points to how "the information about the act is shared yet repressed such that it 'is generally known, but cannot be articulated.'"[101] Nitya Ramakrishnan further explains public secrecy in South Asia: "The trick to the public secret is in knowing what not to know. This is the most powerful form of social knowledge."[102]

Recent ethnographies of police suggest that respondents do not necessarily deny the use of torture.[103] In many of these studies, police responding to ethnographers expressed a need to explain their use of torture, suggesting that its use was exceptional, even for them. An important distinction, however, counterposes routine torture and torture stemming from a desire for justice and order in an inefficient system. A general acceptance of torture and third-degree interrogation thus differs from a defense of such methods in specific high-profile cases. Routine torture remains illegal and so is difficult to defend. It may become visible only in the process of its replacement.

Truth in a legal sense may not be accessible through the deployment of truth machines, but discourse about these techniques can reveal the dynamics of custodial interrogation. Because these methods were seen as scientific, legitimate, and professional, the police readily explained their logic of operation during my interviews. Three themes mark the pragmatic logic of applying the third degree in investigations: duration of custody, distrust of police, and recovery. Here, perhaps my most important departure from previous scholarship (that focus on ideological reasons and/or colonial continuity) is that these are reasons that are internal to police functioning, and they are linked to the original meaning of the third degree that of questioning. The pragmatic logic of third-degree interrogation is thus an articulation of the internal structural contingencies affecting police violence.

According to police accounts, one of the major reasons to turn to third-degree interrogation is the duration of custody. Under the CrPC, the Indian police are supposed to bring a suspect in front of a magistrate within twenty-four hours. Unless the suspect gets bail or an exceptional reason requires continuing police remand, the suspect is then sent to judicial custody.[104] As a police officer based in Ahmedabad pointed out, this short time frame makes the duration of custody crucial for conducting an interrogation:

> Now, in the Indian system what happens is, once you arrest someone . . . And within 24 hours of his arrest, maximum, he has to be produced before a court. . . . So after his arrest the police is expected to complete the investigation, his interrogation within a period of 24 hours. And that 24-hours window is very odd because if you arrest someone this evening or in the night, then . . . the court wouldn't be functioning till around afternoon by and large, and courts also dislike the accused being brought in late or at odd hours. . . . So practically they would get 12, 13, 14, 15 hours with the accused. . . . For investigation you get hardly 3, 4 hours with the accused before he's produced. So these are the things which make it difficult for the police to go by the rule book. So as to those 3 hours, they would rather choose to resort to third degree or abuse and try and get the things out of him under the presumption that next day once he's produced, they are not going to obtain his custody, . . . and once he goes to the judicial custody then he won't speak anything.[105]

Following rules thus poses difficulties that mediate the process of interrogation.

The NPC report similarly attributed shortcut methods of interrogation to the brief period allowed in police custody, as police sought quick confessions or requested further remand to recover stolen materials.[106] As a senior Delhi-based official explained:

> See, torture is taking place essentially for two things in police. One is to extract information; another is to extract money; . . . people also are afraid of that they might be subjected to that kind of routine, so they've been parting money. . . . At least the information part will go immediately [if torture disappears]. And once this need for torture will go, need means perceived need. . . . I honestly feel torture is useless.[107]

In the absence of a change to the provision regarding duration of custody, requests for narcoanalysis or brain scans can become another delaying tactic to extend the period of custody. That may be a principal reason for the increasing number of requests for these techniques, although in practice, very few labs are equipped to conduct them and they now require the consent of the accused.[108] The pressure to deliver results quickly, within the duration of custody, is thus mentioned as a common reason for turning to the third degree.

The second major reason for using third-degree interrogation that was cited by police during my interviews was distrust of their profession. As a police officer in Hyderabad pointed out, whereas CrPC allows for "the constable . . . to investigate and arrest even the president of this country," the system is based on "distrust," because a statement "before a police officer has no evidentiary value, as it reflects a system designed for perpetuation of colonial power."[109] Indeed, one of the police officials I interviewed made the United States a constant point of comparison and suggested that "whereas in a Western country, the accused makes a statement, he signs it. It is verified. If it is found to be untrue, you go back to him and say, 'Look, man, you are telling a lie.' And if it is true, well, it is used."[110]

These accounts of police officers might be understood as justifications for torture or third-degree interrogation. A caution, however, appears in Upendra Baxi's famous essay on torture, where he poses a need to address a lack of trust in the police in recording confessions: "Paradoxically, this very attempt to protect the dignity of the accused tends to create a situation of loss of dignity for the police profession, real or apperceived."[111] Some police officials do indeed connect distrust directly with accountability. For example, the draft antitorture bill, as revised in 2010, appeared to attribute responsibility for torture not just to those who commit it but also to those in charge.[112] One official I interviewed stated that the bill was too harsh because

> in India, the version of the police is not believed in courts of law; . . . whatever admissions are made before the police are not admissible in the courts of law. If that is the situation, if you bring the antitorture bill also, it is very difficult for the police to function. And in that case our only humble request would be to make police versions acceptable in the courts.[113]

When asked how making police testimony admissible would ensure accountability, this official responded, "Well, antitorture bill brings in that accountability. I'm accountable if I do. . . . You do some mischief in investigation or something, use third degree or do some hanky-panky in investigation, I'm accountable for it."[114]

The theme of distrust was prominent among my respondents. A Delhi-based police officer predicated trust and accountability on independence:

> See, if you trust the police, then you have to, at the same time you'll have to take the necessary steps which go along with the trust. You cannot trust somebody who's dependent on others. If you trust the police the way they are now, only under the thumb of politicians, and if you trust them, there will be havoc in society. So if you really want to trust them, you have to make them independent.... But along with the trust, they should be given the independence so that they're independently accountable for whatever they are doing. Then they cannot say, "I got an order from this quarter," or that thing, or this and that.[115]

Trust, accountability, and independence from political control are linked in this narrative, which emphasizes the risk of retaliation and political pressure, even for high-ranking officers.[116] These police officers clearly convey their experience with both lack of trust and incentives to use third-degree interrogation, despite recognizing that anything suspects say in their interaction is inadmissible in court. Their accounts thus present a contradiction: if they perceive (or know) that they are not trusted and cannot use the statements they gain in custody, why use torture?

A third theme that emerged from my interviews—recovery—addresses this question. Torture in India is used in a range of cases, from terrorism and murder to theft, even though confessions and evidence acquired under torture are inadmissible in court and policy prevents police from legally recording confessions (a remnant of colonial practice that has often been a sore point for the Indian police).[117] Yet Section 27 of the Indian Evidence Act allows material discovered as a result of a confession, along with the part of the confession that led to its discovery, to be admissible. A senior police official based in Mumbai expressed a sentiment echoed by many other police officials:

> Now, here a case has come to you of theft, all right. Now I cannot say that "My lord, here is the thief. He has admitted before me." The court is not going to accept that, all right. What the court will accept is, if that man says that, "Look here, I will show you where I have disposed or hidden that property." ... The law itself is saying that, "Look here, I'm not going to believe you unless you produce this" and that "produce this" is not going to come voluntarily. The law also knows. I also know. The judge also knows that no recovery, no discovery of fact as is known in the legal parlance, can take place voluntarily.[118]

One primary incentive for torture in extremely routine cases, therefore, appears to be recovery of evidence. As another police official said, "Courts don't insist on recovery, but recovery does ensure culpability."[119]

In my interviews, theft and property offenses are the main categories of crime to which third-degree interrogation is attributed in routine cases. As one officer noted, "Unless the accused tells us, we cannot go ahead with it."[120] This officer did claim that other methods, such as call detail analysis, help provide evidence, but, ultimately, recovered property is most often used to confront the accused. As the Hyderabad-based police officer explained, when the conviction rate in criminal cases is so low, success depends on recovery rates.[121] A Bangalore-based police official elaborated: "If some person comes and gives a complaint of theft, . . . a lot of tricks are there by the police to find out. Nearly we succeed, only 80–90% we succeed in [getting] the truth of the accused, and we will get the properties."[122]

Ensuring recovery thus becomes a priority. Indeed, states' rates of property recovery are mentioned separately by the National Crime Research Bureau, and even some stories in the media point directly to states boasting about their lead in recovering property.[123] At least two police officials speculated that this trend would stop only if the Indian population, especially the rich and powerful who exert pressure, could insure their property so that they were not dependent on police recovery.[124] My interviews, however, also revealed a lack of police training in interrogation, so much so that the National Police Academy lacked an interrogation module until the 1990s.[125] Police accounts thus reveal the pragmatic logic of third-degree interrogation, which has otherwise been linked to a normalization of torture and receives close scrutiny only in cases of custodial death or "severe" torture.

Reform initiatives have recognized some police concerns and have recommended changes. For instance, both the NPC and the Malimath Committee suggested that the police should be allowed extended custody and that senior police should be permitted to record confessions.[126] Acknowledging the colonial origins of regulations and risk of continued malpractice, the NPC report noted that society had changed to encompass a vigilant media, a citizenry aware of rights, and the possibility of constant supervision by higher officials and magistrates. The report further noted that recording confessions was allowed for income tax and railway officers, causing a lack of parity among officers, and suggested a change to these provisions because they challenged the "image and prestige" of the police when a "large village community" learned later that even a voluntary confession in front of the police was not accepted by the court.

The NPC report thus recommended a change to the rules, allowing confessions as supplementary evidence to "largely remove the present feeling of the police that they have been unjustly discriminated against in law."[127] The Malimath Committee reiterated the theme of trust, noting that, whereas the police are the "foundation of the Criminal Justice System, . . . [the system] does not trust the Police."[128] These recommendations, however, ignore reality: "police remand" is a metaphor for torture.[129] The recurring reliance on supervisory officers or even magistrates is also surprising, because they are recognized for approving torture (see chapter 6).[130] As Pratiksha Baxi argues persuasively in her study of rape trials, state discourse on trusting Indian police to record statements and confessions fails to acknowledge how "police documents are written and how police documents can inspire trust."[131] The state also fails to recognize that often the "practical operations of power . . . actualize corruption, political pressure by powerful offenders, and systemic bias."[132]

Acknowledging the pragmatic logic of third-degree interrogation, therefore, need not lead to acceptance of all the recommendations for police reform or even to remove the constraints on them. Rather, reports and officers' narratives show that torture is justified not by any external, higher purpose or colonial continuity but by the conditions that produce it. Police logic in custody cases thus counters both an ideological and a unitary, bureaucratic understanding of violence and instead forces us to confront the structural contingencies that inform the pragmatic logic of third-degree interrogation. Discussions of the reform discussions and the police experiences from their everyday operations indicate a need for developing theoretical frameworks that acknowledge the impact of these structural contingencies, which is the subject of the concluding section.

THEORIZING POLICING AND VIOLENCE

Scholars such as Beatrice Jauregui and Santana Khanikar have recently focused on legitimacy and the Indian police.[133] In her provocative book *Provisional Authority*, Jauregui contends that the Indian police lack the legitimacy sometimes attributed to them and that their provisional authority is instead "questionable, negotiable, and inconsistent."[134] She points to how "culturally based notions of the authority embodied in familial elders . . . configures relations between the police and the public, throwing into question the true sources and capabilities of state legal authority."[135] The police, she suggests, may at times be "situationally hyperempowered," but they are "structurally disempowered" by many cultural and political forces.[136] Khanikar notes that police enjoy legitimacy despite the violence that they routinely inflict on people due to their everyday interaction with people's lives.[137] Upendra Baxi, while recognizing India's "colonial-repressive police organization," deems the country's police repression possible only because of "colonial-repressive political regimes."[138] He declares the subordinate police the most "vulnerable, exploited and neglected minority group in the nation," calling them a "despised minority" for good reason. Yet he also recognizes that the police have been deprived of basic rights, with inadequate wages, amenities, and conditions and with senior officials facing political pressure and arbitrary transfers that limit their power.[139] These institutional constraints appear as well in my interviews, although their effects on the use of violence in policing may differentially affect police officers in different hierarchical positions.

Institutional constraints, however, need not challenge the police monopoly over legitimate violence in custody cases. Both torture and custodial deaths during investigations remain unabated. Nonetheless, a number of reform efforts do recognize the use of third-degree interrogation, acknowledge its pragmatic logic, and reveal difficulties in police use of violence. Measures to mediate repression include the introduction of truth machines and the emergence of the human rights movement. Institutionalized in India in the 1990s with human rights discourse, the Human Rights Act of 1993 established the National Human Rights Commission and led to a number of Supreme Court cases on custodial deaths and torture, among them the *D. K. Basu* case.[140]

The advent of truth machines coincides with these developments. The retired police officer from Coorg whom I interviewed linked the human rights movement with narcoanalysis.[141] A police officer in a training academy similarly connected the human rights movement, the NHRC reports, and the *D. K. Basu* case; these, he believed, collectively made the police much more nervous about deaths in custody. "His [the suspect's] safety is in your custody," this officer noted. "You don't want him to die, so you take care of him, your brother. . . . You are scared of death."[142] The pastoral role in policing thus emerges alongside the repressive.

An ideologically driven framing of policing that justifies violence in the service of public welfare or explains it as a continuation of colonial practice fails to capture this convergence. Rather than a loss of legitimacy, a willingness to give up torture, or its justification for a greater purpose, violence in police custody reflects the pragmatic logic of torture and third-degree interrogation. The police thus involve semi-state actors, in the form of forensic psychologists, to extend custody, gain trust, and participate in generating information for recovery, all in an effort to address the structural contingencies that constrain them.

Their repressive and pastoral roles are both important here. The new police science points to the pastoral in community-related work; others point to the repressive in pursuit of justice or social order. The pastoral, however, need not challenge police control over violence. Ensuring the safety and security of individuals in custody need not stem from a concern for human dignity (although individual police officers may harbor such concerns) but may instead stem from a utilitarian need, first for productive information and then to escape liability. Dubber's analogy between police power and the patriarchal household may explain the transition to less brutal methods of interrogation.[143] For Dubber, a patriarch, historically, had failed if he used so much brutal power that he rendered his household labor useless. Given the scrutiny of custodial death in police and judicial custody in India, individual police officers may thus want to share custody with forensic psychologists and laboratories in order to prevent custodial death and to protect a suspect's utility for producing information.

Dubber's model explains the relationship of the police to violence with a concept of constraint limited to "malice"—that is, police who apply more than a proportionate degree of force are equivalent to the master who loses his right over the household. Historically, Dubber elaborates:

> the householder worthy of his title enjoyed virtually unlimited discretion in his use of disciplinary measures; the unfit, however, were stripped of their authority.... The householder who acts out of malice has revealed himself to be merely mean. As a mean person, he is unworthy of the elevated position of the householder, unworthy of respect, and unworthy of disciplinary authority. As a mean person he deserves to be disciplined, rather than to discipline.[144]

Proportionality, for Dubber, constitutes an internal limit on the powers of the police: "So an excess of violence and correction that is manifestly excessive and disproportionate to the fault is said to exceed the bounds of police."[145] The Indian police must avoid causing custodial death, which exceeds the threshold of violence that the state can defend, especially in routine cases.

To gain information and prevent custodial deaths to the extent possible, the Indian police play an ostensibly pastoral role. If the number of deaths in police custody, reported by the National Crimes Research Bureau, or if the number of deaths in police or judicial custody does not appear to be extremely high in proportion to the population, the measure underscores, in its dark recesses, the pastoral police function that may have prevented some cases. Together, therefore, the pastoral and repressive represent the relationship of the police to violence. Decisions to send someone into the custody of forensic psychologists, even just to delay an investigation, not only reflect structural contingencies or the pragmatic logic of the third degree but also become manifestations of the pastoral role of the police. The discretion of one officer, then, is part of the structural contingency in which all police must find ways to avoid custodial deaths, sometimes successfully, sometimes not.

CONCLUSION

In this chapter I address two themes: the everyday functioning of the police—a visible site of state power that challenges its rational, rule-based functioning—and the relationship of the police to violence. An analysis of the police, as state actors, and forensic psychologists, as semi-state actors, suggests more contingency than theories of policing as either an ideological institution or a unitary, bureaucratic body allow. Drawing from interviews and from reports on police reform, I reveal the pragmatic logic of this contingency, evident as officials seek access to truth and information. Rather than defend torture and third-degree interrogation as required for justice, social order, or efficiency, officials decry torture in cases of custody that can lead to custodial death. The police thus assume a pastoral role that mitigates their repressive role.

Chapter 3

TRANSNATIONAL BORROWINGS, SCIENTIFIC CONTESTATIONS, AND CULTURAL PRODUCTIONS

> No such magic brew as the popular notion of truth serum exists.
> —CIA REPORT, 1961

Immediately after the 9/11 attacks, the U.S. media reported that one of the methods considered for interrogating suspects was truth serum. Indeed, two widely quoted articles, one by scholar Alan Dershowitz and the other by journalist Jonathan Alter, specifically mentioned truth serum.[1] Reporting was sporadic but led to a debate among legal scholars about the constitutionality of using narcoanalysis in investigating alleged terrorists.[2] Evidence of drugs used to control and treat detainees also surfaced, amid allegations of their use for interrogations, suggesting that drugs were part of the repertoire of the post-9/11 regime.[3]

As I conducted interviews in India, forensic psychologists confidently asserted that narcoanalysis was used in "your U.S." and insisted that its use had continued after 9/11. "It was used on Saddam Hussain as well," respondents confidently told me. I heard these arguments in Gandhinagar (Gujarat), Mumbai (Maharashtra), and Bangalore (Karnataka), where laboratories were known to have used narcoanalysis. These conversations prompted me to check with the human rights activists and scholars most closely following the U.S. torture debate. Through a torture Listserv, I confirmed the lack of evidence for use of truth serums, although a CIA report that surfaced in November 2018 indicated that the agency had considered drugs for interrogation but had ultimately decided against them.[4]

The second season of the popular U.S. TV show *Making a Murderer*, based on the *Steven Avery* case, features brain fingerprinting (BFP). Avery was convicted of the murder of Teresa Helbach, and his postconviction relief petition includes an affidavit from BFP founder Lawrence Farwell presenting evidence of Avery's innocence.[5] Researchers in India associated with both BFP and brain electrical oscillation signature (BEOS) tout their success in solving murder cases.[6] Polygraphs, or lie detectors, also continue to appear in important cases, among them the 1984 Sikh killings case in India, the *Adnan Syed* case in the United States, and, most recently, in the Brett Kavanaugh U.S. Senate hearings.[7]

Despite widespread reporting in the 2000s about these techniques—whether rumor or reality—their scientific validity remains refuted and their results legally inadmissible. Scientific and legal debates are thus distinct from their origin stories and popular representation, which continue to show truth found in the body.

Narcoanalysis, brain tests, and lie detectors originated in the United States and promised to revolutionize the criminal justice system by offering more humane methods than physical torture and third-degree interrogation to extract information. Eventually, however, these new techniques were either rejected (as with narcoanalysis in the United States) or met with legal skepticism (as with polygraph and brain tests in the United States and India and narcoanalysis in India). Scientific claims from experts and the courts, however, played only a marginal role in the wider understanding of these techniques. Instead, the confluence of media, law enforcement, and commercial interests constituted the cultural production of truth machines.

Cultural production establishes an edifice based on a "spectacle of science,"[8] but it is usually sustained by those who seek to use science for forensic or commercial purposes. Truth machines thus appear and reappear in different forms, never disappearing despite long-standing challenges to their scientific and legal validity. Their persistence reflects the quest for truth, however elusive. Truth machines appear to apply science to replace torture, yet, like torture, they posit that the body can betray the conscious will and reveal the truth. The validity of their results, therefore, depends on law, culture, and society.

LYING, TRUTH TELLING, AND THE BODY

The challenge of extracting truth from a lying body has long been a legal and political concern. Indeed, the history of torture is marked by fire, the wheel, the rack, and the torture chamber, all linked by the desire to extract truth from a body. As Page duBois notes, the ancient Athenians tortured slaves in part because they believed that "truth resides in the slave body."[9] Slaves, according to Aristotle, can apprehend but not possess reason; hence their bodies had to be tortured to reveal the truth.[10] In *Discipline and Punish*, Michel Foucault argues that torture in France from the fifteenth to the eighteenth century had to be spectacular, because its terror could both enshrine the power of the sovereign and deter the people from crime.[11] Judicial torture, according to Foucault, was also central to truth production in legal proceedings: "The search for truth through judicial torture was certainly a way of obtaining evidence—the most serious of all the confession of the guilty person; but it was also a battle, and this victory of one adversary over the other, that 'produced' truth according to a ritual."[12]

Over time, of course, the spectacle of torture was delinked from executions and judicial systems. Its traces remained, however, with an emphasis on disciplining the body, even as the soul became prominent as well. This shift is explained in a variety of ways: the humanitarian concerns of Enlightenment philosophers, such as Beccaria and Voltaire; the early influence of human rights;[13] changing conceptions of pain;[14] and, famously, the transformation in legal requirements.[15] New forms of torture—psychological and non-scarring/clean/stealth torture, as Darius Rejali explains[16]—still required a body as an object of focus and a docile subject. Science and experts thus became prominent, though without necessarily challenging the body's differential construction and the targeting of marginalized people: slaves, women, minorities, and colonial subjects.[17] And despite all evidence that torture never works, rationales for the extraction of truth from the body were extralegal—religious, social, or cultural.[18] Information may not be the sole purpose of torture, but it has often been the motive.[19]

As narratives of abolition of torture emerged in the West, colonial strategies outside the West provide insights into the differential constitution of bodies. "Uncivilized" colonial bodies, socially and racially produced, were assumed to be prone to lying.[20] The colonial "rule of difference," which Partha Chatterjee theorizes, thus plays a central role in determining the relationship between the colonial powers and the colonized.[21] Elizabeth Kolsky traces views of "Indian human nature" as inherently deceptive and therefore a constant source of British anxiety. She points to the British perception of a "notorious disregard for truth" among Indians, which mediated legal codes in the late nineteenth century and in the use of scientific evidence in criminal trials in India.[22] Oaths, affirmations, and solemn declarations were deemed inadequate for discovering truth, so experts had to glean evidence from the bodies themselves. As Kolsky explains, citing Norman Chevers, the authority on medical jurisprudence in India, "For Chevers, Indians and their inherent deceitfulness were the biggest obstacles to the fair and impartial administration of colonial justice."[23]

Kolsky analyzes a number of cases concerned with white violence—for example, planters beating Indians, often to death, for minor infractions such as a delayed response to a summons. Because Indians were defined as "pathologically untrustworthy," she writes, colonial medical experts provided the "truth," primarily to let the whites off. Deaths were commonly attributed to a characteristic "diseased spleen," leading to the classic "spleen defense" and only petty fines or minimal punishment for whites. As these cases indicate, the "particular circumstances of the colony were deemed to demand special legislation that departed from contemporary legal rules and practices in England."[24] Scientific evidence thus had to be interpreted by experts and based on an ethnological understanding of native bodies and culture.

According to the colonial framework, raped women lied, as did natives more generally. As Pratiksha Baxi explains, "Native women who complained of rape bore a double burden, suspected as liars being women, and presumed to be untrustworthy being native."[25] Kolsky notes a further irony: civilizational discourse is based on the understanding that brown women needed saving from brown men, yet the "brown" and "women" could not be believed to be telling the truth. The consequence of this double burden on women meant that rape cases in the colonial period routinely dismissed women by relying on class and caste considerations, previous sexual history, delays in filing complaints, and demands for evidence of "violent resistance and physical injury," which considerably enhanced the role of doctors and experts.[26]

Baxi discusses the origins of the two-finger test, its continued use in the postcolonial period, and the medicalization of falsity and consent premised on native women's propensity to lie. The women's movement in India, she notes, led to a change in the standards of evidence such that after the 1980s, character and sexual history were no longer admissible at trial. Yet evidence from the two-finger test, medicalization of falsity, and self-inflicted injury continue to introduce a victim's personal history:

> In other words, the medico-legal certificate issued after a medical examination of the victim becomes a means for a defence lawyer to bring in past sexual history, now no longer permissible in the law, during the trial. The characterization of a woman as a *habitué* or as "habituated," which we routinely come across in appellate judgments, is used to transform a testimony of rape into a statement of consensual sex.[27]

Science and experts thus reproduce a fabricated social truth. Women in Britain historically faced similar disbelief in cases of rape, although without the double burden of colonized subjects.[28]

Of course, the assumption of a lying body is not restricted to women or to a colonial history. For instance, the lie detector in the United States has been closely associated with the conception of the lying woman or a lying Black man, and fingerprinting is associated with a lying immigrant.[29] Chronicling the history of the lie detector, Geoffrey Bunn notes that deceptiveness has been linked more directly to women, almost as if women had "a physiological incapacity for truth telling and were thought to be habitual liars."[30] Furthermore, he writes, their emotions were believed hidden, requiring instruments to access their "invisible" criminality. Presumed criminality and lack of credibility were also applied to Blacks subjected to the lie detector.[31] Similarly, the "perceived need to identify 'faceless,' racially unfamiliar hordes of people who came in successive waves to the shores" led to the popularity of fingerprinting in the United States, just as a similar impulse to distinguish among the natives led to the initial use of anthropometry and later to fingerprinting in India.[32]

All kinds of forensic evidence could be linked to truth production, with claims to expertise and scientific innovation, often racially and socially produced. But these three techniques that I term the truth machines—narcoanalysis, brain tests, and lie detectors—rely on words or brain signals as the source of information and depend on a person's conscious ability to speak or withhold the truth. In contrast, fingerprinting, serology, and DNA analysis read imprints of the body, whether successfully or not. Truth machines, therefore, represent continuity with classical forms of torture, now mediated by science and expertise with its emphasis on a person's will to lie. All three techniques enable a machine or a drug to force a person to speak the truth, through physiological/autonomic indicators (polygraph), by inhibiting conscious will (narcoanalysis), or bypassing speech and directly reading brain signals (brain tests).

As Melissa Littlefield notes, a basic assumption underlying lie detection is based on Hugo Munsterberg's idea that "the hidden feeling betrays itself."[33] This betrayal occurs in a sequence: the autonomic indicators suggest lying, the brain tests signify pertinent information about involvement, and narcoanalysis forces the body to betray the information in words. The origin stories of these techniques can thus reveal the innovative claims of scientific experts, along with the techniques these innovations ostensibly replaced. Specific individuals were involved in the origins of narcoanalysis, polygraphs, and brain tests. All three techniques, however, quickly became linked to the needs of the law enforcement community, and the spectacle of their scientific origins resonated in both law and criminal justice. This overemphasis on science and innovation is, of course, belied by the contested utility of these techniques and by the overpowering role of nonscientific factors in their continuation and resurgence.

ORIGIN STORIES: TRUTH SERUMS, POLYGRAPHS, AND BRAIN TESTS

Narcoanalysis

The drug scopolamine was a German invention. It was considered useful because it was effective in erasing the memory of pain (or pain itself) during labor.[34] Historically, therefore, narcoanalysis has principally involved barbiturates such as scopolamine, Sodium Pentothal, sodium thiopental, hyoscine, and Amytal Sodium. The history of narcoanalysis in the United States is closely related to both Dr. Robert E. House, who discovered its properties and its potential to transform police interrogation, and to media fascination with his attempt to popularize the technique. House, who worked as an obstetrician in Texas, noticed that the drug could put his patients into a "twilight sleep," in which they were deeply unconscious but susceptible to answering questions.

The idea for a "truth serum" came from an incident in 1916. As the famous story goes, one of House's patients could identify the precise location of the scales to weigh her baby, even when in a scopolamine-induced sleep. Following this observation, House sought to determine whether the drug could promote accurate answers to any question asked of someone in this twilight state.[35] Under the auspices of a district attorney, sheriff, and grand jury, he experimented with the drug in the Dallas County Jail in 1922, on two convicted men: William Scrivenor, who was serving fifteen years for a robbery, and Ed Smith, who was convicted of murder. Scrivenor was given scopolamine three times, along with morphine and chloroform at different times, until he clearly had no memory left. Under the drugs' influence, he denied his guilt, and subsequent information from a DA seemed to confirm his innocence. Ed Smith's conviction was also found to be a case of mistaken identity, and charges were dropped.

As House explained the drug, "Scopolamine will depress the cerebrum to such a degree as to destroy the power of reasoning. Events stored in the cerebrum as memory can be obtained by direct stimulation of the centers of hearing."[36] In his account, the drug was meant to communicate directly with the centers of hearing such that the person simply answered the questions heard, without conscious mental processing or the possibility of lying. House named the stage between injecting the drug and the suspect's becoming unconsciousness the receptive stage. "When the will and the power to reason are nonexistent," he elaborated, "then man is too unconscious and too helpless to protect himself by inventing replies to questions propounded."[37]

When asked about his experience with the drug, Scrivenor declared, "Answers to questions slipped from my mind without any apparent desire to stop them... and I felt that I couldn't formulate any imaginative trimmings to them." Scrivenor claimed that he had been able to "distinctly hear the questions being asked, and having no ability to do anything else, I answered them truthfully, knowing that I was telling the truth, and that it was impossible to do otherwise."[38] Alison Winter considers this trial a key moment, when the amnesiac properties of the drug shifted to "retrieve memories."[39] Yet she also identifies a contradiction: Scrivenor's experience appeared to strengthen House's claim about the possible use of the drug, but the drug was also supposed to have disabled the conscious mind, and Scrivenor *knew* he could not lie. A constructivist notion of memory, Winter further notes, would also challenge assumptions, including distinctions between long- and short-term memory.[40]

Between 1922 (the year of the first test) and 1930 (the year House died), regular newspaper reports created much stir about truth serum in both the medical and the legal communities and in the popular discourse. The successful use of scopolomine in these two Texas cases thus generated a halo of success for the drug. The DA even claimed, "If the scopolamine experiments are as successful as they appear to be, it would be the biggest medico-legal discovery since the application of the X-Ray or the use of finger prints. It is virtually a *painless third degree* which will make useless unlawful brutal methods sometimes employed to extort confessions."[41] The optimism was indeed so great that the DA went on to state, "Administration of public justice will be advanced 100 years if 'truth serum' is successful."[42]

Mentioning both lie detectors and truth serums, a number of newspaper articles refer to replacement of third-degree interrogation by "humane" or "gentler" methods.[43] The 1920s also saw much attention focused on the prevalence of the third degree in many states as well as in cities, as the Wickersham Commission, appointed by President Herbert Hoover in 1929, was soon to expose.[44] Newspaper articles in the 1920s routinely termed narcoanalysis a "painless third degree" that was a "new challenger" to the "fistic third degree employed throughout the Anglo-Saxon world, and the torture rack of the Orient."[45] Truth serum was thus "powerfully represented as a sophisticated, scientific, and nonviolent alternative to unsavory police methods,"[46] a more humane and gentler third degree, compared to more physical and mental forms of interrogation then routinely used. The physical methods, in turn, were slowly rejected by the courts, notably in *Brown v. Mississippi* (1936).[47]

Despite concerns that truth serum was a milder form of torture (though without an explanation), House saw it as a way to deal with the problems of the criminal justice system.[48] The "rights of society are greater than those of the criminal," he reportedly said, so "it therefore stands to reason, that where there is a safe and humane method existing to evoke the truth from the consciousness of a suspect society is entitled to have the truth."[49] Just the threat of narcoanalysis was, for some commentators, deemed adequate: "It would accomplish more than any other type of 'third degree' in obtaining confessions, for the reason also that many would prefer to confess than take the medicine; the drug would serve as a positive check and a 'club.'"[50] The drug's popularity thus coincided with a need for both the police and society at large to appear more humane.

After the trial cases in Dallas, House continued to be in the news. In 1923 he engaged in experiments on the West Coast of the United States. In his presentation at the American Medical Association meeting held in San Francisco, he illustrated the use of scopolamine at the San Quentin prison, where a number of prisoners revealed new information ranging from one prisoner's identity to confessions of murders and robberies.[51] Conducting many such experiments all over the United States,[52] House claimed that he did not have a single failure in five hundred cases.[53] Many prisoners took the initiative and asked for the drug, under which they occasionally confessed to a crime but often reiterated their innocence.[54] House would then be quoted in newspapers claiming, for example, "An innocent man is serving a term in the Oklahoma penitentiary."[55] In the 1920s, therefore, the drug seemed to have taken society by storm, gaining House and narcoanalysis acceptability.

Polygraph

As narcoanalysis became popular in the United States, another technique addressing some of the same concerns for law enforcement was also widely debated. A polygraph usually includes an instrument that records physiological responses: respiration, heart rate, blood pressure, and electrodermal activity.[56] To participate in a polygraph test, an individual sits on a chair and is connected to wires that record physiological responses. These are then interpreted by an examiner. A polygraph is used in multiple ways: some examiners use the relevant/irrelevant technique, others use the guilty knowledge test, and still others use the control questions test.

With the relevant/irrelevant technique, the examiner asks "relevant" questions directly related to the crime along with others that are unrelated and hence irrelevant. A physiological response to the relevant questions indicates deception.[57] The guilty knowledge test refers to questions based on knowledge that only the investigators or a person involved in the crime would have, and a greater physiological response to this knowledge indicates deception. The control question technique involves asking questions that normally cause an anxious response in anyone (for example, Did you steal something?), together with questions relevant to the crime, which generate a stronger response in a deceptive person.[58] In each technique, examiners conduct the test and often interpret the results manually.

Chronicling the social history of the lie detector, Bunn notes that the machine's origins in the United States stem from several people and detection instruments. Tracing their creation from the 1860s to the 1880s, he identifies the emerging popularity of the machine from 1920 to 1950.[59] Psychologists and scientists as well as novelists and journalists contributed to its use, but four central figures developed, promoted, or enabled the use of lie detectors in law enforcement: John A. Larson, a professor at the University of California, Berkeley, who served as an expert for the Berkeley Police Department; inventor Leonarde Keeler, Larson's student and protégé; August Vollmer, the area's chief of police; and William Moulton Marston, a Harvard-educated psychologist based on the East Coast. Although a single polygraph inventor is a "myth," Bunn suggests, "invention has nevertheless played a constructive role throughout the instrument's history."[60]

Over time, Keeler became prominent for his work in the Scientific Crime Detection Laboratory at Northwestern University, where he filed a patent for the Keeler polygraph and started a school for examiners using lie detectors. Marston became known for his creation of Wonder Woman, whose lasso of truth represented a version of the lie detector. Vollmer, known for his efforts to professionalize the police, tried to systematize the use of lie detectors in law enforcement. As Ken Alder notes, police chief Vollmer's encouraging Larson to use the lie detector was an important move away from police brutality and third-degree interrogation.[61] Indeed Vollmer referred to the lie detector as "a modified, simplified, and humane third degree."[62] The lie detector even emerged in 1931 as one solution to the findings of the Wickersham Commission, since Vollmer was associated with the commission.[63]

Emphasizing these individuals, Bunn argues, "In the case of the lie detector, charismatic authority was intimately tied to the myth of invention that was in turn the source of the machine's mystique and power."[64] The lie detector, however, also found acceptance in popular culture, as Bunn elaborates:

> For the scientists the aim was to uncover the correlates of criminality within the criminal self, to assess the depth of depravity with a view to treating it. . . . To a considerable extent, the lie detector was an invention of those fiction writers for whom the key issue was simply the presence or absence of guilt within one individual among many. . . . It materialized not from the laboratory but from the story.[65]

Bunn mentions a number of detectives in magazines and pulp fiction that helped to establish the lie detector, such as Luther Trant (created by Chicago journalists Edwin Balmer and William MacHarg).[66] The origin story of the polygraph thus has as much to do with charismatic individuals as well as the fascination of novelists and journalists.

Brain Scanning

Suspicion of the polygraph's reliability, together with breakthroughs in neuroscience and brain research, led to the emergence of new techniques related to reading the brain. Three brain-scanning methods appeared in public and legal discourse from the 1980s and 1990s: functional magnetic resonance imaging (fMRI), brain fingerprinting (BFP), and the brain electrical oscillation signature (BEOS) test. BFP and BEOS have been significant in India, where discussion of these techniques has been connected to experts who have generated research results and occasionally have commercial interests in the instrument's success. Perhaps the broad stakes in the global market in an era of pathbreaking neuroscience research makes such endeavors attractive.

fMRI focuses on brain functioning and captures "the difference between oxygenated and nonoxygenated blood cells due to their magnetic charges, so more active neurons can be distinguished from less active ones."[67] The instrument helps in analyzing conditions such as Alzheimer's and schizophrenia, and some scientists have claimed its utility for detecting deception. Daniel Langleben, among others, argues that when a person is given a task, the fMRI can differentiate between oxygenated and deoxygenated blood, producing a blood-oxygenated-level-dependent (BOLD) effect, which indicates neuronal activity. At least two companies, Cephos and NOLie MRI, tried to convince U.S. courts to accept the results of fMRI. With little verification of validity, however, Langleben and others remained wary of advocating its use for forensic purposes, despite the companies' aggressive marketing.[68]

Lawrence Farwell is most closely associated with BFP, including promotion of its legal and commercial use. The term owes its name to fingerprinting evidence and to DNA matches of an individual to biological samples from a crime scene. As Farwell and his colleagues explain, "'Brain fingerprinting' matches information stored in the brain of the suspect with information from the crime scene."[69] The technique requires investigators to give all relevant information to the examiners, who then divide it into target and probe stimuli. Target stimuli are based on information revealed to the person during interrogation; probe stimuli are based on unrevealed information, known only by someone who committed the crime. Also developed are stimuli that are unconnected to the crime.[70]

To distinguish between relevant and irrelevant information, a subject wearing an electrode cap is shown a familiar stimulus, and an EEG captures the subject's brain waves. As the marketing literature on Farwell's technique explains, "If the suspect recognizes images, words, phrases, audio and videos displayed on a computer screen[,] a P-300 MERMER (Memory and Encoding Related Multifaceted Electroenchephalographic response) will occur."[71] A processor then analyzes the information and determines "information present or absent." As Farwell elaborates, "For brain fingerprinting, ground truth is whether or not the relevant information is stored in the subject's brain at the time of the test."[72] But he is careful to explain that this distinction indicates only awareness of information, not innocence or guilt: "Ground truth is not whether the subject is guilty of a crime." Guilt, however, may be confirmed during posttests.

Indian clinical psychologist C. R. Mukundan is associated with BEOS, a "technique used for the detection of the presence of knowledge of participation in any action committed in the past, in an individual."[73] Initially excited by the Farwell technique in the 1990s, Dr. Mukundan found it inadequate and in the 2000s created BEOS. Recognizing that "remembrance is not at the same speed in all individuals," he argued further that BFP merely identified a suspect's retrieval of information, which is autonomic and involuntary, rather than memory, which involves some participation. "Knowing and remembering are two neurocognitive processes," he said, "of which knowing refers to the cognitive process of recognition with or without familiarity, whereas remembrance is the recall of episodic and autobiographical details from a person's life."[74] "See, for example," a clinical psychologist elaborated,

> if you find that a person has recognized an umbrella, that umbrella which was there in the crime scene, you'll say that he's the only one who has recognized, so he's the one who has done that crime. This is too far-fetched a thing ... [or] Another subject comes, looks at that knife, and there's an increased P-300— "You know what? My grandmother had a similar knife." Not that he knows anything; his grandmother had a similar knife. So he also produces this thing, higher P-300.[75]

BEOS, like BFP, involves multiple electrodes attached to a person's head through an electrode cap. With eyes closed, the person then listens to probes meant to trigger remembrance of the event. Probes appear in a determined sequence that links different parts to provide context. As with BFP, three kinds of questions are target probes, meaning those related to the crime; control probes, related to the person's life and irrelevant to the crime; and neutral probes, which serve as baselines. Here target probes include target A, the investigator's version, and target B, the suspect's version. The dual versions are designed to ensure some neutrality.[76] The origins of BEOS are linked to the guilty knowledge test used with polygraphs, but here the suspect says nothing and all probes are auditory.

The company associated with BEOS, Axxonet (run by Chetan Mukundan, C. R. Mukundan's son), created the Neuro Signature System (NSS) to determine whether a suspect has "experiential knowledge" of participation in a crime, here termed the "signature." With NSS, recordings are done by an EEG, and analysis deems experiential knowledge present or absent. According to C. R. Mukundan, "The scores elicited by neutral probes help to view those probes from the Target section, which have elicited the most significant 'Experiential Knowledge' (EK) scores."[77] Mukundan and BEOS have been central to the implementation of this truth machine in India, where Axxonet aggressively markets the technology.

CULTURAL PRODUCTION OF TRUTH MACHINES

Early Use of Narcoanalysis in the United States

In the 1920s narcoanalysis in the United States had mixed responses from the legal and scientific communities, with the discretion of individual judges determining use of the drug. For instance, in 1923 truth serum was allowed for two Louisiana prisoners, but for three others the drug was disallowed, "because Judge Robert Ellio[,] before whom the cases were tried, [had] given specific orders that they be not experimented with in this manner."[78] In the *George Hudson* case (1926), the court clearly threw out the evidence obtained under truth serum. Hudson, a Black man, had been convicted of criminally assaulting an elderly woman who had identified him, but he claimed mistaken identity.

In this case, the results of the serum test (supported by House) had at first resulted in a mistrial but had not been introduced in a subsequent trial. When Hudson and his attorney challenged the conviction and thirty-five-year sentence using the test results, the Missouri Supreme Court called the appeal "clap-trap": "Testimony of this character is in the present state of human knowledge unworthy of serious consideration,"[79] the court stated:

> Its origin is as nebulous as its effect is uncertain. A belief in its potency, if it has any existence, is confined to the modern Cagliostros, who still, as Balsamo did of old . . . cozen the credulous for a quid pro quo, by inducing them to believe in the magic powers of philters, potions, and cures by faith. The trial court, therefore, whether it assigned a reason for its action or not, ruled correctly in excluding this clap-trap from the consideration of the jury.[80]

Law enforcement thus appears uneven, with occasional mention of courts allowing the tests, other courts rejecting the evidence, and some DAs and sheriffs dropping charges.

At times the selective use of narcoanalysis against Blacks became prominent, as it did in Alabama in 1924 with the so-called axe murders. Twenty-four people had been killed in three years, and four men and one woman, all Black, were picked up and, according to the *Chicago Defender*, subjected to third-degree interrogation and forcibly injected with truth serum.[81] Even though by then House had compared the impact of the serum to a person affected by drinking alcohol, critics argued that the truth serum negatively impacted the bodies of these suspects. The tests were used to gain confessions, and based on that, Johnson, one of the men, was actually given the death sentence.[82] In a subsequent article, the *Chicago Defender* notes that when truth serum was used against whites, they were usually let off by the law enforcement officers anticipating court skepticism.[83] Black bodies thus remained subject to experimentation, here ostensibly to see whether narcoanalysis suppressed their ability to lie.

House argued that the media had unnecessarily exaggerated his claims and expressed doubts, noting that the success of the drug depended on "experience and individuality."[84] The American Medical Association's support was required for the drug's success, but the medical community, too, remained skeptical.[85] In the 1930s and 1940s, doctors cautioned against using the drug for criminal justice purposes, a practice of using drugs then common in Britain mainly for hypnosis. "The term 'narco-analysis,'" one doctor noted, "was first devised by J. S. Horsley (1936) for the technique which utilizes a narcosis artificially induced by a barbiturate for the express purpose of facilitating the analysis of a patient's mental content."[86]

The debate among medical professionals continued, but narcoanalysis was largely deemed unsuited for legal purposes. J. F. Wilde, a psychiatric specialist, distinguished between its uses, although he thought the technique might be improved:

> No doubt, in time, this technique may be perfected so that one can be sure whether the truth is being revealed or not, and this will be a great medico-legal advance, but from the psychotherapeutic standpoint it is not so important to be sure *that the repressed material is absolutely true*. The hidden fears of the neurotic may be sheer fantasy and the wildest confabulations of imagination. They are none the less terrifying, perhaps more so than real dangers. Yet these fantasies are the phenomena with which we as therapists have to deal in helping our patients to adjust themselves to themselves and to their hidden fears.[87]

The same skepticism led others to test the veracity of truth serum induced by subjecting themselves to it, with mixed results. For instance, three members of the International Association for Identification, seeking to prove that truth serum would not really work, were pleasantly surprised to find that they apparently correctly answered all questions put to them, despite their conscious desire to lie.[88] In 1924, however, two prisoners and a newspaper reporter in St. Louis, Missouri, reported unsuccessful tests, which House attributed to the number of people (about fifty) present and the nervous condition of the subjects.[89]

After House died in July 1930, Winter suggests, the technique became used less for finding "truth" than for aggressive policing, aided by the Scientific Crime Detection Laboratory (SCDL) at Northwestern University.[90] Indeed, in one news account of Chicago law enforcement officers, SCDL was reported to be "at the service of all the law enforcement agencies."[91] By 1931, students and laboratory staff who were willing to "lend themselves to the service of science" had participated in successful drug tests at the SCDL, with claims of an 80 percent success rate with the 20 percent failure attributed to students who were not drunk enough. The effects of truth serum were thus compared to half a dozen drinks of gin.[92] As Colonel Calvin Goddard noted, however, once a suspect answers questions under the influence of truth serum, "he usually confesses after he recovers consciousness and sees the record."[93]

Studies continued at Northwestern University into the 1930s, with tests of truth serum by experts with different purposes, among them questioning in murder cases,[94] memory restoration in amnesia cases,[95] freeing persons charged with murder,[96] charging persons with murder,[97] and freeing persons suspected of robbery.[98] Use of narcoanalysis seemed to decline, however, in the 1940s and 1950s. It did emerge during the Cold War but was used less in the criminal justice system than in psychotherapy. Professionals, Darius Rejali says, had come to recognize its unreliability for interrogation.[99]

Even without courts and experts willing to accept the validity of narcoanalysis, truth serum had captured the popular imagination. Much like the polygraph, truth serum received attention in the popular press, although without necessarily engaging the medical claims made by House and others. In the 1920s, soon after its attention in the legal and medical community, a variety of articles contemplated its use in everyday contexts. Many columnists suggested that truth serum might be generally useful in society. The famous journalist Dorothy Dix, for example, wrote at least two columns about truth serum. In one, she responds to its discovery to note that its broad use would completely change the rules of polite society: "Picture an evening party with everybody standing around looking as bored as they feel," she writes, or "when Mr. Jiggs begins to sing, . . . there is a general exclamation that it is time to go home," or instead of an "amiable looking hostess . . . there is a weary woman who ejaculates from time to time, 'Thank God, this is nearly over, and when I've fed these brutes, I will have paid off the last of my dinner debts.'"[100] Dix concludes, "That serum won't do in real life. Our system wouldn't stand it."[101]

In another humorous column, Will Rogers speculates about the influence of truth serum on Hollywood stars, who would be forced to tell their real salaries; female stars, who would remember their maiden names; and politicians in that era of Prohibition, who would be forced to admit that they drank.[102] His only exception was a notorious Los Angeles real estate agent: "They broke three needles trying to administer the stuff to him," Rogers told his readers, "and it turned black the minute it touched him, so they had to give it up. He sold Dr. House three lots before he got out of the operating room."[103] These pieces are humorous commentaries, but they merged with stories of House's claims to successful use of narcoanalysis in jails. As commentary, Rogers writes, "Everybody in jails are for it, for they want to prove their innocence, but everybody out of jails are against it, for they fear they will get themselves under its influence."[104] Rogers underscores his skepticism in asserting that using truth serum to claim innocence is unsurprising, because a suspect would say the same thing under the influence of hydrant water.[105]

Polygraphs and Brain Tests: Sustaining Narratives

Just as narcoanalysis was never fully accepted for forensic purposes by the medical or legal communities, the use of polygraphs raised similar questions of reliability and validity. Brain techniques are more recent developments, but evidence suggests much ambiguity regarding their forensic use. Why, then, does the fascination with these techniques continue? Two arguments seem to have sustained it. First, researchers and forensic scientists closer to law enforcement are engaged in continuous exploration. Second, claims of success are reported so aggressively that they seem to obviate the need for validation by science or the courts. Legal evidence and scientific validity are thus distinct from the cultural production of these truth machines. Indeed, the tension between the legal and scientific communities appears to be resolved in the realm of the cultural.

In the case of the polygraph, its origin in the United States offers a fascinating story over time. Bunn chronicles the cultural history of the lie detector, but its use in law enforcement and other security contexts has been the subject of much speculation. Despite studies dating from the 1920s, it has always been a controversial technique, with an extensive amount of literature documenting its unreliability.[106] A 2003 report by the National Academy of Science, charged with inquiring into the utility of the polygraph for security screening, discusses its challenges and close relationship with law enforcement. The report reviewed past research on the use of the polygraph in crime investigations and found that much of it lacked the reliability or validity desired in scientific studies. The committee thus recommended further research.[107]

Despite its use for almost a hundred years, together with the results of the polygraph determined inadmissible in the U.S. courts (as supported by the 1923 *Frye* case), questions regarding the polygraph recur. Indeed, its status is still open in some jurisdictions, with defendants trying to use it.[108] Ken Alder, for instance, cites studies by the National Research Council in 1941, a Congressional Office of Technology analysis in 1984, and the 2003 National Academy of Science report. "Each concluded that the techniques of lie detection, as used in investigative work by polygraphers, do not pass scientific muster," he wrote. "Yet lie detection lives on."[109]

Consequently, the technique has been neither rejected nor fully accepted.

The 2003 NRC report, however, identified a reason for the ongoing use of polygraph tests in interrogation, despite the difficulty of admitting the evidence in court: anecdotal evidence of confessions continues to suggest the technique's success. "From a scientific standpoint," the report states, "these anecdotes are compelling indications that there is a phenomenon in need of explanation; they do not, however, demonstrate that the polygraph test is a valid indicator of deception."[110] The needs of law enforcement, rather than science, have also directed research on the polygraph, with claims of accuracy ranging from 70 to 90 percent.[111] The report further explains, "Polygraph research has been guided, for the most part, by the perceived needs of law enforcement and national security agencies and the demands of the courts, rather than by basic scientific approaches to research."[112] A decision to use a polygraph is thus driven by policy, not science.

The 2003 report directly acknowledges the cultural production of this truth machine: "The polygraph, perhaps more than any other apparently humane interrogation technique[,] arouses strong emotions. There is a mystique surrounding the polygraph that may account for much of its usefulness: that is, a *culturally shared belief* that the polygraph device is nearly infallible."[113] Littlefield similarly defines the lie detector as "an imagined instrument, an accumulation of the lore, desires, hopes and dreams of the scientific, journalistic, and lay communities."[114] Spectacular science thus becomes the basis of such sustained interest. For Bunn, "Spectacular science is a mode of scientific inquiry that is created and sustained by popular culture."[115] The cultural reasons for the origins and perceived infallibility of the polygraph, together with anecdotes of admissions and confessions, explain its ongoing application, despite lack of either legal acceptance or strong evidence of scientific reliability and validity.

Brain testing has been a much more recent phenomenon, and experts in both the United States and India have claimed major successes in criminal cases. U.S. experts in BFP, for example, claim to have gained admissible evidence that led to bringing a "serial killer to justice" and freeing "a man accused of murder after 24 years in prison."[116] In reality, U.S. courts have been hesitant to accept brain test results as evidence. Nonetheless, continued attempts to introduce brain tests in court suggest that these techniques have some ostensible utility, despite the critiques. Notably, for example, BFP has reportedly been used in three major criminal cases in United States.

In 1999, when J. B. Grinder, accused of killing a fifteen-year-old, had recanted his confession, the police asked Lawrence Farwell to use BFP in the prison where Grinder was held. Farwell concluded that Grinder had concealed information: "'There is no question that J. B. Grinder raped and murdered Julie Helton,' Farwell told a local newspaper after the test. 'The significant details of the crime are stored in his brain.'"[117] In another case, Jimmy Ray Slaughter was convicted of murder and sentenced to death, and BFP was used to ask for postconviction relief. But in *Slaughter v. Oklahoma* (2005), the appellate court deemed the evidence unreliable:

> Secondly, beyond Dr. Farwell's affidavit, we have no real evidence that Brain Fingerprinting has been extensively tested, has been presented and analyzed in numerous peer-review articles in recognized scientific publications, has a very low rate of error, has objective standards to control its operation, and/or is generally accepted within the "relevant scientific community."[118]

As this case suggests, the use of a technique can elide a claim to its success in marketing, especially by Farwell.

The case that appears most often in discussion of BFP is the *Harrington* case. Terry Harrington was convicted of murdering security guard John Schweer in 1978, mostly on the basis of testimony from an accomplice. The physical evidence was minimal.[119] Harrington was sentenced to life imprisonment without parole. In his 2000 attempt at postconviction relief, new BFP evidence was introduced with other materials. In a footnote the court stated, "According to Dr. Farwell, his testing of Harrington established that Harrington's brain did not contain information about Schweer's murder. On the other hand, Dr. Farwell testified, testing did confirm that Harrington's brain contained information consistent with his alibi."[120] Without other evidence, however, the court found that "because the scientific testing evidence is not necessary to a resolution of this appeal, we give it no further consideration."[121] Thus, while Harrington did receive a new trial, the basis of the court's decision was not the BFP tests.

Regarding BEOS, Dr. Mukundan and a number of scientific officers have defended the technique, especially in legal cases. In an article on the Axxonet website, written before the Indian Supreme Court intervened in 2010 to clarify that brain techniques should be voluntary and evidence not directly used, a multiauthored piece notes the courts' mixed response to BEOS.[122] On the basis of ten cases that range from murder by arsenic poisoning to murder of women and children in a village, the article argues that the evidence is corroborative, and in some cases the court refused to accept BEOS as the sole evidence:[123]

> So far, there has been not even a single case, in which the court has convicted a subject based only on the results of the BEOS test. In fact, in the cases, wherein results of the BEOS tests and other Psychological tests were Positive but were not supported by other oral or documentary evidences, the subjects in those cases have been acquitted of the charges against them.[124]

Farwell's instrument also continues to be used in India. It was adopted in the 2000s by S. Malini in Bangalore and more recently in the Raksha Shakti University under a memorandum of understanding with Brainwave Science, the company promoting and marketing BFP, for work on unsolved cases of the Central Bureau of Investigation.[125] A researcher at Raksha Shakti University shared with me some of the research team's thirty cases to explain the way BFP can help to solve cold cases.[126] One was a missing woman (Sarla) whose husband, father-in-law, and husband's friend (purported to be the missing woman's boyfriend) were questioned. After addressing issues regarding language, the father-in-law was found uninvolved, and the suspicion turned to the husband and his friend. The researcher found the husband suspicious because of his aggressive behavior during questioning, but the test revealed no information present. As the researcher explained:

> That first test—"his wife was murdered," no information was present. "His wife got missing," ya, information was present; ya, his wife was missing. But the result was that "indetermined present" means the information is present but it will not determine that this person knows about her missing.... But in a subsequent test, the husband showed the strong belief that his friend had killed her, that the suspicion became focused on the friend.[127]

After several rounds of testing, the examiners found that the husband's friend actually had awareness of the murder:

> After that "Sarla was murdered," the second test. Now, there's a turning point of the case. In this case, ... when some particular probes are appearing, that subject got a little unconscious, and the instrument's ability to identify those suspicious

activities, ok; in fractions of seconds it reads . . . records the waves which are generated by our brain, you can say, when we see any image in our conscious and subconscious mind, recalls that information which are related to that particular image, whatever we have. And that is different for the innocent, different for the professional, different for the criminal, ok.[128]

The instrument can thus ostensibly determine whether the suspect knows information relevant to the crime (here about Sarla's murder), and if the examiners have any doubts, the test is repeated until they are sure, as this researcher elaborated: "So this test said the test shows [the] same results, ok, and [the] aim was 'she was murdered,' and we found that information is present [with] more than ninety percent [accuracy]."[129] Faith in the technique thus emerges from the instrument's ability to gain information, especially in cases that lack physical evidence. The suspect's losing consciousness, although not acknowledged here, probably adds to the suspicion.

In India forensic psychologists attribute their attraction to this technique to bad management of crime scenes, which makes relying on physical evidence impossible. As Dr. S. L. Vaya, the foremost forensic psychologist credited for popularizing truth machines, explains, "[An] increasing number of crimes are being committed in which physical evidences left behind [at] the crime scenario are nil or negligible[,] and it is important to extract information from suspects about their suspected involvements, as well as make the perpetrator admit to the deeds committed by them."[130] Marketing materials for Brainwave Science note the limits of DNA: "Fingerprints and DNA evidence are uncovered in only 1% of all cases. And DNA fingerprinting can only be successfully applied when investigators collect and preserve fingerprints and biological samples in a time-consuming and expensive labor-intensive way."[131] The Indian researcher I interviewed thus had absolutely no doubts in proclaiming that BFP is 99.4 percent accurate in the two cases he described to me. For him, the impossibility of working with fingerprints or DNA, in India or more generally, became the basis for a strong need to believe in BFP.

However, observers continue to criticize both BFP and BEOS. Some cite a dearth of studies that independently verify the validity of these tests. Some scientists in the field, such as J. Peter Rosenfeld and others, do concede that the brain responds to stimuli, thereby suggesting concealed information, but they posit a difference between such responses and evidence of memories, which are much more difficult to ascertain.[132] Rosenfeld notes further that the test protocol is based on the assumption that crimes are always planned and the memory of the planning stored. The misconception, he asserts, is that "the brain is constantly storing undistorted, detailed representation of experience which the BF method can extract from the brain just as easily as real fingerprints can be lifted from murder weapons; (hence the misleading term, 'Brain *Fingerprinting*')."[133]

Rosenfeld refers instead to literature pointing to the fragility of memories and the possibilities for their construction.[134] Referencing the *Harrington* murder case, he argues further that a test conducted twenty years after the crime would be unable to distinguish between a "rehearsed and [a] recalled alibi."[135] Individuals may also commit crimes while under the influence of alcohol and drugs, which the test fails to take into account. Nor do the studies consider countermeasures that might invalidate the test results.[136] Furthermore, the originators of both BFP and BEOS refuse to reveal the mode of calculation on which each test is based.[137]

Those who defend brain testing over the polygraph tend to make a clear distinction between the two methods. In response, Littlefield argues that while brain testing appears as mechanical mind reading as opposed to the body betraying the self in words, the process underlying the technologies is much the same.[138] Brain imaging, she elaborates, is marketed "as a more direct indicator of consciousness than secondary autonomic markers. Nonetheless, like their polygraph counterparts, brain-based techniques are *indirect* measures of mental and emotional states based on changes in physiological processes."[139]

Claims of success by those most closely working with the techniques, together with aggressive marketing and promotion by media and popular culture, have thus been crucial to their acceptance. Science and inadmissibility in court matter less. Indeed, while polygraphs and even narcoanalysis are said to be beatable, Brainwave Science claims that BFP is unbeatable: "We offered a $100,000 reward to anyone who could beat a Brain Fingerprinting test and even then, no one was able to succeed,"[140] company literature claims, noting further that the technique has been "*tested by several U.S. federal government agencies and found to be over 99% ACCURATE.*"[141] Commercial interests are, of course, paramount for Brainwave Science (and Axxonet), which in 2015 was expanding to sell its instruments in Singapore, India, and potentially six other countries, with marketing that featured testimonies of its success.[142]

Touting the validity and reliability of BFP, Farwell also claims an accuracy rate of 99 percent. He agrees, however, that the test indicates only awareness of the information presented and is not necessarily an indicator of guilt:[143]

> A brainfingerprinting test shows that the subject does or does not know the specific details about the investigated situation embodied in the probe stimuli. It is up to the attorneys to argue, and the judge and jury to decide, based on brain fingerprinting and all other available evidence, whether a crime took place, what the crime was, and who is guilty or not.[144]

In 2001 a U.S. congressional report rejected BFP "because use of the technique requires a unique level of detail and information that would be known only to the perpetrator and the investigators."[145] Citing connections to security agencies, however, Brainwave Science remains aggressive in claiming the technique's success for solving cases and finding the guilty.

Farwell, in turn, has appeared in controversial media portrayals of criminal cases, such as the popular Netflix show *Making a Murderer*, based on the case of Steven Avery, convicted of killing of Teresa Halbach in Manitowoc County, Wisconsin. After the show aired in 2015, the case was much discussed in the media. In 2016 Farwell conducted BFP on Avery, and in his 2017 court affidavit defended the technique: "Fingerprinting [h]as been tested and proven at the FBI, the CIA, the US Navy, and elsewhere."[146] Farwell then concluded that Avery showed no signs of knowing the newly discovered evidence, as the tests indicated "information absent" with 99.9 percent statistical accuracy. His website also posted the test, along with media stories on the case.[147]

The media has thus played a supportive role in BFP. As Paul Wolpe and his colleagues argue, media approval and aggressive marketing of brain-testing technologies have contributed to their popularity, despite reservations among science and legal experts.[148] Indeed, the websites of both Farwell and Brainwave Science highlight BFP's capabilities and constantly update its use in key cases or in different countries: "'Truth and Justice, by the Blip of a Brain Wave' was the headline in one *New York Times* article . . . while the *San Francisco Chronicle* simply announced 'Fib Detector' . . . in the year that Farwell was mentioned [in] the Time 100: The Next Wave innovators—the Picassos or Einsteins of the 21st Century."[149] BFP thus appears to be following the path of the polygraph, just as Alder predicted: "The lie detector cannot be killed by science, because it is not born of science. Its habitat is not the laboratory or even the courtroom, but newsprint, film, television, and of course the pulps, comic books, and science fiction."[150] In an era of reality TV, *Making a Murderer* became a major vehicle for touting the success of BFP, with Avery's lawyer promoting it aggressively.[151]

Attempts by both Brainwave Science and Axxonet to defend brain testing became more aggressive than the earlier, more tentative claims by scientific officers.[152] Axxonet posted on its website, "Unlike other technologies which have been used in 2 or 3 cases, NSS has been used in over **700 cases** reported by independent Forensic laboratories in areas such as Murders, Insurgency, Poaching, [and] Illegal immigration to name a few." The website then reflected efforts to distinguish BEOS from other methods: "Unfortunately the court confused BEAP/BEOS with the outdated and minimalistic P300 technique with which BEOS has no connection."[153] Axxonet asserted further confusion caused by the court's decision to consider three methods collectively. In these defenses of brain testing, marketing materials, aspirations of the tests' originators, and sometimes their relationships with law enforcement produce a cultural defense of truth machines with little support from science or the courts.

Truth Serum: Cold War and the War on Terror

Questions of national security have long been linked to continued fascination with truth machines.[154] In the United States, discussion of narcoanalysis has occurred not only in the criminal justice system but also in the context of intelligence gathering. As Winter explains, "It has attracted consistent controversy, recurrent rejection, and also recurrent resurgence."[155] The Central Intelligence Agency (CIA) experimented with truth serum, along with other drugs, in the 1950s and 1960s, prompting congressional hearings in the 1970s, which may have contributed to its demise as a Cold War relic. The intervention of the U.S. Supreme Court in the *Townsend v. Sain* case in 1963 may also have contributed to its rejection.

The most substantive information about the CIA experiments emerged from the Church Committee and the Rockefeller Commission reports in 1975 and from a number of documents released in 1977 under the Freedom of Information Act (FOIA) and congressional inquiries.[156] By then the CIA had claimed that it had stopped using drugs for experiments by 1967 directly and indirectly by 1973 and that many related records had been destroyed.[157] The CIA experiments included a number of methods, among them hypnosis, polygraphs, narcoanalysis, behavioral change, and drug testing, particularly with LSD. Unlike the longer history of these techniques, especially narcoanalysis, in the criminal justice system, the CIA emphasized possibilities for intelligence gathering.

The materials presented by the CIA during the congressional hearings included a brief history of truth serum dating from the 1920s and the experiments done by House. According to the CIA report, the drug became widely used until both psychological and physical side effects became evident and drastically undermined using the drug for interrogation.[158] Side effects not mentioned in the newspaper reports of the time included "hallucinations, and disturbed perception" and "dry 'desert' mouth."[159] The report points out concerns from the very beginning about whether it was a form of "psychological third degree." The CIA report tries to distinguish between a well-protected criminal justice system and unprotected intelligence gathering for national security. The agency cites the possibility of enemy use of truth serum, which would require resistance, despite the courts' hesitation to allow it. The report further illustrates four stages of response to the drugs, the fourth of which could lead to death,[160] but points to the second stage (hyperactivity) as useful in police work and intelligence gathering.

Two major studies were quoted in this report. One involved soldiers who were neuropsychiatric patients. They were first questioned about their crimes, then injected with amytal (either delayed or administered repeatedly) and encouraged to confess; later, when they regained consciousness, they were asked to repeat their confessions. About seventeen subjects repeated their confessions and eight recanted. The report states, "With respect to the reliability of the results of such interrogation, [Gerson and Victoroff] conclude that persistent, careful questioning can reduce ambiguities in drug Interrogation, but cannot eliminate them altogether."[161]

In another experiment, at Yale University, F. C. Redlich and others concluded that lying under the influence of truth serum is possible, depending on the individual's mental state:

> The results, though not definitive, showed that normal individuals who had good defenses and no overt pathological traits could stick to their invented stories and refuse confession. Neurotic individuals with strong unconscious self-punitive tendencies, on the other hand, both confessed more easily and were inclined to substitute fantasy for the truth, confessing to offenses never actually committed.[162]

This report ends by stating, "No such magic brew as the popular notion of truth serum exists."[163] Each study suggested further research to explore possibilities, and the CIA and the U.S. military thus initiated Projects Artichoke, Bluebird, and MKUltra to study the impact of truth serum. These efforts, however, were subsequently abandoned.[164] Alder notes that some of these programs used the polygraph as a pretext for introducing polygraphers, who would also monitor the effects of psychological methods involving drugs.[165]

The congressional hearings included very little detail about House's experiments, the courts' response, and the CIA's own studies. The CIA report instead poses a problem of hesitation in the West to study such interrogation methods: "The general abhorrence in Western countries for the use of chemical agents 'to make people do things against their will' has precluded serious systematic study (at least as published openly) of the potentialities of drugs for interrogation."[166] This statement suggests a basis for future studies without acknowledging that truth serum had been used again and again and generally treated with a fair amount of skepticism.[167]

After 9/11, discussion of truth serum resumed, along with a number of interrogation techniques, although there is no clear evidence of its use.[168] Some scholars and state officials argued for use of truth serum, both because it was not physical and because they distinguished between intelligence gathering and use of evidence in criminal trials.[169] In the post-9/11 period, debates on truth serum emerged among those who argued for torture or for "torture-lite." Commentators suggested ways of either institutionalizing torture or leaving it to the discretion of individual state actors, rejecting the use of torture or of cruel, inhuman, or degrading treatment (CIDT) as morally and legally unacceptable and historically unreliable.[170] Lawyers of the Bush administration found ways of either bypassing national and international laws or reinterpreting them to make methods of "harsh or enhanced interrogation" appear sanitized and more acceptable.[171] Debates and policies thus yielded a regime of torture, CIDT, and other excesses in prisons such as Abu Ghraib in Iraq, Guantánamo Bay in Cuba, and a host of extraordinary rendition sites.

Narcoanalysis and truth serum did receive public attention after 9/11. According to Alter, "Short of physical *torture*, there's always sodium pentothal ('truth serum'). The FBI is eager to try it, and deserves the chance. Unfortunately, truth serum, first used on spies in World War II, makes suspects gabby but not necessarily truthful."[172] A story in *Time* noted the use of truth serum on Abu Zubaydah (a high-value detainee) mentioned in a book by Gerald Posner, who wrote that "an unnamed 'quick-on, quick-off' painkiller and Sodium Pentothal, the old movie truth serum—in a chemical version of reward and punishment [was used] to make Zubaydah talk."[173]

Media discussion also considered whether the drug could be used as an effective mode of questioning in the war on terror, and some U.S. officials considered it a possibility, especially with al Qaeda suspects, who were considered unprotected by the Geneva Conventions. Alternatively, officials suggested that detainees could be sent to countries that condoned truth serum, suggesting that even if these drugs did not get to the truth, they would at least break prisoners' defenses.[174] The 2018 report from the Office of Medical Services reveals an explicit discussion over two to three months in 2002 about using Versed (generic name midazolam), a more recent benzodiazepine, even though Project Medication was shelved in early 2003.[175] Apparently, my respondents in India's forensic laboratories were correct in reporting a reevaluation of the use of truth serums in the United States after 9/11.[176]

Debates over the legality of truth serum date from 1963, in the U.S. Supreme Court decision in *Townsend v. Sain, Sheriff, et al.*[177] The case involved murder suspect Charles Townsend, who claimed at trial that his confession should be inadmissible because it had been coerced. Townsend was a heroin addict, and when he exhibited signs of withdrawal during questioning, a physician gave him 1/230 grain hyoscine (similar to scopolamine), and 1/8 grain of phenobarbital to alleviate the symptoms. Soon afterward Townsend "talked."[178] Townsend claimed that the interrogating officer beat him and gave him drugs that made him feel better but also sleepy and dizzy. After the questioning, he was made to sign statements both at the station and in front of the state's attorney (after the administration of more pills). The prosecution, in turn, insisted that Townsend had been awake and coherent when necessary, and the physician claimed that the hycosine was intended only to pacify him, failing to mention its properties as a truth serum.

The Supreme Court's majority opinion, written by Chief Justice Earl Warren, rejected Townsend's confession as inadmissible. Most of the majority opinion and the dissent focused on whether the district court should have held a hearing to reconsider the facts in the case, but the Court did address the status of truth serum, arguing that its admissibility depends on whether the confession is voluntary. Volition, the justices opined, is integrally linked to whether the "will was overborne" and whether the confession was a product of "rational intellect and free will." Beyond questions of physical or psychological coercion, the court focused on the "drug-induced statement" and said,[179] "It is difficult to imagine a situation in which a confession would be less the product of a free intellect, less voluntary, than when brought about by a drug having the effect of a 'truth serum.'"[180]

The court addressed the validity of the technique only briefly, in a footnote, where the justices acknowledge a raging debate about truth serum. Rather, the court's focus on the inadmissibility of the confession was central to the decision: "Whether scopolamine produces true confessions or false confessions, if it in fact caused Townsend to make statements, those statements were constitutionally inadmissible."[181] And it is precisely this focus on inadmissibility of evidence in a criminal trial that advocates of truth serum for intelligence gathering cited after 9/11. Kenneth Lasson, for instance, claimed that the technique was unlike torture because it was a "relatively painless, less intrusive method" and, despite problems of reliability, could be extremely useful in "ticking bomb scenarios."[182] The *Townsend* case, Lasson further suggests, applies only to admissibility in court, not to any use of such techniques. During the Bush administration, this line of argument was mentioned explicitly in memos from the Office of Legal Counsel regarding other techniques.[183] Necessity thus became an element of analysis as scholars came to suggest truth machines for interrogation, even though evidence remained inadmissible at trial.

To assess whether truth serum would be disallowed by the Supreme Court in the future, scholars have compared its use to other invasive procedures.[184] Alan Dershowitz, a major figure of the post-9/11 torture debates, famous for suggesting "torture warrants" to ensure accountability in the system, asserted that, constitutionally, the act of injecting a liquid into a person without consent is little different from withdrawing blood for testing a person's alcohol level.[185] "The involuntariness of the injection itself does not pose a constitutional barrier," he explained. "No less a civil libertarian than Justice William J. Brennan rendered a decision that permitted an allegedly drunken driver to be involuntarily injected to remove blood for alcohol testing. Certainly there can be no constitutional distinction between an injection that removes a liquid and one that injects a liquid."[186]

The debate about whether U.S. laws prohibit the use of truth serum is linked to whether truth serums are prohibited by the UN Convention against Torture and Other Cruel, Inhuman, or Degrading Treatment, especially since mind-altering drugs are specifically mentioned in the federal torture statute (FTS).[187] The focus here is often on whether the impact of the drug will lead to prolonged mental harm or whether its use reflects a specific intent to create such harm. The 2018 Office of Medical Services report similarly states two potential legal obstacles for use of truth serum during the discussions in 2002 for detainees: a prohibition against medical experimentation on prisoners and a ban on interrogational use of "mind altering drugs" or those that "profoundly altered the senses."[188]

The legal question is important but reflects a mode of debate in the aftermath of 9/11, a clash between what I have elsewhere called "aggressive hyperlegality," where the intent is to narrow protections against torture, and to avoid a more substantive conception of law that protects from all forms of excessive violence.[189] Even as the Counter Terrorism Center (CTC) decided not to seek explicit approval for use of truth serum after 9/11, it did note a lack of clarity as to whether the provisions of the FTS applied only to LSD, given that truth serum was banned only from use as evidence in court.[190] The CTC's position may reflect rigorous debates in the Church Committee and the decision in the *Townsend* case, all of which may help to explain why truth serum did not substantially return with other methods after 9/11. Truth serums in the United States are more visible as the fantasies of Hollywood films[191] or in the war on terror, as a means for inducing helplessness.[192]

Representation of Science in Law and Media

The stories of truth machines are centrally linked to their originators and to the responses of media, culture, and society. Fascination with the process of forcing the body to betray itself—through autonomic indicators in a polygraph, a drug-induced confession, or an imaging study of the mind—is distinct from judicial and penal torture. The emergence of truth machines is often related to a narrative of progress, science, and civilization meant to distinguish the present from the past. The spectacle of science supports this cultural production, despite challenges to the legality, validity, and reliability of these techniques.

And yet, with forensic techniques like fingerprinting or truth machines, this narrative is linked to particular bodies—often racialized and gendered—especially at the time of their origin. Over time, questions of scientific and legal validity recede, and the narrative of truth machines is culturally produced, in media, popular culture, law enforcement, and commercial marketing, the latter especially for brain-testing methods. The transnational circulations of the scientific techniques, in turn, depend on the circumstances—most notably national security though not restricted to that—in which truth machines achieve acceptance, rejection, or resurgence. Unifying these efforts is an underlying goal: to find ways for the body to betray itself.

CONCLUSION

In this chapter I recall the origin stories of the three truth-telling techniques in the United States (and India in the case of BEOS), and I recount some of the debates about these techniques in the scientific and legal communities. Despite concerns about the scientific validity of truth machines and the legal admissibility of the evidence they produce, I argue, these techniques resonate in the media and in product marketing, driven by experts and commercial interests. Rather than science or law, therefore, cultural production validates these techniques and sustains interest in them. Nonetheless, the disdain of science can challenge sustaining narratives, as with narcoanalysis in the United States.

As Dean Wigmore reflects on the power of science, "If medical science or psychic science, represented by an accord among the experts of the science, establishes the trustworthiness of a confession induced by some artificial means known to such science, then a confession so induced should be admissible."[193] Above all, the search for new techniques and the resurgence of those once discredited are reminders of the ongoing need for producing truth. This search then leads scientists, courts, and law enforcement to a focus on the body, whether through conscious speech or through access to the conscious mind.

Chapter 4

THE STATE FORENSIC ARCHITECTURE

Forensic Psychologists and the Art of Scientific Interrogations

Field Note 3: The new forensic science university had plush corridors. As I sat comfortably in the personal assistant's room, the curious men helpfully handed me glossy brochures about the university. I entered the director's room a little nervously since the interview was unexpected based on a random email unlike some of my other interviews. The brief interview confirmed everything I had found about the techniques, but the question that was most difficult to answer in the conversation was why I, as a political science professor who had no background in psychology, criminology, or physiology, was interested in studying these techniques.

This chapter is a long answer to that question and considers the reasons these techniques matter for political theorists, legal scholars, and human rights activists.

In India lie detectors have been used since the 1960s and 1970s, although they were not well publicized. Narcoanalysis and brain scanning became more visible in the early 2000s. Over time, these techniques became the purview of forensic psychologists, who in turn became prominent as part of the state forensic architecture.[1]

Operating in hospitals and forensic science laboratories (FSLs), forensic psychologists unofficially replaced the police as interrogators. The emergence of truth machines in India was thus closely related to forensic psychologists' efforts to attain legal recognition, both individually and professionally, and to join the states forensic architecture, where they became embedded almost like cyborgs.[2] This change has implications for understanding state power and legal violence in liberal democracies.

Three public figures appear in the story of expansion of truth machines: Dr. S. L. Vaya, Dr. C. R. Mukundan, and Dr. S. Malini.[3] Vaya, a pioneer in forensic psychology in Gandhinagar, Gujarat, received the 2011 C. S. Kang Oration Award from the Indian Association of Clinical Psychologists.[4] Mukundan, mostly based in Gandhinagar, Gujarat, invented the brain electrical oscillation signature test, the Indian counterpart of brain fingerprinting, which he successfully patented. Malini, a psychologist based in the FSL in Bangalore, Karnataka, was visible in the emerging popularity—and notoriety—related to truth machines.

In deploying these techniques, the forensic psychologist mediates the relationship among science, the police, and the legal system. This expert's legal and scientific status, however, was at first unclear. Unlike scientific experts who present bodily evidence gleaned from DNA, autopsy, or serology, forensic psychologists interact with live suspects. Indeed, as one explained to me, psychology is one of few sections in an FSL where live suspects enter.[5] Scientific literature may suggest little validity or reliability for truth machines, especially for criminal justice, but early on, forensic psychologists expressed excitement about their potential for helping the overloaded criminal justice system. Invoking science, alongside the ability to read a suspect therapeutically, the forensic psychologist becomes an expert unconstrained by law. Indeed, only when attempting to define their expertise legally, the scientific falsity and unreliability of truth machines get revealed. Once exposed, they become subject to debate. The notoriety of forensic psychologists is also linked to interpersonal rivalries amongst them.

The Indian police, as agents of postcolonial state power, remain closely connected with torture, the technique that most directly inscribes a sovereign's power on the body of the accused. In contrast, the forensic psychologist, with a combination of science and art, appears to enable an innovative regime of interrogation that avoids the travails of torture. Ultimately, however, forensic psychologists reinforce the structure of Indian policing, which long emphasized violence and confession. The state forensic architecture thus reflects the convergence of contingency, materiality, and expertise that fits a modernizing discourse marked by uncritical claims of progress by the postcolonial state and police.

FORENSIC PSYCHOLOGISTS AS EXPERTS

Truth machines—narcoanalysis, brain scanning, and lie detectors—have origins associated with specific individuals (see chapter 3). In India the police came to accept the claims of experts. Forensic psychologists, as experts, then became part of the state's planned expansion and development of the police, the bureaucratic agents of state power. The process encompassed changes in legal procedures, legitimation through media and state initiatives, and a range of material conditions, including drugs, courses, machines, and laboratories. These constituted the state forensic architecture, a unitary structure derived from contingent conditions.

Here I draw from Timothy Mitchell's classic work, *Rule of Experts*, where he relates the role of expertise in creating a narrative of progress to the development of science in postcolonial Egypt. "From the opening of the twentieth century to its close," Mitchell argues,

> the politics of national development and economic growth was a politics of techno-science, which claimed to bring the expertise of modern engineering, technology, and social science to improve the defects of nature, to transform peasant agriculture, to repair the ills of society, and to fix the economy.[6]

Forensic expertise in India emerged to resolve the ills of policing and the criminal justice system, notably the courts' overload and the high incidence of third-degree interrogation. Analyzing experts and techno-politics, Mitchell emphasizes contingency and both human and nonhuman agency: "The expertise was hybrid, not an exterior intelligence applied to the world, but another artifactual body" such that "solutions were worked out on the ground."[7] Experts on the ground in India were responsible for the adoption, innovation, and continued development of truth machines. Verification by science or the state was initially deemed irrelevant.

The experts working at the interface of forensics and healing play an important role in this story. An analogy is Sameena Mulla's *The Violence of Care*, a detailed ethnography of forensic nurses in Baltimore, Maryland, in the United States.[8] As Mulla shows, despite these nurses' intent to care therapeutically for rape victims, the institutional context—time, persistent rape myths, documentary and visual practices—shapes their professional practice to conform more to the needs of the legal system. Nurses know that few cases ever go to trial, but they nonetheless enact "violence of care" for the victims. "This violence is born not from the intentions of individual forensic nurses who consciously set out to alienate the victim-patient with whom they are working," Mulla explains, "but rather from the particular institutional, professional, and historical location of forensic sexual assault intervention."[9]

The forensic needs of a legal system, therefore, determine forensic practices. Forensic psychology is a feminized profession, and, like nurses and clinical psychologists generally, practitioners claim to be involved in therapeutic care.[10] Here, however, the intent is not to preserve evidence to fit a client's narrative but to glean a confession or information to solve a case. Forensic psychologists have a peculiar relationship to the machines and drugs they use. Mitchell applies the notion of techno-politics to experts, an alloy of human and nonhuman, intentional and not, that emerges from a process of manufacture in which the intentional or the human always gives way to the unintended.[11] For forensic psychologists, I apply the term "cyborg," a merging of human and machine, constantly morphing into one or the other, sometimes emphasizing the mechanical (science), at other times the human (therapeutic art). Distinguishing themselves from police, forensic psychologists, as cyborgs, help create the state forensic architecture.

Emergence of Forensic Psychology and the Polygraph

Lie detectors gained prominence in India primarily because of the advocacy of forensic psychologists, who vouched for their utility. These efforts eventually gained recognition from the Central Bureau of Investigation and the Ministry of Home Affairs (MHA), and they featured in complaints to the National Human Rights Commission. The claims of individual forensic psychologists first connected the components of forensic architecture: drugs, machines, laboratories, and the police. In the process, these semi-state actors claimed expertise in addressing the ills of the criminal justice system, especially the prevalence of third-degree interrogation.

According to one of the forensic scientists I interviewed, the earliest use of the lie detector in India can be traced to the late 1960s.[12] In 1968, the Central

Forensic Science Laboratory (CFSL) in Delhi, under an eminent psychologist Dr. A. K. Ganguly may have been the first to use the machine. Once its "potentiality" was confirmed, other laboratories started acquiring it.[13] But even Ganguly was uncertain about its full potential, claiming that only recovery after a confession could confirm the machine's veracity. Otherwise, he cautioned, a suspect's answers could be affected by fear of the machine.[14] As one of his colleagues explained:

> In fact, many of the people, the investigating officers, unfortunately they say that, you know, we could not get information; now this machine will tell you, and if you don't do that one, it will be deleterious to your health, . . . so the people, you know, do confess under duress though they have not committed a crime.[15]

Information from a polygraph test was never admitted as evidence, he elaborated, but recovered items could be admitted under Section 27 of the Indian Evidence Act (as discussed in chapter 2).[16]

Subsequently, a number of FSLs acquired forensic psychology and polygraph divisions, which generally functioned without controversy. In its 2013–2014 report, the MHA confirmed that the polygraph in CFSL was first set up in 1973.[17] A study on the use of lie detectors between 1974 and 1976 in 115 cases and 263 suspects concluded, "The polygraph does render valuable help to investigating officers in detecting the guilt of a suspect and *inducing him to admit guilt*. It can also reveal the innocence of a suspect and check the veracity of the statement of a complainant."[18] A. K. Ganguly, father of polygraphy in India, and S. K. Lahiri, his senior scientific assistant, write revealingly about the examiner as interrogator:

> [The] polygraph examiner's most important task and responsibility consist in the diagnosis of deception from an examination of the physiological changes recorded by the instrument which makes absolute sense. Along with his skill in that respect, he must, however, be able to perform the next most important task to interrogate a subject skillfully with a view to obtain a confession from him in case he is guilty.[19]

In 1976 Ganguly and Lahiri published an article titled "Polygraph" in the journal of the American Polygraph Association and reported fifty cases in India between January 1974 and December 1975, involving 120 suspects, witnesses, and complainants. Of these, 41 suspects had been questioned about theft and roughly 30 suspects about murder. About 28.3 percent of suspects were found to be deceptive, and 69.2 percent were not. In at least eight cases involving 11 suspects, the "lie detection test proved useful as the suspects admitted their guilt to the Police."[20] The study thus reports the prevalence of polygraphs without discussing their reliability.

Forensic psychologists gained some recognition in the 1980s, with the development of their profession most evident in Gujarat, where Vaya authored a report during her time in Gujarat's FSL and India's first forensic university (its website claims it to be the first such university in the world).[21] Widely known as Vaya Madam, her name came up constantly in relation to truth machines in all the laboratories I visited. The lie detection division was founded in Ahmedabad's FSL in 1982, but the need to "widen the scope of the investigation while examining suspects" led to a forensic psychology branch in 1988.[22] The lie detector was inserted into the *Gujarat Police Manual* in 1992, with guidelines for its use:

> In important crimes wherein no direct evidence is available and it is suspected that witnesses/suspects are suppressing the truth, the investigating officer [IO] can avail the facility of *scientific techniques of interrogation* of such persons through the lie detection, hypnosis[,] etc. at the forensic science laboratory in their forensic psychology division.[23]

An effort to promote lie detectors to mediate police practice thus involved a forensic psychologist, administrative permission, and modifications to a local manual.

Courts' recognition of forensic psychologists provided additional incentives to innovate. Some cases involved rape victims, reflecting the emphasis on using the polygraph on complainants, with the expectation that it would help both the innocent and the police in noncustodial situations.[24] The cases gradually extended to theft and *dacoity* (armed robbery by gangs) and to murder and terrorism. The use of lie detectors in criminal cases thus gained momentum from the 1980s onward. By 1988 the courts had come to recognize that polygraphs could be helpful. With them, investigative officers gleaned more information. Even the CBI started sending cases to the FSL in Gujarat.

Attempts to highlight the significance of the polygraph appeared in the CBI journal explaining its use as a good alternative to third-degree interrogation. Two authors associated with the lie detector division in Karnal, Haryana, concluded:

> Polygraph examination is a scientific method of interrogation.... (a) It is effective in such cases where [the] third degree method does not work. (b) Where the third degree method cannot be applied, and (c) It can help in eradicating the use of third degree methods which is a cognizable offence as defined under various Sections of the Indian Penal Code.[25]

These conclusions were based on five cases ranging from theft, to murder, to death by lightning, all solved through polygraph where the third degree had failed. For example, the complainants in a murder case were subjected to the polygraph, and its results led to confessions of their own involvement in the murder of the wife of one of the complainants.[26]

These reports highlighted the role of forensic psychologists.[27] As Vaya and J. M. Vyas explain, "In the whole process, [the] mental set of a person taking the polygraph test play[s] an important role which needs psychological handling."[28] Commentators further noted the difference between the United States and India: in the U.S. "lie detector examiners usually have [a] police background; rarely, if ever, do they have [the] training required of psychological and medical specialists."[29] In India, however, forensic psychologists emphasized that most polygraph examiners had postgraduate degrees in psychology and six months of in-service training.[30] A legally ambiguous argument further asserted that polygraph tests conducted by psychologists, rather than police, would render admissible confessions.[31]

The confessions heard and deceptions ascertained during pretest and post-test interviews further highlighted the role of forensic psychologists. As Bibha Ray and S. R. Singh report in one case, "On the basis of the polygraph examination, they revealed in the pre-test interview they confessed their and their parents' involvement in the murder which they had been denying prior to the polygraph examination in spite of the third degree methods used by the police.[32] Posttest interviews similarly revealed deception or led to recovery of stolen items.[33] With psychological training, one forensic psychologist asserted, questioning involved no touching, privacy issues, or drug contraindications. Although most cases involved corroborative, not central, evidence, she noted, forensic psychologists had solved cases, notably an ATM burglary and a case of infanticide.[34]

Eventually, the NHRC received complaints. In May 1997, Inder Choudhurie lodged a complaint about the use of lie detectors along with mental and physical torture, including the injecting of an intravenous drug, while he was in the Shimla jail. Choudhurie wanted both the NHRC and the CBI to conduct an inquiry.[35] The NHRC reports focused on the lie detector and drug, not on mental and physical torture. Perhaps the illegality of torture required no comment, but its casual mention is striking. The NHRC acknowledged both its failure to take up the case and the high court's rejection of Choudhurie's petition but did create guidelines, in the absence of law, for the use of lie detectors. Finally approved in November 1999, the guidelines mention other complaints regarding the use of a lie detector after injecting a drug.[36]

In the official circular sent to all states and union territories, the NHRC notes two concerns. First, the tests had been conducted under coercion and without informed consent, making them violations of the self-incrimination clause of Article 20 (3) of the Indian Constitution. Second, these techniques violated Article 21 (procedure according to law and expanded conception of due process), which requires techniques of interrogation to be noninvasive. In making these determinations, the commission also makes a very important distinction among three kinds of volition: one where the accused voluntarily asks to take a lie detector test to prove innocence versus a second and a third kind where the police implicitly or explicitly link taking the test to freedom. The commission reiterated the importance of voluntary consent. According to the guidelines, consent is to be recorded in front of a judicial magistrate, who would explain that it amounted not to a confession but to a statement before the police, because, in India, confessions to police in routine criminal cases are inadmissible in court.

While the NHRC guidelines are in line with the conditions for interrogation and confession, two are particularly noteworthy:

> (vii) The actual recording of the Lie Detector Test shall be done in an independent agency (such as a hospital) and conducted in the presence of a lawyer. (viii) A full medical and factual narration of manner of the information received must be taken on record.[37]

The emphasis on a hospital setting and medical narration suggests a concern about a pattern of cases in which drugs had been injected, yet the commission sidestepped the ambiguous medical impact:[38] "The Commission had been receiving a number of complaints pertaining to the conduct of this test, said to be administered under coercion and without informed consent. The test is allegedly conducted after a certain drug is administered to the accused."[39] Not until narcoanalysis emerged as a distinct method of "scientific interrogation" was drug use with the lie detector explored. Also unaddressed were questions of inherent coercion and unreliability.

Meanwhile, lie detectors continued to be used in laboratories. Vaya's report from Gujarat mentioned a record of about 5,504 cases from 1983 to 2007 in which lie detectors were used, with the highest numbers, 520 and 644, in 2004 and 2006, respectively. The machine was used principally against suspects (3,323 cases) and those accused (643 cases), but it was also used against witnesses (383 cases) and complainants (474 cases). Thirty percent of the cases came from in the city of Ahmedabad. The results of these cases appear to be mixed.[40] Deception was identified in 1,269 cases but none was observed in 2,585 cases, while results were doubtful or inconclusive in 248 and 139 cases, respectively.

Questionnaires were sent to police stations to assess the usefulness of the polygraph in criminal investigations. Results suggested utility for the investigating officer in 118 cases and lack of utility in 104 cases. In 88 cases the report was presented in the court, and in 22 cases it was just considered but not presented. While data from all laboratories are not available, the MHA does note in its 2013–2014 report that, at the CFSL, "since 1973 to-date, examination of approximately 11,500+ subjects have been conducted for detection of psychophysiological deception."[41] All five laboratories that I visited noted procedures, and at two sites, staff pointed to forms that ensured consent from the accused. The tests, however, were considered noninvasive and hence were conducted in a laboratory. I heard no mention of drugs other than those used in narcoanalysis.

Forensic psychologists sometimes appeared as experts in court, but before the Supreme Court's intervention in 2010, courts determined the validity of evidence on a case-by-case basis. So from 1973 to the early 2000s, only sparse evidence suggests the use of lie detectors, the duress the machines might create, or the concomitant use of drugs.[42] Nonetheless, this period not only acknowledged the role of lie detectors in investigations but also, more importantly, foregrounded the partly hidden role of psychological experts who could resolve one of the major issues concerning the Indian police. Forensic psychologists explicitly promoted solving cases with scientific machines rather than third-degree interrogation. They considered their skills more psychological than technical.

Disputes in other parts of the world over the validity of the polygraph (as indicated in chapter 3) make no appearance in these discussions. By itself, however, the lie detector seemed insufficient for the police to embrace wholeheartedly—until, that is, forensic psychologists pointed to additional truth machines.

Innovations in Forensic Psychology: Claims and Visibility

In the early 2000s, forensic psychologists gained more public visibility as two other methods—BFP and BEOS—were increasingly used alongside polygraphs and the more controversial and invasive narcoanalysis. Techniques began to be used consecutively: first the lie detector, then brain scanning, followed by narcoanalysis, although sometimes in reverse. Polygraphs were used in a number of laboratories, both public and private,[43] but only three state FSLs—in Mumbai, Maharashtra; Bangalore, Karnataka; and Gandhinagar, Gujarat—could conduct all three tests.[44]

Forensic psychology and forensic psychologists gained importance as claims to the revolutionizing potential of truth machines became public. By 2005–2006, officials were proclaiming the success of these techniques. For instance, Dr. B. M. Mohan, former director of the FSL in Karnataka, argued that these techniques are not only useful but have "revolutionised the causes of crime investigation."[45] Despite refusing to show any statistics Mohan (and Malini, a former coworker) claimed to have a 96 to 97 percent success rate in three hundred to five hundred cases.[46] Vaya pointed to the utility of all three techniques in gaining information in many high-profile cases of murder and poaching, and she received awards for her ostensible successes.[47] Indeed, even former home minister Shivraj Patil said in a 2006 conference on terrorism that "rather than solely depending on oral evidence, I think we must use scientific evidence which is derived using [the] latest technologies [widely reported as referring to narcoanalysis and brain mapping]."[48]

My interview with a senior police official confirmed a widespread belief about the usefulness of truth machines in cracking difficult cases, especially those related to terrorism. Details were not shared publicly, however, because of national security concerns.[49] Growing support for these techniques was also evident in news reports about the CBI's planning to no longer rely on the three existing FSLs but to create a state-of-the-art facility, with the necessary infrastructure, in Delhi.[50] Scholars and practitioners associated with Bangalore's National Institute of Medical Health and Neuro Sciences (NIMHANS), one of the most prominent Indian research institutes, shared with me their conversations about using narcoanalysis for interrogations. They were skeptical about its use for legal purposes, they said, having considered it appropriate mostly for therapeutic reasons.[51] One doctor in Karnataka, associated with a government hospital where narcoanalysis was conducted, further shared news of meetings and documented plans for expanding forensic psychology through mobile units at the district level.[52]

Forensic psychology thus appeared to become the mainstay of the state forensic architecture, from the central to the local level, to solve criminal cases. Almost all high-profile cases from 2000 to 2010—the Aarushi and Hemraj murder cases, the Telgi stamp case, the Mumbai blast terrorism case, and the Arun Ferreira and alleged Naxalite case—seemed to have involved all three truth machines, and many high court cases contested their constitutionality.[53] Forensic psychologists' efforts also appeared to be gaining traction. For example, in 2004 the forensic psychology division of the Directorate of Forensic Science (DFS) in Gujarat was declared the National Resource Center for Forensic Psychology, and in March 2005 the MHA awarded the DFS, which had taken a lead in establishing forensic psychology in India, 38 lakhs (about 50,000 US dollars) for research, training, and documentation.[54]

A major effort ensued to introduce the police and judiciary to "scientific aids as modes of interrogation" that would parallel the introduction of truth machines to the CFSL and to other state forensic science laboratories.[55] During 2005–2006 alone, 97 judicial officers, 52 investigating officers, and 23 forensic experts participated in the training and reportedly found it impressive. Another set of judicial officers associated with fast-track courts, civil judges, and session court judges—totaling 419 individuals—also underwent training. A memorandum of understanding (MOU) with the Maharashtra FSL was signed, and a new certificate program on forensic psychology with NIMHANS included six months of theory at Bangalore and six months of practical training at the DFS in Gandhinagar. Delegations from the Singapore Ministry of Home Affairs also visited Gujarat to learn about the use of forensic psychology.

From the late 1960s to the early 2000s, therefore, psychologists and forensic scientists transformed the hidden role of forensic psychology as they sought to gain greater visibility and legitimacy in the criminal justice system. As truth machines increasingly became embedded in everyday police practice, however, both the techniques and the practitioners needed the external sanction of the media and state agencies. To launch more widely, truth machines and the forensic psychologists who claimed expertise using them required the state to establish a forensic architecture. This new system appeared as BEOS and narcoanalysis became increasingly prevalent.

Clash between Science and Forensics: Brain Scanning

The prominence of forensic psychology as well as the most public clash between science and forensics occurred with BFP and BEOS. The clash over these techniques also revealed the high stakes for the MHA in creating the state forensic architecture. The first reported use of BEOS was in 2003 in Gujarat. There, between 2003 and July 2007, BEOS was used in 329 cases, including 167 suspects, 83 accused, and apparently also 12 complainants and 4 witnesses. Cases seem to have come from all over India but mostly from Gujarat (203) and Delhi (61). According to a prominent forensic psychologist, the inadequacy of the polygraph rationalized use of the other two methods.[56]

The origin of BEOS is thus the source of both a critique of the lie detector and close collaboration among the police, forensic laboratories, and the psychology community, together with NIMHANS. Apparently the FSL in Bangalore received its polygraph sometime in 1995 or 1996 but had no one to operate it. A NIMHANS clinical psychologist was then asked to help out. "Then I got . . . their lie detection machines to my lab and started seeing the subjects," he told me."

> Then I found that there was a lot of support, lot of interest from the police department. Only thing what I found is that they'll bring a case then; . . . there will be half a dozen policemen also coming with them, and they all will be standing around inside my lab. . . . My students are doing PhD work, other work, everything will be affected. We were all very tense. *See, people were not friendly with the police as we are today.* . . . So I went and requested my director and other people, we'll shift this lie detection machine to [the] forensic lab itself. And I had trained one of the students with me in using it also.[57]

As this psychologist recounts, the lie detector was first introduced to serve the police, and their needs became the basis for expansion and innovation. He had spent decades studying P-300 brain waves in alcoholics, schizophrenics, and head injury patients and was initially excited about Farwell's BFP (see chapter 3). As he explained, however, the P-300 instrument offered sensitivity but not specificity, so in 1994–1995, with a grant from the Ministry of Information Technology, he introduced BEOS.

The initial phase was extremely time-consuming, he explained, because of a lack of software for computing the results, but eventually a group of "boys from IBM" developed digital analysis software for signal computing of EEG results.[58] Nonetheless, by 2002–2003 the Bangalore FSL had decided to buy the Farwell machine, thereby stopping this psychologist's efforts. He was forced to sign an MOU with Gujarat Forensic Science University (GFSU), the principal laboratory for BEOS, the polygraph, and narcoanalysis. By the time he moved to Gujarat, BEOS was ready. "And we had just set up the model [for BEOS]—okay, the whole model," he recounted. "We knew that was working. We had worked on several cases, and we found that if you can trigger remembrance in a person, that's a different type of activation, which is absent if there's no remembrance."[59]

A more pragmatic reason for inventing an Indian version of BEOS was the high cost of Farwell's machine. Farwell himself had gone to India to demonstrate the technology (in Hyderabad, March 27, 2004), and experts were asked whether the machine actually worked. But it was too expensive, so Indian practitioners turned to BEOS and, ultimately, to two different methods. In Bangalore, Malini used the P-300 method, or BFP, invented by Farwell. In Gandhinagar and Mumbai, Mukundan's BEOS was used. The difference between the two brain-scanning methods was somewhat controversial, although the success of Mukundan's patent application resolved the controversy.

A clinical psychologist associated with BEOS claimed that the polygraph and the P-300 machine were inadequate indicators of deception, leading to several years of research and the creation of BEOS. Yet because of lack of support for the project and threats from the United States questioning the ability of Indians to come up with the technique, patents were difficult to file in India,[60] even though some of the scientific propositions used in developing brain scanning are found in ancient Indian philosophy, or Sankhya theory.[61] Indeed, a clinical psychologist I met sullenly asked whether I had been sent as an informer by the U.S. government. A little more than three years later, after approval of a patent, the same psychologist was euphorically willing to share the success of BEOS. As a research associate working at GFSU explained:

> If the system is sold by some U.S. company, people will start buying it. That is also one of the limitations. It is developed by an Indian. *Indian ne banaaya hai*

kuchh theek thaak hi hoga [If Indians have made it, it may just be ok]. That is also one of the mentality. They don't promote Indian products.[62]

One truth machine was thus linked to national recognition as well as to local innovation for police reform in a postcolonial state.

Yet broader appeal, legitimation, and availability beyond a limited function required MHA-sponsored development, which, together with individual efforts, established the state forensic architecture. Only with such state support could BEOS play a modernizing, transformative role in police practice. In 2007 the MHA set up the D. Nagaraja Committee to look into neuromapping—that is, brain mapping and BEOS.[63] The committee was charged with "technical peer review of the technologies developed and used in forensic interrogation" for the purpose of presenting credible results in court.[64] More visibly supported techniques, the committee reasoned, might strengthen and legitimize the state forensic architecture (though not termed as such). The Nagaraja Committee conducted the most public government-sanctioned review. Besides an overview of peer-reviewed publications, committee members heard presentations from companies promoting the two methods (including Axxonet, headed by C. R. Mukundan and his son Chetan Mukundan) and presentations about their use in FSLs.[65]

In its scathing report, the committee found no peer-reviewed evidence showing effectiveness of these techniques:

> Review of the brain electrophysiology based techniques (brain mapping used in FSL Bangalore and BEOS used in FSL Gandhinagar) suggests [a] sub-optimal scientific basis for them to be used as evidence in [a] court of law. Hence they cannot be used as evidence in the court of law.[66]

The Nagaraja Committee did recommend further research but was critical of brain scanning (with a critique that coincides with some of those noted in chapter 3). Without much explanation, however, the MHA chief forensic scientist dissolved the Nagaraja committee, though not before the chair managed to leak the formal report to the media.

Given the report's damning conclusions, the clash was perhaps unsurprising, but the MHA chief scientist's memo dissolving the committee, written in October 2008, reveals the prominence of forensic psychologists and the state's investment in a forensic architecture.[67] The memo associated Mukundan with

BEOS while he was affiliated with the FSL in Bangalore, Karnataka, where the ministry had initially funded his project. Mukundan eventually left that job and joined the DFS, Gujarat, and continued the work after the DFS signed an MOU with NIMHANS.[68] As the memo notes, "As per the MoU terms and conditions, Dr. D Nagaraja and NIMHANS, Bangalore were actively involved in starting the Brain Electrical Oscillation Signature (BEOS) profiling facilities at DFS Gandhi Nagar."[69]

The minimal valence for Farwell's P-300 technique in crime investigation thus led to further research and to the development of BEOS. My respondents also suggested that NIMHANS was involved in its early stages but withdrew from formal MOUs because, as a premier academic institution, it wanted to avoid legal responsibility for the application of either brain scanning or narcoanalysis.[70] By then the Bangalore laboratory had also bought the Farwell instrument. Although Mukundan's reasons for relocation differ in various accounts, with this move the Gujarat FSL did become the principal center for all three truth machines.

In his memo dissolving the Nagaraja Committee, the MHA chief forensic scientist also repeatedly mentions the high demands of brain scanning. To assess the situation, he had held a meeting with forensic scientists affiliated with the CBI, CFSL, Chandigarh, and FSLs in Gujarat and Maharashtra.[71] The memo notes reasons for dissolving the committee: lack of committee members' visits to laboratories in Gujarat, Maharashtra, and Karnataka, where truth machines were in use; committee members' "incompetence" in deciphering the results; flawed methodology in assessment; and refusal to acknowledge that lack of peer review was linked to patent application. Because Nagaraja had been previously involved in the research on BEOS and was affiliated with NIMHANS, with which the forensic laboratories had initially signed an MOU, the memo also suggests conflicts over patent ownership.

But the two principal arguments against the committee's report were, first, that the state and central investigating agencies were "highly satisfied with the findings of FSL, Gujarat and Mumbai in a number of cases." As the report continues, "A number of courts in Maharashtra and in other states have strongly supported the BEOS findings in their judgments."[72] The second argument was that a study, with one hundred volunteers in Gujarat's FSL, to test the findings and ascertain experiential knowledge showed positive, encouraging results.

Singapore's government committee also found the results satisfying. The memo thus concluded:

> This Directorate doesn't agree with the findings [of the Nagaraja Committee]. The FSLs of Gujarat, Karnataka and Maharashtra are doing good work in helping the law enforcement agencies and courts with their available tools and their roles cannot be underestimated. The courts of Law are there to evaluate the scientific findings of the forensic laboratories on BEOS/Brain Mapping Technologies.[73]

Thus, in a remarkable move, the recommendations of a committee established by the state and joined by some of India's most prominent scientists, some from the highly reputed NIMHANS, were not only disregarded but also delegitimized. Unaddressed as well was the committee's fundamental question about the absence of peer-reviewed publications, as mentioned by critics.[74] With a lack of independently verifiable studies—a hallmark of brain scanning (and, indeed, the other truth machines)—involvement of the FSLs in the decision to dissolve the committee suggests their strong influence in determining the future of these techniques. The public clash between science and forensics appeared to be resolved in favor of forensic psychologists, reflecting the faith of the police and, by extension, the legal system in these experts and their methods.

The two methods of brain scanning in India are thus BEOS and Farwell's BFP, sometimes marketed by Brainwave Science (though not by Farwell, as chapter 3 explains). BEOS is used in Gandhinagar, Gujarat, and Mumbai, Maharashtra; whether other states and the CBI have also acquired these machines remains unclear.[75] BEOS continues to be used much more visibly than lie detectors and narcoanalysis, with hope for admissibility of its evidence, despite the 2010 Supreme Court judgment rendering such evidence inadmissible. One reason for the prospect of admissible evidence is that, unlike the polygraph and narcoanalysis, probes with this technique are questions to which no answer need be given, thereby providing only memory rather than spoken words. Hence the technique may be deemed non-invasive and less a concern for constitutional protections. Furthermore, unlike the polygraph and narcoanalysis, which have long and controversial histories, BEOS appears to be distinct.

The Farwell method is used at Raksha Sakhti University in Gandhinagar,

Gujarat, apparently thanks to either a marketing gift or an MOU with the university.[76] Despite the MHA's claim that the technique may not require validation, attempts to validate it are ongoing. Its success in solving cases, rather than peer review, however, is the basis for claiming validity and reliability. One effort, for example, is to solve about thirty of CBI's old cases with Farwell's technique.[77] Forensic psychologists thus continue to play a key role in determining the future of the truth machines in India. With the Nagaraja Committee, public attempts to legitimate the state forensic architecture apparently failed, but the introduction and medicalized use of truth machines continued unabated.

Narcoanalysis and the State Forensic Architecture

The art of questioning associated with narcoanalysis emphasized the role of forensic psychologists in India. Truth machines no longer remained the province of individual practitioners or laboratories working with the police but also appeared in MHA reports as a planning priority for the state. Forensic psychologists' initiatives merged with the postcolonial state's development plan and a "techno-political solution" to address the ills of policing and the criminal justice system. According to a report on Gujarat, narcoanalysis was first conducted in 1989 in a case of official secrets, then in a theft case in 1990 and a murder case in 1999.[78] One of the field's pioneers explained to me the impetus behind the early use of this technique, together with the polygraph and BEOS, as a "need-based requirement. In cases where there is a dead end—there is no way out for the investigators and with court permissions—the methods were actually used."[79] In private practice, drugs were already used for therapeutic purposes and termed "abreaction therapy." Some police were also using drugs illegally. As my respondent elaborated, "The effort was to make it more ethical, because it was an accountable way, a legal way of doing it."[80]

The presence of medical personnel in prison enabled some of the first test cases. Gradually, however, the team included a psychologist, a psychiatrist, and an anesthetist. By 2003 an explicit proposal appeared in the *CBI Bulletin*, suggesting narcoanalysis as a humane approach to interrogation.[81] Cases of narcoanalysis spiked suddenly, to 38 in 2005, then to 88 in 2006, and to 72 in July 2007. From 2002 to July 2007, 213 cases involving narcoanalysis included 28 accused, 79 suspects, and 1 witness. Eighty-three cases were from Gujarat, 32 from Delhi, and 97 from elsewhere. The report mentions about 99 subjects undergoing narcoanalysis in Gandhinagar, Gujarat.[82] In 2013 I visited an operation theater for minor procedures in Gandhinagar, where narcoanalysis continues to be used. In 2010 the setting saw 51 cases and in 2011 55 cases, with 56 in 2012 and 70 in 2013. Most of these occurred after the Supreme Court decision on these three techniques in 2010,[83] and the tests continued in 2017: a report in July 2017 notes, "Directorate of Forensic Sciences (DFS) in Gandhinagar has performed 42 narco-analysis tests in the first six months of 2017 against the annual average of 60 tests."[84]

The FSL in Gandhinagar was aware of the potential legal issues for an invasive procedure, so consent was taken from subjects, and for those accused it was recorded in front of a magistrate (as per the 1999 NHRC guidelines and after the 2010 Supreme Court decision). Indeed, one pioneer in the field claimed that courts and forensic psychologists preferred suspects coming from judicial custody rather than police remand. Notably, although deaths do occur in judicial custody, police remand is synonymous with torture.[85] One forensic psychologist acknowledged that police often tried to delay the process to complete the investigation but that she preferred suspects from judicial custody because "physical and mental fitness was difficult to ascertain [in police custody] and to be safe, suspects came from the judicial custody." This procedure was also a way to avoid later legal battles and ensure a more open process.[86]

Attempts to legitimize truth machines as a part of the state forensic architecture exceeded both individual efforts and local development initiatives through MOUs, university courses for forensic psychology, and government hospitals' expansion of mobile units. In 2005 even the DFS distributed a laboratory manual for using narcoanalysis,[87] and an attempted explanatory note to Section 53 of the Criminal Procedure Code would have allowed truth machines in medical examinations.[88] The biggest shift, however, was the excitement regarding narcoanalysis expressed in MHA reports from 2008 to 2014. Although the technique had been mentioned in earlier reports, it now appeared, along with community policing, as one of the National Police micromissions for infrastructure development.[89]

The 2008–2013 reports also mentioned BFP as an area in which the CFSL would direct future growth, and the 2011–2013 reports specifically mentioned Chennai and Kolkata as scientific aid units for the CFSL. Despite controversies, especially over narcoanalysis, these techniques appeared important to the CFSL expansion plans. The 2013–2014 Ministry of Human Affairs report, for example, proudly acknowledges the success of the lie detection division both for the CBI, in Delhi, and for other states:

The division has initiated [an] action programme for induction of the state-of-the-art technology for analysis of information present in the brain X of the subject and is making efforts to open (1) Narco Analysis (2) Brain Mapping (3) Computerised Polygraph System (3 units) and (4) Voice Stress Analysis (VSA) facilities. These installations will be helpful in the investigation of crime.[90]

Despite the legal and scientific questions apparent by that time even in the Indian context, enthusiasm for these techniques continued at the highest echelons of the government.

In some ways the MHA report attempts what Timothy Mitchell elsewhere terms "objectivation," here by collecting information, making it public, and marking these techniques as priorities.[91] Lie detectors receive the most systematic calculation; according to the MHA report, "Since 1973 to-date, examination of approximately 11,500+ subjects have been conducted for detection of psycho-physiological deception," but here the polygraph stands for the possible calculability of all techniques.[92] The project report from Gujarat also tries to capture the expanded use of truth machines at GFSU and the Gandhinagar FSL.[93] What existed in the shadow of law, with mention disaggregated, became a state priority for policing. While these techniques are not the exclusive focus in forensic science, their sheer persistence, despite their lack of credibility, is noteworthy.

Attempts to consolidate the state forensic architecture seemed to persist against all odds. In its reports, India's postcolonial state had recognized problems with torture and third-degree interrogation and had recognized truth machines as a scientific way to resolve these problems (see chapter 2). Forensic psychologists seemed to have police support for their use of truth machines. In addition, the psychologists were now poised to be the foundation for a forensic architecture that had state support to permeate to the lowest levels of police administration and a forensic science university with a curriculum to train practitioners who could fulfill some of these needs.

Rise, Fall, and Resurrection of Forensic Psychology

The 2010 Supreme Court decision in the *Selvi* case (discussed further in chapter 5) mediated the development of India's forensic architecture by ruling out the involuntary use of truth machines and rendering evidence inadmissible. As with the 1963 *Townsend* decision in the United States, however, the Court did not rule on the coerciveness of the techniques.[94] Expecting the euphoria over these techniques to die down, some of my respondents, together with other commentators, felt that use of narcoanalysis would diminish. Courts had been important to establishing the state forensic architecture, especially as most high courts, where these techniques had been challenged, had preferred them to third-degree interrogation.

Some of the fissures in the state forensic architecture were revealed after *Selvi*, but the state, together with individual and commercial interests, has mostly repaired the cracks.[95] Forensic psychologists reclaimed their place, as indicated by the number of narcoanalysis cases mentioned since 2010. Indeed, the Delhi High Court's insistence in January 2019 that a narco test machine be made operational within three months in the Delhi FSL indicated the continued significance of narcoanalysis.[96] One prominent strategy for gaining visibility and legitimacy was the claim to replace physical torture with truth machines. In defining the forensic psychology division, for example, Vaya, stated:

> It has been the aim of this division to promote the use of scientific methods on [a] regular basis in all investigations so that it enhances the credibility of police investigations. This automatically discourages the use of third degree in police interrogation[,] which helps in maintaining the dignity of the suspects and preserve[s] their rights.[97]

Stated purposes for expanding the use of truth machines were not only to aid the police scientifically in investigations but also to help the judiciary decide cases when forensic psychologists gave corroborative evidence.[98] The narrative of replacing third-degree interrogation was, of course, difficult to sustain, as it was used in very few cases. Furthermore, many critics considered narcoanalysis a form of psychological torture, and at least in terrorism-related cases, truth machines were used alongside the physical third degree.[99] Nonetheless, one of the principal elements of legitimation from the 1960s to the 2000s was that truth machines, including BEOS, would help replace torture and third-degree interrogation. As a research associate explained, "Why [do] we need to beat up the person? Because that is not giving you any further information in terms of brain activity."[100] I asked whether the police tend to avoid using the third degree, and she replied, "Usually for high-profile cases they don't go for third degree, but if it is [a] normal person, then they go for such things." I pushed her to explain the distinction, and she said:

Usually police officers don't opt for third degree. They're not inhuman in nature, but sometimes they get orders to do such things. Even they share that "we don't enjoy giving third degree. We try to avoid it as much as possible." But in some cases when they're not getting anything, when they think that, they see that the person is very resistant, they go for it. But they also agree that if we have this type of technology, then we'll think about it. Next time we'll not go for third degree.[101]

Critics, however, maintained that only sustained interrogation, not truth machines and not third-degree, was effective.[102] P. Chandrasekharan, an award-winning forensic scientist, was critical of the 2010 Supreme Court decision that authorized these techniques with the consent of the accused. He opposed the arguments by Ashwani Kumar, then CBI director, who argued that the Indian Parliament should sanction the polygraph and brain scanning. "We have to find the truth," Kumar asserted. He went on to say:

> It is high time the Parliament, public and press took it up. Because it is Parliament which has to make the law. The Supreme Court has interpreted vis-à-vis the existing constitutional provision. I respect the judgment but I would like to differ with regard to polygraph and brain mapping. I completely agree with the view on narcoanalysis.[103]

For Chandrasekharan, however, the critique was not restricted to narcoanalysis. "Forensic Science never owned the polygraph," he lamented,

> or the recent science-fictional brain fingerprinting as scientific tests belonging to their armour. Polygraph has always been the tool of the criminal investigator rather than the forensic scientist even before it came to disrepute. Its functions have been handled world over by people trained in the techniques of criminal investigation and interrogation and not by forensic scientist[s].[104]

Indeed, the peculiar combination of truth machines and forensic psychologists appears to be an Indian innovation. A forensic scientist, famous for his role in former prime minister Rajiv Gandhi's assassination case, called these techniques a kind of Potemkin science or the equivalent of an octopus squad—that is, asking an octopus to predict which football team would win.[105] Those associated with BEOS were less enthusiastic about narcoanalysis, claiming that requests for truth serum are only tactics to delay cases (though the continued demand for narcoanalysis belies that assertion to some extent).

Despite the contestation, the state forensic architecture remained part of state planning. Along with MHA reports citing truth machines as strategic policing, the plan for the future of forensics, shared with the MHA in July 2010, notes their ongoing use:

> Similarly, the practice of polygraph, brainmapping and narcoanalysis should be in the purview of forensic medicine [FM] set up since these techniques involve different extents [of] invasiveness and warrant the availability of medical attendance. It is to be noted here that a judgement pronounced on May 05, 2010 by the Supreme Court of India stipulates conducting of such tests only after the subject's informed/voluntary consent; there is[,] however[,] no ban[,] which means that the administration of tests can continue. . . . Therefore these three facilities of the Central/State FSLs should be relocated in phased manner, and made available at FM set up.[106]

To ensure safety and medical supervision, state forensic experts have called for the incorporation of all truth machines within forensic medicine, as with narcoanalysis, but these proposals raise questions about the relationship of the drugs to the other techniques. Ongoing use of narcoanalysis in Gujarat, followed by suggestions for other narcoanalysis test facilities, thus fits the planning for the state forensic architecture.

The state's inability to reject truth machines is also evident in the legal case regarding forensic psychologist Malini, who worked at the FSL in Bangalore and was criticized for her aggressive use of these techniques. Controversy regarding her credentials and some false certificates led to her dismissal, although she had to be legally reinstated because of a faulty process. She also faced allegations that she had sold narcoanalysis recordings to the media, had often beaten up suspects during interrogations, and was not actually trained as a forensic psychologist.[107] When I visited the Bangalore FSL in 2014, the laboratory had no functioning forensic psychology division, even though Malini had been recently reinstated.

Malini and the director, B. M. Mohan, were the most vociferous defenders of truth machines and claimed a high percentage of accurate results. Most of the recordings regarding narcoanalysis that had been leaked to the media—among them videos of Abdul Karim Telgi, Krishna Thadarai (in the *Aarushi-Hemraj* case), and Sister Sefi (in the *Sister Abhaya* case)—involved their laboratory.[108] After the Supreme Court *Selvi* case, therefore, other forensic psychologists claimed that Malini's aggressiveness had delegitimized their techniques. Initially, however, Malini was much sought after, and even suspects who had undergone nacroanalysis elsewhere, including Arun Ferreira, who had been tested in Mumbai, were taken to her in Bangalore for examination.[109]

The contrast between Malini's critics and the Karnataka High Court, which reaffirmed her qualifications, is evidence of the continuing legitimacy of truth machines.[110] The court noted that Malini had master's and PhD degrees in psychology, had greatly contributed to solving crimes, and had been the target of political pressure to remove her from her position without due process. The court spent several paragraphs recounting her awards from the MHA, the police in Hyderabad and Bangalore, and the Karnataka government:

> The fact that she was in service as [a] contract employee for a period of 7 years continuously and during that period she was involved in [a] number of sensitive cases, her hard work and ability was appreciated by various authorities is not in dispute. In fact, she is a National Award winner and renowned researcher, specialized in conducting Narco Analysis and Brain Mapping tests for various under-trials, suspects involved in sensational cases from across the country.[111]

Testimonies of terror suspects, however, mention physical torture associated with Malini's use of narcoanalysis (see chapter 6), and videos related to the *Aarushi* case show her slapping suspects. Yet the court accepted her contributions in these cases, even though much of that narco-induced evidence was suspect.[112] As with the MHA's rejection of the Nagaraja report, the court directly or indirectly reaffirmed the expertise and influence of forensic psychologists in the use of the truth machines.

While the state continued its efforts, companies such as Axxonet aggressively promoted BEOS machines. Axxonet's website, for instance, asserts the following:

> Unlike other technologies which have been used in 2 or 3 cases, NSS has been used in over **700 cases** reported by independent Forensic laboratories in areas

such as Murders, Insurgency, Poaching, Illegal immigration to name a few. . . . Unfortunately the court confused BEAP/BEOS with the outdated and minimalistic P300 technique with which BEOS has no connection.[113]

The Supreme Court's inability to distinguish among methods of brain scanning, this marketing claims, is responsible for the delayed recognition of BEOS's advantages.[114] Facilities vie for attention to their version of brain scanning, and laboratories and institutes associated with either BEOS or BFP continually provide evidence of their success.[115] State and commercial interests are linked to both techniques.

High costs are associated with all techniques. BEOS and BFP machines are backed by strong commercial interests, but polygraphs and narcoanalysis, too, cost money.[116] For instance, a news article in 2009 cited a cost of 30,000 rupees (U.S.$435) (an increase of 20,000, or U.S.$290) to conduct narcoanalysis for agencies outside the state of Gujarat and 50,000 (U.S.$725) for expedited services.[117] As the chief home secretary of Gujarat explained, "The decision to increase the fees for psychological tests was taken considering appreciation in [the] cost of various things, including the salaries of DFS staffers and modern equipment needed for its laboratories."[118]

Occasional media stories appear about understaffing in the Mumbai laboratory. In a murder case where narcoanalysis was allowed, the media reported that the "Forensic Sciences Laboratory in Kalina employs experts and technicians on a contract, which expired in April and is yet to be renewed."[119] One story even reported a BEOS machine lying unused in the Chandigarh FSL, and in January 2019 the Delhi High Court expressed surprise that the Delhi FSL lacked a narcoanalysis machine, requiring that suspects be taken to the Gujarat FSL, and asked that a test machine be made operational within three months.[120] The apparent result was the installation of the BFP machine in the Delhi FSL.[121] The concern is thus an inability to meet demand. Meanwhile, the clash among forensic experts, the scientific community, and human rights activists is all but forgotten in a quest for technical fixes to the criminal justice system.

Just as the NHRC had suggested in 1999 that a medical review ensure safety in the use of truth machines, recommendations to move these techniques into the realm of forensic medicine appears to be the answer to any critics. While the science of these techniques has been the subject of much dispute, elaborate efforts have sought to insert forensic psychologists into the state forensic architecture. The question, then, is why forensic psychologists, as opposed to other forensic scientists, have been so readily embraced by the police and then have become so integral to the forensic architecture of the Indian state.

FORENSIC PSYCHOLOGISTS IN INDIA'S FORENSIC ARCHITECTURE

> You have to understand that irrespective of what a subject has done, we empathise with him. To judge someone is not our job. We leave it to the courts. As a psychologist, we journey with the suspect as he narrates his tale. There are times when we have felt that had we been in a similar circumstance, in which the subject found himself to be, we too would have done the same thing. —Dr. S. L. Vaya, "Meet the Woman Who Bonds with Hardened Criminals")

As experts, forensic psychologists became central to India's forensic architecture. With their machines and drugs, they plied their trade in laboratories, serving police reform with resource expansion, changes in legal procedures, and media support. Their contingent efforts thus applied the material resources to assist the bureaucratic agents of state power. The state forensic architecture came to rely, to a large extent, on forensic psychologists' abilities to define their role, their spatial location, and their unique relationship to truth machines. Just as Mulla's forensic nurses are central to the collection of evidence in cases of rape, forensic psychologists saw themselves as indispensable to finding evidence—whether confessions, information, or aids for investigation—in unsolved crimes, and they tried to convince others to rely on them.

Forensic psychologists, in turn, relied on machines like polygraphs or EEGs and on drugs to detect lies or to tap memories and obtain information. Yet beyond interpreting evidence, as other forensic experts do, they functioned almost as extensions of the machines—in effect, like cyborgs.[122] The January 2019 demand of the Delhi High Court for a "Narco Test Machine" captures this merging of machine and expert.[123] More than other forensic scientists, however, forensic psychologists were often conscious that their work was considered subjective.[124] Therefore, they highlighted their role by distinguishing themselves from police—spatially, professionally, and therapeutically—and sought to supersede the innovators responsible for machine-driven processes, bypassing the need to verify the machine's reliability and validity. The forensic psychologist's skill thus merged with the machine as the expert oscillated between professional autonomy and machine-derived expertise.

Distinction from the Police

Forensic psychologists are highly invested in distinguishing themselves from the police. Their laboratories, for example, are separated from police stations. The forensic laboratories I visited presented the type of hustle-bustle that is common to any bureaucratic office. Gaining entrance to the main building was straightforward, although formal access was required for observing the machines. In one laboratory, I witnessed a woman and her daughter (suspected in a domestic violence case) subjected to a layered voice analysis test in an extremely crowded space.[125] Other tests were conducted in more formal testing rooms.

Both psychologists and psychiatrists claim expertise distinct from the police. As one forensic psychologist said, "Psychologists, medical health professionals should be able to do it [conduct tests] since they understand nuances of [the] mind, the aspects of volition, cognition, and feeling at all levels."[126] Given the importance of the suspect's safety and security, this practitioner elaborated, the police, located at a police station, might be unable to handle the "psychotic breakdown" that a truth machine could trigger. Mental health professionals, in contrast, routinely deal with guilt, sadness, deception, and psychotic breakdown.

Even a drug or alcohol is administered differently in a forensic setting. In police settings, alcohol is a popular means of lifting inhibitions, promoting a desire to "let it all out" in order to avoid physical and mental discomfort. Alcohol may even be a face-saving device, rendering the individual unconscious of the speech act later on. One forensic psychiatrist I spoke with distinguished alcohol used in a police station and a drug administered in a medical setting:

> See, the reason, the difference between alcohol and Pentothal—alcohol you cannot make person to drink. That is [the] first part. Second part, you cannot control the intoxication phase, like we do not know . . . whether the person is going into [a] trance with 1 peg, 1.5 peg, or 3 pegs. So the beauty of this medicine is [that] you can control. In alcohol you can't.[127]

Only a medically trained professional, therefore, can use a drug efficiently. Narcoanalysis has been used illegally on terrorism suspects (see chapter 6), and private doctors have administered drugs in police stations (see chapter 2). For forensic psychologists and psychiatrists, however, the extralegal techniques used by police undermine the legitimacy of their work.

Identifying with their subjects through empathy and association is also crucial in the forensic psychologists' efforts to establish guilt and, in turn, further distinguishes them from the police. As a prominent forensic psychologist explained:

> While torture is an external stimuli [sic], these techniques are internal ones and invite an internal journey. They force you to review your past in a different way, not confess, but ask them to think about their selves and come back. It is a moment of catharsis in the legal system. Unlike the police custody, where there is fear of encounter or custodial death or torture, here there is empathy. There are no doubts about the methods, and [the] system can reach truth regardless of the consequences.[128]

While speaking of the confessions in a particularly horrific case of multiple murders, one clinical psychologist noted that when the murderer (who was subsequently executed) cried and confessed in the BEOS laboratory, he felt guilty:

> CLINICAL PSYCHOLOGIST: I only think that he's a patient. First of all he's a patient.
> JINEE LOKANEETA: He's a—?
> CP: Mental patient.
> JL: Mental patient?
> CP: Otherwise he will not do something like this. But then that testing was done because he's admitting that he has done.[129]

The guilt is accompanied by an attempt to avoid traumatic probes, as the clinical psychologist elaborated:

> No traumatic probe should be presented, not a single word which can traumatize. Everything has to be presented in a nontraumatic way, because you know that you're not going to use this as evidence in the court. What you want to know is that . . . was he interacting with this person? These are the things that

you want to know. And he says he was not there at all. So if you know that he was there, he was interacting with this person, that itself becomes sufficient ... to convince him; see, the test is showing like, "This, you were there." And later you can interrogate him using that.[130]

Trauma must thus be avoided because a practitioner could empathize with a suspect, even while obtaining information. In an interview highlighting her award, Vaya notes, "There are times when we have felt that had we been in a similar circumstance, in which the subject found himself to be, we too would have done the same thing."[131]

The gender typing of forensic psychology also separates these professionals from the police. Forensic psychology, like forensic nursing, is a feminized occupation,[132] and many prominent forensic psychologists have been women. In reference to fingerprinting, Simon Cole notes that historically "95 percent of the 115 identification clerks employed by the [U.S.] Navy were female."[133] Rationales for gender typing include claims that women have "better aptitude" and "attention to detail," but Cole suggests that the predominance of women is instead linked to the "feminization of clerical work" in the early 1900s United States and to women having been restricted to marginalized professions more generally.

A female research associate mentioned to me that the reasons for women's predominance in psychology in India is a common question. "It may be because they're more patient in nature," she speculated, going on to say:

> They have better listening skill[s] because [the] forensic psychology part comes later. It starts with general psychology. When you're interacting with a person, how you're interacting, how you're getting information, women are more reliable, more credible as compared to men. So even [with] phone calls by some company is being "Ah ... the person is female." So if a female is giving you a call, you will rely more on her.[134]

Occupational credentials, however, need not offer professional autonomy. Women forensic psychologists have written almost all articles on truth machines in CBI bulletins and police journals, but these are almost always coauthored with a male director or forensic scientist.[135] And the assumption that women naturally lie was the basis for disbelieving their accounts of rape and turning to the lie detector for evidence (see chapter 3). The police and the courts, in comparison, are male dominated, suggesting a contrast between presumably patient forensic psychologists and more aggressive law enforcement. Elaborating on the virtues of their patience, one forensic psychologist said:

> When you're interacting with police officer[s], you cannot be aggressive in nature. You have to keep your patience. You have to keep your mind calm. And police officers, their profession is such that they're more towards aggression, or they have to behave in that manner; otherwise, people will not listen to them. If, as a forensic psychologist, I start behaving aggressively, I cannot control another person. He will not cooperate with me. I don't want that.[136]

This forensic psychologist sought to establish rapport with suspects:

> There are many reasons, not for therapeutic purpose but when a person is coming, irrespective of whether he's innocent or guilty person, he's anxious. So in order to calm him down, in order to make him more cooperative, you have to be [a] little therapeutic in nature. So it is more like rapport formation and not giving proper therapy to the person. So in order to win his trust, you have to move in that direction; otherwise, he'll not respond; he'll not cooperate. And if you don't get consent, you cannot go for investigation.[137]

Lack of patience among police, this practitioner believed, was a crucial reason for their inability to create rapport with suspects. As Vaya similarly explained, "They [police] usually don't have the patience to make use of the techniques because they are under several kinds of pressure, including fast resolution of a case."[138]

The forensic psychologists I met considered themselves so separate from the police that their conversations focused on differences explaining the dilemma between forensic and clinical psychology. The latter, several respondents told me, is often a voluntary relationship. The forensic psychologist, in contrast, is part of the state forensic architecture. Clinical psychologists can promote "unconditional trust for healing the wound," one forensic psychologist noted; "here the wound that is suppressed may be scratched and may affect the person."[139] The process of obtaining a confession further requires a continuous interview until the information is extracted and committed to paper with a signature (although a suspect can retract the confession). The catch for the forensic psychologist, however, is "But once if you read it to me, I have heard, my opinion can reflect what we talked about. While the intent is not to harm you but I have to report what we talked about."[140]

Thus, all truth machines are deployed to obtain information or confessions, whether directly or indirectly. The purpose of BEOS, BFP, and the polygraph, therefore, is not to detect deception. Even if the technique fails to provide information during the test, the pretest and posttest interviews extract confessions or information. With BEOS, pretest interviews are used to create questions for probes and then for confessions. As a clinical psychologist explained:

> And that's how you find that, even when you ask them, they tell you that, after [the] BEOS test[,] when they present the findings to the subject, so many of them confess straightaway. That self-confession is very large[,] this thing in BEOS. People confess.[141]

As the director of a major forensic lab (not a forensic psychologist) summarized for me, "Whenever they [police] can't use torture, they bring them here for confessions."[142] That is the ultimate motivation for the use of truth machines.

Experience over Validity

If the goal in the forensic setting is confession or information, then juridical truth in courtrooms, or even scientific validity, as explored by the Nagaraja Committee, is not that crucial. Regarding BEOS, one forensic scientist explained validity this way: "The findings in cases have actually proven its validity on its own. You don't need a validation test. It is irrelevant today. More than me, those people [the forensic psychologists] are certain that they can solve a case."[143] Forensic psychologists offer reliance on the truth machines based on experience in thousands of cases. Innovation and proof thus lie deep within the state forensic architecture. The experience of forensic psychologists and the necessity of information thus trump all else, a claim clearly upheld by the state's response to the Nagaraja Committee as well as the decision to continue using truth machines under the aegis of forensic medicine. As one forensic psychologist said, "It helped so from [a] victim point of view. . . . Anything that may help in investigation has to be tried."[144] A forensic psychiatrist made the same point even more strongly: "[Solving] burglary is not going to help [the] nation, but if [a] terrorist is there, it is definitely going to help [the] nation. The worst scenario [is] we can't help, but even if [there is] one one-thousandth of a percent chance that we may get some information that can be helpful, so that was probably the reason that it was started."[145]

Distinguishing themselves from the coercive police—spatially, professionally, and therapeutically—forensic psychologists tout their experience as a mode of legitimation. Unlike police interrogators, however, they feel committed to "make the person accept from within."[146] They see their work as a therapeutic process that helps the patient "work out inner responses of his actions," and they attempt to show empathy and not "leave them wounded." Despite the enormity of some crimes, the forensic psychologist has to "understand with compassion," "without judgment" (until later), and without any conception of "right or wrong." Indeed, one forensic psychologist insisted to me that the "questions are almost like the inner voice." Elaborating, she said, "You cannot pretend, because they will know, and then they will not connect without conscious inhibitions." The process, she averred, is not about gaining answers but about "relief of the patient" so that his "burdens would be relieved" and his health unaffected.[147] The forensic psychologist posits herself as both working for the state and the patient.

Relationship to Machines

Beyond exhibiting empathy with those who have committed horrendous crimes, forensic psychologists mediate suspects' relationships with the truth machines. As the history of the lie detector indicates, the machines can evoke fear.[148] When brain-scanning electrodes are attached or a drug injected, the result is often additional anxiety beyond concern over the test, a problem that has been raised in court (see chapter 5). In response, the forensic psychologist, as a medical professional, ensures that the procedure is safe and spends much effort trying to counter the ostensibly "irrational fear" of being attached to an electrode cap or drugged and emphasize the objective nature of the process.

An early twentieth-century debate on the validity of fingerprinting and anthropometry (the art of observation considered science) offers a parallel. Fingerprinting developed more valence as a technical procedure—"a mechanical quality"—than human observation. Cole writes, "In short, fingerprinting seemed like part and parcel of the new, rationalized bureaucracies, scientific management, ... and methodization of government."[149] Similarly, emphasizing polygraph reports or BEOS/BFP results deemphasizes the subjective aspect of these techniques. The exception, of course, is narcoanalysis, which emphasizes narratives. Nonetheless, discourse about all truth machines promotes their relationship to science, and when compared to the police, they do indeed *appear* less arbitrary and a more modern mode of investigation.

The relation between the machines and the forensic psychologists also lies in the innovation initiated by those who actually use these techniques in the labs. For instance, BEOS-related scientists emphasized that if lack of participation in the crime (experiential knowledge, or EK) appeared more than once, they repeated the tests. One research associate told me the following:

> If the suspect is innocent and on his version he's showing [a] lot of EK, that means whatever [the] suspect is telling, you can go with that and not on [the] IO's [investigative officer's] version. On [the] IO's version he's not showing any EK. On his own version he's showing EK. That means he's towards innocence. Whatever he is telling you about the crime scene is true, correct.[150]

If there is experiential knowledge, on the basis of the inventor's suggestion, the process is repeated to ensure that the suspect actually has knowledge of the crime. Repetition presumably promotes reliability and assurance in the test's objective, scientific underpinnings.

Technicians and forensic psychologists, however, initiated a shift in this practice after finding that constant repetition of the tests, even after a slight indication of experiential knowledge, changed the results not confirmed them. As one clinical psychologist explained:

> So today, even if one probe shows EK, they will test him again [the] next day with another set of formulation. And suppose, then, also they get only one EK; then again they will test him. And you'll be shocked to see that; even I'm shocked; the third day or the third time they test, they get fifteen, twenty probes showing EK, because that was the right formulation. Because the police came and said that this is the way it would have happened, even they thought this is the way it happened. The way it really happened was different. You present that, but for that you have to do a lot of your own brain work. Not that everywhere you may succeed, but this is when they get so many EKs, they tell the investigator, "See, this is the way it happened. Now, you go, investigate." They

go to another location, another place, investigate, and in two days' time they get a phone call saying *saab* (sir), case solve *ho gaya* (case is solved); we got all the evidences.[151]

The inventor was apparently impressed with the forensic psychologists. As my respondent elaborated, "I mean, the other day she was telling '*hum ek mahine ke baad test kiya, wohi finding*'" (we repeated the test after a month and found the same result).[152] The relationship between machines and forensic psychologists thus lies not only in science but also in laboratory innovation, with almost the merging of forensic psychologists and truth machines—the emergence of cyborgs—exceeding the understanding of the machines' originators.[153] The application of the machines, therefore, with forensic psychologists as cyborgs, reveals practices that strengthen their presumed validity.

WHY TRUTH CLAIMS FAIL

The problem with building a state forensic architecture on the work of cyborgs is that even a new regime that ostensibly replaced torture and third-degree interrogation continued to rely on methods of obtaining confessions and information. Here confessions are no longer extracted during police detention but instead are sought in forensic laboratories or hospitals through the misnomer of "scientific interrogations." As Peter Brooks famously explained in *Troubling Confessions*, a confession may be due to a desire to share some guilt about anything with an authority figure—priest, psychologist, therapist, or police officer—and may be true for some wrongdoing but not for the act under investigation.[154] Such confessions are often unreliable, involuntary (volition being an important legal norm), or even false. In this case, the use of machines and drugs by medicolegal experts overdetermine the process of inducing confessions even more.

The inability to dispense with truth machines, despite a constant critique and the availability of other forensic methods, suggests the same logic that propped up physical torture. The scientific techniques that informed investigations when they remained in the shadows became official, but with recovery still the basis for confirming a suspect's account, the need for confirmation led to a continual search for methods to detect lies and discern truths. The transformation of forensic psychologists from hidden to intermediate to visible, then, rendered them central to contemporary Indian policing and the state forensic architecture.

Through narratives and documents, forensic psychologists became the harbingers of truth. Reported documents never represent the entire sequence of pretest, test, posttest, or test repetition, despite meticulous records and CDs recording interrogations. A thick case file shared with me in one FSL with strict instructions not to reproduce any part of it clearly indicated what emerges from a paper record. The expert's report folds out any creases, contradictions, and elements of interpretation.[155] The forensic psychologist's report was often the sole document representing the forensic truth whether formally presented as evidence or not. The Delhi FSL's adoption of BFP in response to the Delhi High Court's recommendation for a narco test machine also reveals that even when some methods are delegitimized, the state forensic architecture remains ready to embrace new truth machines. The criteria for their adoption is that they resemble the truth machines such as the newer suspect detection systems or voice layered analysis, which above all provide a prominent role for forensic psychologists desiring confessions or information through a combination of art and machines.[156]

CONCLUSION

Tracing the state forensic architecture that enabled scientific interrogation reveals that state acts are not as intentional as theories of the state and policing claim but are instead contingent on the initiatives of semi-state actors. Commercial concerns and patent interests mediated the use and legitimization of truth machines. Their use may then have expanded intentionally, but the everyday practices of forensic psychologists—not the action of a unitary state—ultimately determined their application. For example, forensic psychologists applied techniques on their terms, seeking to make suspects less anxious and unscarred physically and mentally.

Forensic laboratories and forensic psychologists thus occupy a space separate from police custody. While still under police charge and working with investigating officers, forensic psychologists are certainly under police pressure. Yet the notion of custody changes between police station and forensic laboratory. Forensic psychologists ensure that suspects are relaxed in the chair before conducting a polygraph test.[157] Or they conduct it several times to discern a pattern and note any signs of anxiety while presenting results. Similarly, BEOS works only if a person is undamaged neuropsychologically, and narcoanalysis requires doctors to ensure that suspects remain physically unharmed. With truth machines intended to replace physical torture, forensic psychologists distanced their work from the secrecy of police custody and operationalized the art of questioning. Ultimately, however, this distancing has failed as it has created another confessional site for interrogation, and become only a symbolic attempt to address physical torture with the help of science and where delegitimized methods can yield to new techniques.

Chapter 5

COURTS AND LEGAL DISCOURSES

The (Flawed) Art of Government

> Such tests are conducted under strict supervision of the expert. It cannot be said that there is any violation of the fundamental rights guaranteed to a citizen of India.
>
> —ROJO GEORGE V. DEPUTY SUPERINDENDENT OF POLICE

The legal discourses of the high courts and the Supreme Court of India in relation to the three scientific techniques have to be considered in the context of a raging debate between human rights critics and state officials defending these techniques. Using a Foucauldian framework to study court opinions on the use of lie detectors, brain scans, and narcoanalysis, I argue that these legal discourses are indicative of both a liberal state's desire to modernize and its specifically postcolonial nature. In the legal and political discourses, one finds a strong desire to modernize and in the process replace the "physical third degree," or torture, which is currently impacting the criminal justice system. I argue that even though the courts defend these scientific investigative techniques as a way to replace torture, the edifice being sanctioned actually allows for a creation of a flawed art of government in a peculiarly postcolonial manner.

LAW AS VIOLENCE: EXTRAORDINARY LAWS, EXTRAJUDICIAL KILLINGS, AND CUSTODIAL TORTURE

As noted in the introduction, the significance of the emergence of the truth machines only becomes clear when contrasted with the levels of state violence in India and the consequent theorization emerging from those challenging that violence. Two major scholars and civil liberty activists who have worked extensively on analyzing the nature of state power, law, and violence in contemporary India are K. G. Kannabiran and Ujjwal K. Singh. Their work powerfully illustrates the violent nature of the Indian state and law. However, while their particular analyses, emerging from the study of extraordinary laws, is extremely insightful, it remains inadequate to analyze the constant innovation by the state and law as seen in the use of scientific techniques such as lie detectors, brain scans, and narcoanalysis.

Kannabiran's conception of the law emerges from his careful analysis of colonial legacies that, according to him, play an important role in determining the nature of the postcolonial state and law. In his book *The Wages of Impunity*, Kannabiran defines law as "a society's consensus for the regulation of human activity in various fields, and the regulation of these activities by the development of state power, a deployment that need not necessarily be violent or backed by the threat of force."[1]

This definition of law is similar to many other liberal conceptions of law (such as those of H.L.A. Hart or Ronald Dworkin) that consider consensus building as the basis of law rather than violence. However, a dominant theme in Kannabiran's essays undermines this conception of the law. As he notes, "expressions like 'law and order,' 'public order' and 'state security' enable the state to employ violence against the people without a corresponding obligation to exercise discretion."[2] He locates the origins of the repressive character of the postcolonial state in its colonial history, which has been consciously preserved by the state in two ways: first, by directly adopting some of the repressive legislations used by the colonial state, and, second, by perpetuating a colonial mentality that is intolerant of people's movements.

An excellent example of how colonial continuities have informed present-day state violence, whether directly or indirectly, appears in the context of the extrajudicial killing of many political activists and organized criminals, known to many in India as a "fake encounter."[3] Kannabiran notes that the legal basis of encounters in Andhra Pradesh is the A.P. (Andhra Pradesh) Suppression of Disturbances Act (1967), which was based on the Madras Suppression of Disturbances Act of 1947 (the year of Indian independence). This extraordinary law allowed the state to identify tribal areas as "disturbed," and, once the area was declared as such, police were authorized to shoot at any party of five or more, since any act of assembly was considered unlawful.[4] Kannabiran further points out that other extraordinary laws, such as the A.P. Preventive Detention Act of 1970, also identified certain persons as targets thus enabling violent state actions.

Ujjwal Singh has built on this violent narrative of the postcolonial state in his systematic study of extraordinary legislation such as the Terrorism and Disruptive Activities (Prevention) Act of 1985 and the 2002 Prevention of Terrorism Act (both laws upheld as constitutional by the Supreme Court of India).[5] Singh notes that even though these extraordinary laws initially appeared for a particular purpose of challenging terrorism or responding to disruption for a specific time, they were vague in scope and tended to persist beyond their designated time period in terms of ongoing cases or as legal provisions that were incorporated into ordinary criminal laws. He calls this phenomenon the "permanence of the exception."[6] Further, due to the undemocratic nature of the provisions of extraordinary laws and the aggressive use of them by the state, Singh puts forward the powerful phrase "violence of jurisprudence" that law in its various forms takes.[7]

In both Kannabiran's and Singh's work, law and state emerge as primarily violent, and there appears to be continuity between colonial and postcolonial law, which is most visible in antiterrorism legislations. Kannabiran indeed explains the actual relationship between law and violence in the following way: "The law, of course, does not provide any guidelines to measure the force used."[8] For him, it appears that the state and law have a particular motivation for not clarifying these terms. This is because, as he puts it, "defining power would limit it and make it accountable and enhance rights."[9]

Even otherwise, human rights reports confirm the high numbers of torture and custodial deaths in the routine criminal justice system, strengthening the theory that law and state in contemporary India are often synonymous with violence in both routine and extraordinary contexts.[10] In these reports, torture is often blamed on the lower-ranked Indian police. As I have argued earlier, "An exclusive emphasis on the . . . [police and other enforcement agents] distracts attention from the continuing ambivalence of the Court towards excess violence."[11] In other words, the law and the state have consistently created space for excess violence, including torture, at all levels, and the courts have largely been unable to curb the violence despite some very powerful judicial interventions.[12]

The significance of such work is to challenge the "rule of law" based framework prominent in the self-presentation of the postcolonial Indian democratic state and instead emphasize its "terror" aspect.[13] However, the question I ask is, Why, even in the context of untrammeled opportunities for terror, does the postcolonial Indian state come up with new modes of scientific investigation such as lie detectors, brain scanning, and narcoanalysis ostensibly to replace physical torture in the context of interrogations; and how do the courts respond to such a phenomenon? I suggest that rather than emphasizing the colonial continuities, it is important to evaluate the emergence of these techniques in postcolonial developments on the relationship between law and violence.[14] The significance of a powerful human rights movement and a formal adherence to human rights norms and values by the postcolonial Indian state in contrast to a colonial state may be important to acknowledge in this narrative. I argue that the tension between a desire to replace physical torture and an inability or unwillingness to challenge the conditions for its persistence reflects the peculiarity of the postcolonial state.

Techniques and Its Critics

As soon as the techniques started appearing more visibly in the early 2000s, all three techniques were collectively challenged in the courts. As discussed earlier, lie detectors or polygraphs involve the use of an instrument to detect physiological changes, such as heart rate, blood pressure, breathing, and sweat patterns, when relevant questions related to the crime are asked.[15] In brain scanning, responses to stimuli are recorded by the EEG to determine experiential knowledge of the crime.[16] Of the three techniques under discussion, the most controversial is narcoanalysis, which involves the use of drugs to elicit specific information. The use of such a drug then enables a trained psychologist to ask certain questions and get "truthful" answers; the entire process is often videotaped.[17] Here it may be helpful to reiterate some of the criticisms that the human rights activists and scholars put forward in response to these techniques that prompted the courts to respond in particular ways.

Human rights groups and scholars focused on these new modes as violative of human rights and have unequivocally termed narcoanalysis a form of torture. For instance, medical ethics scholar and activist Amar Jesani characterizes narcoanalysis as a form of "pharmacological" torture. As he puts it, "Torture, in fact, remains torture even if it does not spill blood, break bones and is done in sterile, airconditioned operation theatres."[18] Jesani's criticisms are two twofold: first, he criticizes the scientific acceptability of these methods, and, second, he questions the ethical concerns in the use of these methods. Jesani argues that until now the scientific validity and reliability of these methods has been highly suspect. For instance, he notes that even if a person's brain responds to certain questions in brain scanning, it could easily be due to environmental factors (comparable to a physiological response to a doctor's office or to an intimidating MRI machine) or even from a fear of being called a liar. Similarly, although it is well known that a person becomes more excited and lucid due to the injecting of Sodium Pentothal in narcoanalysis, that does not necessarily lead that person to speak the truth. Indeed Jesani suggests that the person could equally be responding to hypnotic suggestions by the interrogator.[19] In the absence of clear scientific studies indicating that these methods work, the eliciting of truth through the P300 wave or the inhibition of GABA (gamma amino butyric acid) are mere assumptions.[20] Indeed, an early developer of electroencephalogram-based methods in the United States, Dr. J. Peter Rosenfield, a psychologist and neuroscientist at Northwestern University, told the *New York Times*, "Technologies which are neither seriously peer-reviewed nor independently replicated are not, in my opinion, credible."[21] Similarly, P. Chandra Sekharan, president of the Forensic Science Society and former director of the Forensic Sciences Department of Tamil Nadu points out that narcoanalysis is mainly a form of psychological third degree:

> The outcome under a "sleep-like state" . . . could be contaminated by deception, fantasy, garbled speech and so on. Sodium pentothal, a drug used in this test, helped a person to extract repressed feelings, memories and thoughts. It only revealed "psychological truth" and not "probative truth," which the police looked for.[22]

Along with the scientific reliability of these tests, Jesani notes the importance of ethical concerns, especially the role of doctors in the process. Since the drug can have dangerous effects, small doses have to be tested on a person to check for "allergic anaphylactic reaction," and careful and constant monitoring is required to avoid sudden lowering of blood pressure, "cessation of respiration or apnea, constriction of the larynx, or a laryngeal spasm."[23] According to Jesani, participation in such a dangerous procedure, without informed consent, is a serious violation of medical ethics as reflected in the World Medical Association's 1975 Tokyo Declaration against the participation of doctors in torture, a declaration formally strengthened even further in the post-9/11 context.

In addition to emphasizing the medical effects of narcoanalysis, the Delhi-based civil liberty group Peoples Union for Democratic Rights characterizes "Narco-analysis . . . as a form of torture" because they see the test as a violation of the self-incrimination clause of the Indian Constitution (Article 20 (3)) and the corresponding 161 (2) of the Criminal Procedure Code:[24]

> These are fundamental principles of criminal law ensuring that the accused has the right to keep silent during the course of investigation. Narcoanalysis negates such protections by making redundant the right to silence of the subject. If interrogated when in his/her full senses, the subject may choose to remain silent. However[,] by breaking down rational defences, narco-analysis undermines both an individual's right to remain silent and the principle behind this right.[25]

Thus, PUDR emphasizes that these constitutional and procedural protections are meaningful only when the person's volition is not impacted by the use of these techniques. Furthermore, they point to the fact that despite some attempts to emphasize consent in the use of these techniques, the latter is often less meaningful for the more marginalized sections in society. PUDR is also critical of the dissemination of results of these techniques, particularly of narcoanalysis, in the media that led to a media trial, thereby affecting the actual fairness of the trials.[26]

Overall, the specific criticisms of human rights groups and legal scholars refer to the extraordinariness of these techniques in a liberal rule-of-law-based constitutional system and labeled them essentially legal and state violence in another form. The use of BEOS (not even narcoanalysis) to convict Aditi Sharma in a murder case led Professor Rosenfield to argue, "The fact that an advanced and sophisticated democratic society such as India would actually convict persons based on an unproven technology is even more incredible."[27] Thus, the critics portrayed the use of these techniques as an extraordinary moment in the Indian criminal justice system to be resolved conclusively by the different courts.

While the human rights activists and scholars have rightly criticized the medical, ethical, and constitutional concerns connected with these techniques and play an important part in explaining them, I suggest that it may not be adequate to exclusively focus on the violence of these forms. Instead, one has to situate the emergence of these techniques within a legal and political regime that does exhibit certain moments of introspection and self-transformation however limited that process may be in practice.

Interpreting the Political and Legal Discourses: A Desire to Modernize at All Costs

State functionaries who are in the business of narcoanalysis and brain mapping publicly defended the need to use these techniques. As mentioned in chapter 4, the individual efforts of forensic psychologists such as Dr. Vaya, Dr. Malini, and Dr. Mukundan, encouraged by the forensic lab directors and welcomed by the police for a range of reasons, stood poised to build a state forensic architecture articulated in the Ministry of Home Affairs reports.[28]

The high courts therefore had a crucial role to play in this public contest between human rights groups (and some forensic scientists), who mostly rejected the techniques, and state and semi-state officials, who mostly defended the scientific investigative techniques and the apparent growing consensus in their favor.[29] Here, I am particularly interested in the response of the courts to one specific claim made in the state discourses—namely, that the use of these scientific techniques would replace the physical torture and custodial deaths that are prevalent in the current criminal justice system. As mentioned earlier, this claim was consistently made to defend these techniques as replacing physical torture. In the *State of Andhra Pradesh v. Smt. Inapuri Padma and Ors.* (2008), for instance, the court notes:

> In the accusations made in India, the Police are attributed with applying third degree methods in eliciting information and there are instances of the culprits or suspects dying in lockups during the course of interrogation on account of application of third degree methods, therefore, *there is a blame* that the Indian police are flagrantly violating the human rights and fundamental rights guaranteed under Article 21 of the Constitution of India. Therefore there is every need to apply scientific tests to elicit the information from the culprits.[30]

This is a remarkable admission by the courts of the state's inability to address custodial torture and death despite decades of progressive jurisprudence on the subject. This impulse is clearly echoed even in the statements of state officials regarding the expansion of the use of these techniques (which I have systematically traced in chapter 4). For example, a senior official at the Central Forensic Science Laboratory, Delhi, was quoted in newspapers as saying:

> The use of forensic science for modern-day investigation has become imperative. One cannot use third-degree methods for extracting confessions. Many of the witnesses even turn hostile in front of the court[,] which defeats the purpose. Scientific investigation and tools like brain mapping and narcoanalysis are the only way to prove guilt and bring justice.[31]

This assertion is a clear attempt on the part of the high court and other state officials to create limits on the state's violence on one hand and allow the use of scientific investigative techniques for the welfare of the population on the other. One could read this as an attempted Foucauldian move that would replace visible sovereign power by an art of governing. In other words, in a context where there are high numbers of custodial deaths each year and routine torture/third degree, any such shift would mean that social control is not just realized in the form of top-down sovereign (or even disciplinary) power but also is visible in the harnessing of the productive capacity of individuals within a population. Foucault writes, "Government has as its purpose . . . the welfare of the population, the improvement of its condition, the increase of its wealth, longevity, health etc."[32] This allows for the emergence of a different form of power—almost a "pastoral power" aimed at the welfare of the entire population (something I discuss in chapter 2).

However, in order to make this goal legible and persuasive and to present these techniques as forms of welfare not repression, the high courts had to do two things: first, they had to create a discourse that could counter the challenges made by the critics and the petitioners in these cases about constitutional violations. And, second, they had to present the techniques as completely safe and thereby a mere modernizing of the means of investigation for its citizens similar to the introduction of techno politics that Timothy Mitchell notes in the context of Egypt (discussed in chapter 4).[33] Indeed, one could say that the high courts are so convinced of the necessity of the scientific techniques for the welfare of the accused that they do not even require the consent of the accused or the application of the usual constitutional safeguards.

As indicated earlier, one of the main criticisms of these techniques was regarding the violation of Article 20 (3), the self-incrimination clause of the Indian Constitution. The high courts very creatively sidestepped the applicability of the article to the use of these techniques by parsing the meaning of the term "statement" in the article. The judge in *Ramchandra Ram Reddy v. The State of Maharashtra* (2004) explains that the results of neither polygraphs nor brain mapping are in the form of verbal responses.[34] Since the results indicate only whether you are lying (in polygraphs) or possess knowledge (brain scanning) and do not specify the information, the results of these tests cannot be considered statements and thus cannot be subject to the protections provided by the Constitution. This immediately draws the focus onto narcoanalysis, where statements are made in response to the questions asked during the procedure. The high court, however, addresses this by simply maintaining that the Constitution prohibits only inculpatory or incriminating statements. It asserts that whether a statement would be incriminating or not can be apparent only after a test is conducted. The court thereby did not consider whether the initial utilization of these techniques is unconstitutional itself.

The second major issue of contention is a related yet distinct one of whether these techniques can be constitutionally applied by the investigating agency without the consent of the accused. Here the argument on consent appears to emerge both from a right to silence enshrined in the Constitution as well as due to the use of medical procedures on the body of the accused (although not explicitly discussed as such). In general, the high courts suggest that consent of the subject is not necessary in these instances based on a range of reasons: one, application of these techniques does not constitute compulsion; two, they do not affect the health of the person; and, three, and most significantly, they are represented as a necessary part of the investigation. The combination of these arguments is best illustrated in the *Selvi* case in the High Court, where the Court explains that the use of narcoanalysis could not be said to constitute compulsion because of the way compulsion or duress is defined in the English law dictionary. The judge writes, "Duress is where a man is compelled to do an act by injury, beating or unlawful imprisonment (sometimes called duress in [a] strict sense) or by threat (of the aforementioned and to a family member)."[35] Here the emphasis is primarily on actual injury or a threat of the same and reiterates how establishing veracity of state violence continues to rely on the impact on the physical body with the court reiterating, in the process, the contrast between these techniques and physical third degree.

In addressing consent, the courts also evaluate the alleged negative medical implications of the procedures. In addition to claiming that lie detectors and brain scans do not directly violate the body, the high court in *Selvi* takes great pains to explain why the medical concerns are not sustainable challenges with regard to narcoanalysis. The court points to Section 53 of the CrPC that allows medical practitioners to *"make such an examination of a person arrested as is reasonably necessary, and to use such force as is reasonably necessary for that purpose."*[36] The court argues that this section clearly suggests that "some pain or discomfort" "caused (in injecting the drug)" is inadequate for disallowing narcoanalysis. Here the emphasis is on the act of injecting the drug as a criterion for causing compulsion or duress, not so much on the impact of the drug on the person. In other cases the possible medical effects of these techniques have been addressed more directly and ultimately rejected by the court. In the *Dinesh Dalmia* case, where the accused claimed that these techniques posed a "health hazard" or "an indirect physical torture," the court denied any such understanding. The court basically supported the state's counsel that these tests were safe, since they were similar to other scientific tests such as MRI or CT scan and other medical procedures.[37]

In a subsequent case, a twenty-four-year-old accused was particularly concerned about long-term consequences, since narcoanalysis was a "complicated procedure" and had "drastic side effects and sometimes it may be even fatal."[38] Because the procedure involved injecting a drug that "depresses the central nervous system, slows heart rate, and lowers blood pressure" and dosage varies by "age, sex, physical constitution and also mental attitude and will power," a "wrong dose could send a subject into coma or even cause death."[39] The court acknowledges that, similar to other methods, narcoanalysis does have a danger of "adverse reaction" but points to the fact that a person is checked for medical fitness with a complete lab workup before being injected, which thereby minimizes adverse reactions. The court further writes:

> As I have already stated[,] narcoanalysis is a *scientific* test conducted by the experts in the subject after taking all *possible precautions*. It is true that it has got adverse reactions also. But such adverse reaction can happen while administering any medicine prescribed by doctors practicing modern medicine. So merely because there is a remote possibility of adverse reaction, use of such technics [sic] in conducting investigation cannot be prevented.[40]

Here the constant comparison of these techniques with routine medical tests such as CT Scans, x-rays, MRIs, and other modern medical procedures is an obvious attempt to normalize their use. After all, the adverse reactions that accompany all modern medicines and tests are often ignored due to the "lifesaving" nature of these techniques. The reference to lab work to ensure subject fitness again points to an explicit concern for the welfare of the population in the use of these techniques while ignoring the specific critiques made by human rights activists.

But the most obvious way that these techniques were normalized and institutionalized by the high courts is the way in which the question of consent is organically linked to the process of investigation. Time and again, the courts insist that the question of consent is unimportant, since these tests are a natural part or a mere extension of the scientific investigation. The court explains this in *Santokben*:

> The aforesaid two tests are scientific methods in furtherance of the investigation. . . . The investigating agency cannot be prevented to interrogate the accused at the stage of investigation[,] and restraining the Investigating Agency to further investigate the crime through the aforesaid two tests would [be] tantamount to interfer[ing] with the right of the investigating Agency to investigate the crime of which it is statutorily authorized.[41]

Quickly linking this to the question of consent, the court writes that since these tests are a part of the investigation, they do not require the consent of the accused, "otherwise the Investigating Agency will not be in a position to further investigate the case."[42] Indeed, inverting the argument about the involuntary nature of these techniques, the court ends up blaming the accused for these turn of events:

> When the accused/person has not told the truth during the investigation, naturally, that accused/person would not be voluntarily giving consent for the aforesaid two tests[,] as he is always apprehensive that if the aforesaid two tests are conducted than [sic] the same might go against him[,] therefore, he is bound to not give consent.[43]

The court thus squarely rejects any need for gaining consent since the tests are seen to be a normal part of an investigation.

In all, the legal discourses presented by the high courts pointed to the ordinariness of these scientific techniques. Focusing on new forms of knowledge about the subjects once they are drawn into the investigations and the comparison of these truth-seeking techniques to lifesaving ones suggests a major shift in the paradigm of state control—that of replacing physical third degree or torture. In fact, the emergence of these techniques is portrayed as a response to past criticisms from the same human rights activists. As B. M. Mohan, former director of the Forensic Science Laboratories in Karnataka, writes in response to medical activist Jesani, "When the public and human rights activists protest that investigating agencies adopt 'third degree' methods to extract information from the accused, it is time the agencies took recourse to the scientific methods of investigation described above."[44] There is almost a suggestion that any criticism of these techniques would make the activists themselves responsible for the reversal to third degree. This shift is also apparent in reports that suspects themselves consent to these techniques primarily out of a fear of being subjected to the third degree (and indeed requested the tests to be used for exculpatory purposes).[45]

The Supreme Court's intervention in such a context becomes extremely significant. In a landmark judgment, the Indian Supreme Court in May 2010 declared the *involuntary* use of the polygraph, brain scanning, and narcoanalysis unconstitutional.[46] The Court declared the involuntary use of such techniques as both a violation of Article 20 (3), or the right against self-incrimination, as well as of "substantial due process" under Article 21. As the Court emphatically writes, "The compulsory administration of the impugned techniques violates the 'right against self incrimination,... unjustified intrusion into mental privacy,' and amount[s] to cruel, inhuman or degrading treatment."[47] Thus, the Supreme Court not only reasserts the significance of the right against self-incrimination but also goes a step further to suggest the integral relationship between Article 20 (3) and the interpretations of Article 21 regarding right to fair trial and substantive due process, which had completely been ignored by the high courts.

By rejecting the involuntary use of these techniques, the Supreme Court reversed their uncritical acceptance and embraced one of the major criticisms of these techniques by human rights activists. The Court frontally struck down one major contradictory impulse in the high court decisions—that of modernizing at the cost of constitutional violations. Consent had to be ensured in the use of these techniques, dismissing the assumption that they were a natural part of the investigation for the welfare of the subjects. At the same time, it is important to note that the Supreme Court does not reject the techniques themselves, perhaps accepting the basic premise of the high courts that they do represent a shift in the nature of state power. As the Supreme Court writes, "We do leave room for the voluntary administration of the impugned techniques in the context of criminal justice, provided that certain safeguards are in place."[48] Indeed, recent interviews and news reports indicate (and as I mentioned in chapter 4) that while there was an expectation that the number of narcoanalysis cases would be reduced after the Supreme Court judgment, they continue to be used, and the Forensic Science Labs continue to build on their plans to expand the use of lie detectors and brains scans.[49]

If the courts collectively suggest that these techniques reflect a shift into an art of government, the question I ask is, What is the edifice that will ensure the replacing of custodial physical torture? I follow the logic of the legal discourses to explore whether the courts are able to create an art of government that can actually free subjects from torture. Here it is important to clarify that I am merely following the logic of the legal discourses without assessing or elaborating on the nature of the techniques themselves. In other words, I am exploring whether the courts, in defending the techniques, are able to question the conditions that allow for custodial torture or deaths ("state terror") to actually take place in India. Even if one were to accept that these techniques themselves were reliable and they were being used only with the consent of the accused (after the Supreme Court's intervention) are the courts able to create an edifice that replaces torture?

A FLAWED ART OF GOVERNMENT

I explore the contention of the Indian courts that the introduction of the investigative techniques under discussion is a shift in the nature of state power to introduce an art of governing. I take seriously the claim by the high courts that the main reason they have considered these techniques as organically acceptable means of investigation is because they are meant to replace torture. It is important to clarify that methodologically I do intentionally take the claims made by the state seriously on its own terms. I do that for two reasons: First, just as the claims of a state are taken seriously when the focus is on critique, a similar approach has to be adopted when there is a state articulation of an adherence to rule of law or human rights as opposed to a prima facie rejection of the state claims. Second, and a related point, is that such an approach allows one to identify the tensions within the state and legal discourse and not outside of it.

In this case I note that even if the use of these techniques represents a shift in state power as the courts claim, there is a fundamental flaw in the way the art of governing is being introduced. Although the courts are defending these techniques ostensibly to replace torture, as I will show below, the edifice that they have sanctioned is drawing upon precisely those elements that have supported the persistence of torture in postcolonial India.

The new art of government built by the courts in allowing these scientific investigative techniques has three different elements: the techniques are seen as superior to physical third degree without a clear explanation of what makes them so, doctors and medical professionals become defined as custodians of safety despite their dubious role historically, and the meaning of custody itself is transformed despite the continuing reality of custodial violence.

Human rights activists have pointed to lingering questions about the scientific validity, reliability and safety of the techniques (the safety mainly for narco-analysis). Yet the *need* for scientific techniques trumps any doubts that the high courts have as they organically become a part of the investigation to protect the subjects from the third degree. Just a mention of a scientific basis for these techniques appears to be sufficient evidence for the courts to see all three as safe alternatives to physical torture.[50] After all, from colonial to postcolonial times, the need for scientific means of investigation has been a dominant desire of prevailing states. In colonial times, science played a twofold role in the context of law: in introducing new forms of evidence, particularly medical testimony despite its highly contradictory character; and in the form of early experiments that took place in the colonies before those new scientific methods were introduced in the West.[51]

There appears to be some identifiable differences in the way postcolonial courts consider the question of due process. The Supreme Court has not uncritically accepted scientific techniques at all costs. It does seem to have some regard for voluntariness and substantial due process in considering the use of these techniques, as opposed to the high courts that have blatantly defended them even if ostensibly for the welfare of the accused. That said, the mere invocation of the term "science" still appears to be adequate to authorize the techniques. This may be the case because faith in scientific techniques as substitutions for torture has been a recurring feature even in the past. As Justice Markandey Katju, a Supreme Court justice wrote, "In western countries scientific methods of investigation are used.... Hence, in western countries torture is not normally used during investigation and the correct facts can be usually ascertained without resorting to torture."[52] As I have argued in chapter 2, police reform efforts such as the Gore Committee Report in 1971 also reflected the uncritical embrace of science and scientific experts. Similarly, the Malimath Committee in 2003 deliberately connected the police investigation to the truth machines. Thus, the focus on scientific investigations has clearly reverberated not just in the police reform efforts but also judicial decisions.

Some of the contradictions in the Supreme Court's decision on these investigative techniques can only be explained if one considers this unrelenting faith in science. For example, the Court states, "It is also quite evident that all the three impugned techniques can be described as methods of interrogation which impair the test subject's 'capacity of decision or judgment.'"[53] Yet the justices claim, "Going by the language of these principles, we hold that the *compulsory* administration of the impugned techniques constitutes 'cruel, inhuman or degrading treatment' in the context of article 21." Similarly, although the Court rejected the admissibility as evidence of even consent-based test results in a criminal case, it did allow for the admitting of "information or material that is subsequently discovered with the help of voluntarily administered test results."[54] This argument is based on Section 27 of the Indian Evidence Act that has long been a source of abuse, because it even allows evidence gained as a result of physical torture as discussed in chapter 2. Thus, in upholding the *voluntary* use of these techniques, the Supreme Court ends up reflecting a general faith and openness in the reliability of these scientific techniques despite noting its contradictory effects.

The special status given to science may be further explained by the second element of the art of governing—namely, an attempt to make new semi-state actors appear as custodians of life, safety, and health. The high courts attempt to portray medical professionals as creating a responsible regime. In the Rojo case, the high court writes, "such tests are conducted under strict supervision of the expert. It cannot be said that there is any violation of the fundamental rights guaranteed to a citizen of India."[55] The belief in the medical expert is even more visible in this statement: "[In the] . . . supervision of medical experts, the likelihood of complications are very rare and fatality is very remote."[56] It is precisely the medical professionals who are meant to ensure the safety of the accused.

The role of medical professionals in this art of governing is akin to what Foucault has talked about in other instances. Foucault notes how law and medicine work together in what he identifies as the juridico-medical complex and represents an extension of state power with extra-state actors. In an interview in 1976, Foucault says, "Medicine has taken on a general social function: it infiltrates law, it plugs into it, it makes it work. A sort of juridico-medical complex is presently being constituted, which is the major form of power."[57] Here it appears to be a transformation in the nature of both state power as well as its actors.

The faith expressed in medical personnel on the part of the Indian high courts while discussing the scientific techniques, however, elides the well-documented role of state medical agencies in the investigations of custodial deaths. Doctors have a long history of complicity in the continuation of physical torture and deaths. As human rights reports have constantly shown, many of the doctors working for these medical agencies are not independent of the police, which has become apparent in controversies surrounding postmortems after custodial death cases, and in those instances the medical professionals are only involved after the fact.[58] In chapter 6 I discuss the role of doctors in enabling torture. In these particular investigative techniques, the medical actors (forensic psychologists and psychiatrists) are directly involved in performing the interrogations during investigations or monitoring their health (doctors), which raises questions about their independence from the process. Indeed, as I note in chapter 4, these semi-state actors are ultimately committed to the state forensic architecture to gain confessions.

There are also alleged instances of medical professionals using physical violence in order to use these scientific techniques effectively.[59] The use of psychologists and other medical professionals at Guantánamo and the CIA dark sites suggests a similar role for science and scientists in the post-9/11 U.S. context. The presence of medical professionals represents "scientific reliability" and ostensibly an ability to regulate techniques, but instead of combating torture, they end up either participating in torture[60] or ensuring that the techniques do not reach the official definitions of torture.[61] Therefore, the undue faith of the Indian courts in medical professionals as a way to combat torture raises many unanswered questions.

In this regard, even the Indian Supreme Court has not clearly defined the role of medical professionals in investigations in the *Selvi* case. While clearly striking down the notion that the scientific investigative techniques can be considered to be allowed under Section 53 of the CrPC, which permits the use of some force during medical investigation, the Court does not go beyond that critique. More important for our purpose, the juridico-medical apparatus appears intact primarily because medical professionals are not barred from participating in these tests. As Jesani explains, the Court falls short of explicating the relationship between "medical ethics and human rights," indicating only that doctor participation in criminal investigation is an exception to physician-patient privilege.[62]

The articulation of the exception to physician-patient privacy does indicate an openness toward medical participation in such techniques and almost a faith in them without addressing the past role of medical professionals in the continuation of torture. The courts never really explain what exactly transforms the role of medical professionals in this new paradigm. As discussed in chapter 4, after the Supreme Court decision in 2010, the Perspective Plan for Indian Forensics presented to the Ministry of Home Affairs suggests that the three techniques should be transferred under the realm of forensic medicine as if the mere supervision from medical professionals will address all the concerns with these truth machines.[63]

Finally, the courts have tried to suggest that these new modes of scientific investigation will change the very meaning of custody converting it into a safe space. This is significant because police custody is consistently the very space notorious for death and torture as noted in chapter 2. The strong distrust of the police in India has always been visible in the laws disallowing them to record confessions and is reflected in the Supreme Court's powerful jurisprudence on custodial violence in routine interrogations (except in extraordinary laws relating to terrorism cases). For instance, in 1992 the Supreme Court stated in a custodial death case, "If a person is in police custody[,] then what has happened to him is peculiarly within the knowledge of the police officials who have taken him into custody."[64] In 2003 the Supreme Court noted that despite strong initiatives in custody jurisprudence developed from 1990 onward, it "seems to have caused not even any softening attitude to the inhuman approach in dealing with persons in custody."[65] A Supreme Court case in 2019 took up the subject of an anti-torture legislation.[66] Thus, since the 1990s, the postcolonial Supreme

Court has repeatedly come up with custodial safeguards and proclaimed a right of compensation in torture cases, especially when torture leads to a custodial death. And yet failure of the state is apparent in the large number of custodial deaths that occur each year and in the continuation of custodial torture in routine cases, let alone extraordinary cases where there is more explicit impunity for state violence.

Despite this long history of being unsuccessful in checking physical torture, the new scientific techniques are used by the high courts to redefine this custodial space as safe by highlighting the role of medical professionals. As an Indian high court writes in defending the truth-seeking techniques in 2008, in the "constant surveillance of the state of the accused . . . the element of risk is minimal."[67] What ultimately legitimizes the police is the presence of "modern medico-forensic aides for [the] larger good of [a] larger number of persons— the community on the whole whose such individual is a member."[68] Or as stated earlier, the courts believe that the custodians of safety, security, and health can be the medical professionals in this mode of investigation and that they emerge as a perfect solution to the trials and tribulations of the criminal justice system: using scientific techniques to supervise the notorious police and thereby redefining custody as a safe space. The courts and other state officials highlight the changed meaning of custody, and custodians, and point to these techniques as proof of the progress being made moving away from a more "brutal" regime.

However, I argue that this edifice actually allows for at best a flawed art of governing allowing for torture to persist. I call it a flawed attempt because it does not address the conditions necessary for an explicit shift in the mode of state power. In other words, only if the courts had addressed the question of scientific reliability, validity, and safety of these techniques and addressed why these particular medical professionals will ensure safety in custody, that would have reflected an explicit intent to address the conditions of "state terror," custodial deaths, and torture, at least in the context of interrogation. Here I should clarify that "flawed" does not refer to an ability of the state merely to correct/reform the system; rather, "flawed" refers to the precise way the state often attempts and courts often respond to efforts that really are ways of accommodating violence. Here it is also important to acknowledge that in my earlier work, I have noted that my own understanding, similar to that of other scholars, is that for Foucault sovereignty and governmentality coexist. Thus, one is considering only the elements that dominate a particular context and time to determine its implications for violence but those shifts in configurations of state power and legal violence are important to note.⁶⁹

In this regard the Supreme Court's intervention in the *Selvi* case is a major break from most of the high court cases, especially since the lack of consent in previous cases had been a major source of concern for human rights groups and scholars. The Supreme Court even raises concerns about the violation of constitutional rights in its opinion. But the overemphasis on consent by the Supreme Court is a little arbitrary considering that these techniques are being used in custodial situations, the techniques exist to overcome the will, and ideas of consent have particularly less meaning for marginalized sections of society.⁷⁰ In addition, even the Supreme Court does not explain how a voluntary use of these techniques will counter the other conditions for state terror and avoid the possibility of using the information from these techniques indirectly.

LIMITS OF THE SUPREME COURT DECISION: TWO CASES

The limits of the Supreme Court's intervention can be understood by briefly drawing on two criminal cases: the Aditi Sharma trial and the *Aarushi-Hemraj* double murder case regarding the two main implications of the Court opinion regarding consent and inadmissibility of evidence.

Aditi Sharma, along with her husband Pravin Sharma, was convicted in 2008 of murdering Aditi's former boyfriend, Udit Bharati, and both were subjected to a polygraph. Aditi was additionally subjected to the BEOS, which showed experiential knowledge of the crime. According to the session court judgment, Aditi "showed experiential knowledge on a number of target probes presented to her indicating her involvement in the murder of Udit Bharati."⁷¹ While the convictions were stayed by the High Court, it is noteworthy that consent was taken before the technique was used, and the judge stated that she was relying on the scientific results only as supplementary evidence not primary evidence. In fact, by procedurally focusing on consent and inadmissibility of results as evidence, the Supreme Court decision allowed these techniques to remain a part of the arsenal of the process of investigation and interrogation with more legitimacy. Consequently, the techniques may undermine the very rights that the Court claims to uphold—namely, voluntariness and right against self-incrimination. In Aditi Sharma's case, neither a focus on consent nor inadmissibility was adequate to protect her from the violation of her constitutional rights. Thus, I argue that the courts collectively have not only failed to challenge the conditions for physical torture that remain even in the introduction of these scientific techniques as noted earlier but also, in the process, fail to ensure the rights that could be undermined by the very use of these techniques.

The second case concerns the double murder of fourteen-year-old Aarushi Talwar and a domestic helper, Hemraj. The complete lack of forensic evidence in the case (primarily due to the inefficiency of the police) meant that Aarushi's parents were convicted on primarily circumstantial evidence. The main argument was that four people were in the house the night before the murder, and two ended up dead (Aarushi and Hemraj) with no evidence of outside entry, thus, the murders must have been committed by the two people left alive—namely, the parents. A key aspect of the revisiting of the case relies on three other suspects in the double murder: the friends of Hemraj who were also aides for the family and the friends of the Talwars. They were Krishna, who was a helper in Rajesh Talwar's clinic; Rajkumar, a domestic helper in the Durrani household–friends of the Talwars; and Vijay Mandal, who worked in a neighbor's house.[72] In a very detailed analysis of the case, a senior journalist by the name of Shoma Chaudhury pointed to the significance of these techniques, noting the guilt of these helpers that appeared to be ignored in the case.

> During this time, both the Talwars and these aides were put through two sets each of polygraph tests, brain mapping tests, lie detector tests, and narcoanalysis. Mark this: both Nupur and Rajesh Talwar showed absolutely no deception in their tests. They also showed no knowledge of the crime. The aides, on the other hand, particularly Krishna and Rajkumar, showed deception in their lie detector tests. Even more crucially, their narco tests pointed to their involvement in the crime. They admitted to their presence in the house that night, described the sequence of the crime, the murder weapon, and how Aarushi and Hemraj's phones were disposed of. Arun Kumar, the head of the CBI team investigating the murder, held a press conference on 11 July 2008, sharing cautious details of these tests with the media.[73]

According to many journalists, the alternative story that was never fully explored was regarding the three aides. One of the primary arguments of the trial court and the police has been that the parents failed to explain how the murders occurred if there was no evidence of forced entry. The part that doesn't appear to be explored by the prosecution is, What if Hemraj had actually allowed the aides to come in?

Here is where the results of narcoanalysis emerge most clearly. In the press conference, police officer Arun Kumar reportedly shared that based on the narco interviews, the aides confessed to how they had been invited by Hemraj to come over and how the murders took place.[74] As Avirook Sen puts it dramatically in his book *Aarushi*, "The story contained in the scientific reports of the servants has never been told. The documents were buried. Until now."[75] Sen presents evidence from the narco tests, lie detector tests, and brain tests from Krishna, Rajkumar, and Vijay Mandal to counter the trial court's narrative. While acknowledging the inconsistencies in the stories, he does write:

> Whatever the contradictions, including those related to the admissibility of the evidence, it seemed possible that the three men were at the scene of the crime. If they were innocent[,] why would they even unconsciously place themselves there? Unless that is how it was.[76]

An innovative podcast series, *Trial by Error*, based on the Aarushi case also reiterates this focus on narcoanalysis.[77] The podcast is a perfect example of the obsession with criminal cases in the media as well as the desire to shift the media discourse on the case.[78] In the podcast, journalist Nishita Jha, while rightly criticizing the botching up of the evidence by the police, the CBI, and the judge, does end up suggesting that the lie detector tests, the brain tests, and the narcoanalysis seem to be in favor of the parents and not the servants. For instance, in episode 2 of the series, the narrator Jha notes:

> The missing piece of the puzzle in these murders is evidence gathered from three scientific tests: narco test, brain mapping and polygraph. The narcos results are obtained under the influence of a drug[,] which is why its results are inadmissible in court. But let's not forget the fact that the narco, brain mapping and polygraph test have this weird coincidence. None of the Talwars' tests show any signs of deception. Meanwhile all three of Vijay Mandal, Rajkumar and Krishna's tests show deception. Also, all three admit to being in the house on the night that Aarushi and Hemraj were killed.[79]

In this particular narration, suddenly the legal inadmissibility that the Supreme Court proclaimed and trial court followed became merely a technicality (for narco and not for the other two even though the Supreme Court *Selvi* decision applies for all), and the lack of verification of their being scientific and accurate became irrelevant. In the realm of media construction, suddenly the evidence from these truth machines became more crucial. "So should we just forget about the evidence found in the scientific tests?" asks Jha, along with Avirook Sen. While not demanding admissibility, they do ask for using the evidence gleaned from the narco and others tests—the "confessions" as they refer to this evidence.[80] It is not surprising that when the high court overturned the parents' convictions in October 2018, the forensic psychologists associated with these techniques. like Dr. Vaya (who I discuss in chapter 4) and Dr. Shukla, appeared in the media claiming their success in the techniques, which had been ignored earlier, giving them and the techniques a renewed life altogether. Thus, both the Aditi Sharma case and the Aarushi case reveal the limits of the Supreme Court interventions on the truth machines and how the state forensic architecture based on the truth machine continue to find valence. Above all, as I note in chapter 4, the constant desire to gain confessions with the help of the forensic psychologists or "cyborgs" as I characterize them become the basis of a continued search for such truth machines that focus on the body to betray itself.

CONCLUSION

The Indian state's commitment to a "rule of law" and democratic practices and institutions has often been used by its defenders to deny the violent actions that it routinely accommodates and enables. The response from civil liberty scholars and activists is to squarely challenge this claim by theorizing its law as primarily violent based on their study of extraordinary laws and fake encounters. However, this critique may be inadequate to explain the introduction of these scientific investigative techniques as an apparent anomaly given the widespread impunity for physical custodial violence. This is particularly significant since the techniques are presented precisely as a way to replace the violence, at least in the context of interrogation. The state's desire to limit its own violence is important to note, even though as I have shown, the edifice currently used to introduce the scientific techniques ends up creating at best a flawed art of government. Thus,

I argue that these techniques represent a liberal state's desire to modernize along with a reluctance to challenge the conditions for the persistence of torture—a phenomenon that is peculiarly postcolonial.

I term this phenomenon "peculiarly postcolonial," not because there are no parallels in other democracies; rather I use that term because of three major arguments: First, the gap between the legal rhetoric and ground reality appears particularly stark in the Indian case. The pressure to represent itself as a liberal democracy for global recognition perhaps underlies some of the political and legal rhetoric. Even though the jurisprudence is extremely critical of torture in routine contexts rhetorically, the court is actually unable to challenge the conditions of torture again and again. Second, the postcolonial aspect is visible in the framing of modernization and science apparently mimicking the Western countries, yet it is able to accommodate a colonial legal framework associated with the most brutal forms of physical torture, such as the Armed Forces Special Powers Act and other extraordinary laws. Finally, it is peculiarly postcolonial because it allows for the coexistence of physical, mental, and other forms of excess violence in all spheres.

The courts do reflect a desire to do away with physical third degree or torture, although the high courts appear less consistent when they refuse to recognize any constitutional violations. While the Supreme Court has rightly raised the question of consent, it fails to challenge the techniques themselves despite all the doubts that remain regarding them. The desire on the part of the courts to transform custody into a safer space and develop ways of dealing with violence inherent to the system is important precisely because this marks a difference between colonial and postcolonial state's modes of power to some extent. Yet the Court's intervention in this context remains limited. Even if the inadequacies in the interventions are not deliberate, at the very least, the legal discourses surrounding these techniques reflect a powerlessness in creating conditions to challenge the terror and torture that impact the postcolonial Indian criminal justice system. Even when there is a distinct desire to do away with physical torture, there appears to be an inability to challenge all the conditions responsible for its persistence.

Chapter 6

SCAFFOLD OF THE RULE OF LAW

Terror Suspects and the Experience of Violence

> Waheed was on a flight to Bangalore and he was being taken there for a narcoanalysis test. He remembers being excited and yet feeling remarkably relaxed. The narco-test, he believed, would clear the "misunderstanding" and he would be spared the ordeal. It would prove him to be innocent, he was convinced. He, in fact, greeted Dr. Malini in Bangalore and blurted out, "I am innocent, Ma'am." But the Doctor ignored him and did not seem to have taken any notice of what he said. That was when he began worrying.
>
> —VIKRANT JHA

In May 2017 Abdul Wahid Shaikh released a book in Hindi—*Begunah Qaidi* (Innocent Prisoner)—that describes his ordeal as a detainee.[1] Shaikh was charged in the 2006 Mumbai blasts, in which 189 people were killed and over 800 injured. Out of the thirteen Muslim men charged in the case, Shaikh was the only one acquitted. A special court pronounced the verdict nine years after the tragic event. In the book, Shaikh shares his experience of narcoanalysis, characterizing it as a continuation of the third-degree interrogation long used to coerce confessions.[2] Here I focus on two prominent terrorism related cases—the Mumbai blasts case and the *Mecca Masjid* case, in Hyderabad[3]—that represent the experience of suspects like Shaikh.

Narcoanalysis and other techniques have been used in a range of cases across different states in India, but those related to terrorism reveal much about truth machines. My focus is on the rule of law discourse, which becomes the foil for any discussion of violence in interrogation. Like other liberal democracies,

India is based on the rule of law, and the state claims that torture cannot be used in investigations and interrogations. Rather, the police must follow the law and therefore must either hide torture or use more scientific techniques. These terrorism related cases illustrate the lack of even the semblance of replacing physical torture. Truth machines thus become visible parts of the toolbox for extracting confessions, often in a laboratory or a hospital staffed by figures with scientific authority.[4]

Three themes emerge from my interviews with lawyers and activists and my analysis of documents related to these cases: first, technique of police investigation and interrogation; second, failure of doctors and magistrates to ensure safeguards against torture; and, third, violence that is brutal as well as racialized and feminized. Discussions on narcoanalysis reveal these processes with important implications for theorizing the rule of law. In India, I argue, the rule of law represents a scaffold that relies on procedures to mask violence. The scaffold, in turn, depends as much on doctors and magistrates as on the police to perform the work of interrogation.

The definition of "rule of law" often focuses on formal procedural safeguards and the judiciary's role to ensure individual rights. The accounts of terrorism suspects in India, however, underscore the need to shift the frame of reference away from formal procedures to practices imposed on those who experience the rule of law. These experiences reveal the tension between formal safeguards and their application. They help to dismantle the scaffold and challenge those who keep it in place. Only when this scaffolding is identified can the underlying violence be revealed and contained and a resistance mounted. A substantive rule of law can then potentially be created.

RULE OF LAW, RULE BY LAW

Discussions of the rule of law are deeply tied to violence and coercion. Especially important are limits to the powers of state officials and the role of judges in ensuring the law's implementation. As Brian Z. Tamanaha explains, "The rule of law means that government officials and citizens are bound by and abide by the law."[5] Elaborating, he identifies three central elements: a government "limited by law," "formal legality," and "the rule of law, not man." A divided government, where power is dispersed, allows checks on the law and its application.

Formal legality requires knowing the rules in advance, which in turn provides equality and predictability. And "rule of law, not man" avoids arbitrary application, as well as biases and prejudices that may undermine trust in judges' legal interpretation.

For Tamanaha, the government coercion is related to the rule of law. "When the government exercises coercion against a citizen, it must do so in accordance with legal rules stated in advance," he explains,

> in a manner consistent with the dictates of formal legality. Legal rules must affirmatively authorise the government action. The government action cannot transgress any standing legal restrictions. At some point there must be recourse to an independent court dedicated to upholding the law that will make a determination of the legality of the government's action. And the ruling of the court must be respected by government officials.[6]

Established legal rules thus check the coercive power of government, and an independent court determines the legality of government actions. Randall Peerenboom considers this view a thin version of the rule of law, as opposed to a thick version, which may be substantively determined by the goals of a particular system.[7]

Jothie Rajah uses Singapore as an example to argue that the notion of rule of law versus rule of man can ultimately become "rule *by* law."[8] Singapore, she explains, is a paradox, a state ostensibly based on the rule of law even as it has few political liberties and has instead introduced legislation targeting freedoms and political dissidents. According to Rajah, rule by law is "'law' which, in content and in institutional execution, is susceptible to power such that the rights content of 'law,' and restraints on and scrutiny of state power, are undermined."[9] In *Opposing the Rule of Law*, Nick Cheesman analyzes Myanmar and suggests that the conception of rule by law lacks clarity: "Rule by Law reduces questions about the rule of law to matters of instrumentality, of empirical degree, of gradation along a sliding scale of practices."[10] He suggests studying the rule of law through its opposite, the law-and-order ideal, which state actors, such as the magistrates, help to uphold.

Scholarship on the codification of laws in India during both the British colonial period and their postcolonial continuation in India is especially pertinent to this discussion. Notions of "rule by law" and "rule of men" are a colonial legacy, as a number of scholars, including Nasser Hussain and Keally McBride, point out.[11] As Hussain notes, limits and exceptions to the law were colonized subjects, even as the British colonial powers claimed to maintain the rule of law. For McBride, "the Aristotelian distinction between the rule of law and the rule of men collapsed; colonialism offered the possibility of having one, or just a few men, write the rule of law."[12]

McBride further points to the impulse behind the colonial codes, chronicling the establishment of the rule of law by James Fitzjames Stephen (legal member of the Colonial Council of India) and others. In the 1860s, she explains, this initiative in codification led to the Indian Penal Code (IPC), the Indian Evidence Act (IEA), and the revision of the CrPC. Radhika Singha, in *A Despotism of Law*, also notes the importance of this period for the consolidation of the British state.[13] According to McBride, despite believing that the colonized were incapable of governing themselves, the colonial power had Stephen "regularize, clarify and modernize the law."[14] Of course, the "codification was uniform, but it did not create equal legal subjectivity; instead it asserted the necessary hierarchy of colonialism in an orderly fashion."[15] For example, as Elizabeth Kolsky has noted (and as I discuss in chapter 3), violence perpetrated by white planters was always treated differently, using medical expertise and defenses such as a weak Indian spleen (to explain away the violence) in order to exonerate accused whites.[16]

Ranabir Samaddar points to the content of colonial codes, especially provisions for confessions and legal evidence: "Rule of law meant being responsible to the law. And law meant due process."[17] For the British, the CrPC, or even just the creation of procedure, thus became a way to focus on reason and self-interest and to ensure equality before the law. On one hand, the IEA was a rational creation of legal process. On the other, the act allowed physicality to become the basis of Indian politics, whether by acknowledging colonial conquest or by emphasizing the body in the construction of a criminal act.

Punishment was also made both public and rational. As Samaddar elaborates, rationality alone can never explain the basis of confession and admission. Rather, rationality remains the most abused part of the IEA, as the evidence act constantly amended from the colonial to the postcolonial period to suit the "political and governmental priorities of the state. That was how reason (and procedure) evolved anywhere and everywhere."[18] Despite attempts to introduce procedure, therefore, judicial power determined facts, proofs, evidence, and relevance and so required a means for producing knowledge of a suspect's actions. Dressed in the garb of reason and rationality, the IEA obfuscated the process of truth production, which is always elusive and must be explicitly constructed.

TERRORISM TRIALS AND THE SPECTACLE OF THE SCAFFOLD

Scholars such as Upendra Baxi and Ujjwal Singh have pointed to the duality of the Indian system—the parallel preventive detention system and criminal justice system—or indeed an interlocking of ordinary and extraordinary laws.[19] The preventive detention system has very few safeguards; the criminal justice system has more formal safeguards and rights. Singh and other scholars articulate the concept of "violence of jurisprudence" that the law and the state represent (discussed more explicitly in chapter 5) similar to the rule *by* law that Rajah notes. Using the Singh framework, Sharib Ali powerfully writes about the *Mecca Masjid* case in Hyderabad: "This discourse of the 'war on terror' today and its powerful evocation of a suspect community as well as the levying of the state of exception against the Muslim minority is not a sudden construct, but rather a definitive moment in political history."[20] The violence accommodated in the rule by law is thus acute in cases of terrorism, which often target Muslim youth, and Muslim identity becomes the foil for a nationalistic discourse based on fear. Extraordinary laws, such as the 2008 Unlawful Activities Prevention Act, further enable torture and detention.

I suggest that more than rule by law or violence of jurisprudence explains developments in these cases. Both extraordinary laws and individual cases may undergo either tests of constitutionality or judicial scrutiny that reveals glaring violations of due process and forces judges to intervene.[21] Occasionally, interventions to protect liberty stem from strengthened statutory procedures, recommended police reforms, and reasserted constitutional protections. Legal discourse, therefore, must contend with its own speech.

As a result, rather than focusing only on jurisprudence and the judiciary, we need to focus on what I term the scaffolding of the rule of law. Taken from Michel Foucault's spectacle of the scaffold, scaffolding signifies not the structure but its continuous formation.[22] For the maintenance of public order and national security, I suggest, everyday state agents ensure the process of scaffolding of the rule of law.

In *Discipline and Punish*, Foucault points to torture as both a spectacular ritual and a regulated technique, part of procedure in ancien régime.[23] My concept of the scaffold of the rule of law, however, explains how the scaffold exists not to create fear or to make sovereign power visible but to make the system appear functional. With scaffolding of the rule of law, the violence associated with spectacle is absent, but the judge still produces truth. As Foucault explains, "In criminal matters the establishment of truth was the absolute right and the exclusive power of the sovereign and his judges."[24] Judges played a major role in determining truth in criminal trials. Confessions, even after torture, had to be "spontaneous," uttered "in full consciousness," and "surrounded by guarantees and formalities." As Foucault continues, "Through the confession, the accused committed himself to the procedure; he signed the truth of the preliminary investigation."[25]

For Foucault, the spectacle of the scaffold, through public execution and torture, confirmed the truth of the crime in public. The scaffold of the rule of law, however, ensures the truth of the crime in public through procedures precisely meant to avoid the theatrical production of torture. In criminal cases, a system based on the rule of law incorporates a presumption of innocence, independent collection of evidence, and constitutional and statutory safeguards to ostensibly protect a suspect from violence. However, alongside the police, doctors and magistrates play particularly important parts in this process, continuously producing this scaffold that masks violence, even in cases of terrorism.

The *Mecca Masjid* Case

On May 18, 2007, a blast took place in the courtyard of the Mecca Masjid, a mosque in Hyderabad. Nine people were killed and forty injured. As the victims were removed from the area, the police initially fired to disperse the crowd but, as later became clear, added to the death toll. As one activist noted, "More people had died in the firing than in the actual bomb blast," a comment that was technically false but nonetheless identified police malfeasance.[26] As the accounts of lawyers and activists indicate, this case points to both the police modus operandi and to the scaffold of the rule of law in terrorism cases.

Following the attacks, more than a hundred Muslim youth were picked up from different areas of Hyderabad, and the police claimed that the Pakistan-supported Indian Mujahadeen was responsible for the blasts.[27] After intervention from activists, many Muslim boys were released over a few days, but others remained missing. Many petitions were then filed in courts, and thirty-nine youth were finally produced in front of the judge.[28] The police claimed that these Muslim boys either had bomb-making materials or had taken arms training in Pakistan or India. As one activist noted, "Everyone was labeled as a terrorist, and according to the police there was irrefutable proof against every one of them."[29] The young Muslims were then jailed, and reports of torture and third-degree interrogation soon followed. Activists checking backgrounds discovered that those incarcerated included medical and engineering students and welders supporting families. They had no connections to arms training.[30]

Hearing complaints of torture, activists approached the minority commission set up in 2004. Fortuitously, the commission's head was retiring and decided to appoint one man, Ravi Chander, an advocate at the Andhra Pradesh High Court, to inquire into the allegations of torture. Chander represented the Bharatiya Janata Party, the Hindu right-wing party in a case regarding quotas and affirmative action for minorities. (The Bharatiya Janata Party gained power nationally in 2014 with Narendra Modi as prime minister.) To determine whether the youth had been tortured in the *Mecca Masjid* case, Chander visited the jail without prior notice and immediately afterward held a press conference. There, according to one activist, he furiously stated, "The torture they are going through is unbelievable, and as of today I'm on their side, and the things they have been asked to confess to are unbelievable. It is extremely clear that it's only been done under duress and force and they have not committed any of this."[31]

As his report later detailed, Chander found that procedures at the jail had violated the Supreme Court's ruling in the D. K. Basu case, which had required the youth to be produced in front of a magistrate and have medical examinations to ensure protections against torture.[32] As his report revealed, "They were stripped naked, severely beaten, administered electric shocks, including the genitals[,] and deprived of food and water. The police used abusive language against their women folk and forced them to hail Hindu deities."[33] The police modus operandi in arrest, investigation, and interrogation in such cases thus became clear.

The police in Andhra Pradesh even otherwise appeared to be especially brutal and ruthless, particularly against the Naxalities, or members of Maoist organizations.[34] Indeed, a prominent journalist working in Hyderabad associated police cruelty with the prevalence of Maoists:

> So, I think, the police in Andhra Pradesh is one of the most cruel police. And they have been using torture for a long time as everywhere else, but . . . the

standards of brutality are far more higher in Andhra Pradesh than anywhere else.... Maoism had been rampant here, as you're quite aware. And when Maoism is rampant, they think they can easily kill somebody without any question being asked. If you do such tortures in the civil society, they will not be allowed. So the easiest way is to discredit somebody as a Maoist and then pick him up and torture him and kill him. In fact, of course, now things are much better in the sense that things were far more worse, say, in the 1990s and all when the Maoist problem was very rampant, even earlier.... Now ... I think that scientific techniques are not there at all. They are very crude tortures, because scientific torture will only take place where you want to prove a case and use ... what the admission that guy has made and you want to use it against him. But if you don't want, your idea is to utilize somebody, bump him off or scare him; then you don't need those torture, na. So narcoanalysis is not, I don't think, is so common here, so, straight bashed ... torture.[35]

Both journalists and lawyers have similarly characterized the Andhra Pradesh police as brutal, as have advocates for civil liberties and democratic rights.[36]

In the *Mecca Masjid* case, police behavior represented standard procedure in cases of suspected terrorism. According to one lawyer:

They would take these boys. First they will come to their houses and say, "Oh, there's some small investigation; can you come up?" Then they'll take him in a Jeep. There [are] a lot of heavily built guys in the Jeep. Then first thing is your eyes are folded, blindfolded. Then it is a long drive. You don't know where you are. And after you go wherever, you're beaten up, electric shocks on genitals. And this was examined. I had this forensic man to physically examine those boys and tell me. And in one or two cases even I had to stand and see that, though I don't know if that in itself is a human right violation, but I said, for the ... for the purpose of moving on with the investigation, it needs to be done; something, that sense ... sense of nausea even now to me.[37]

A longtime woman activist similarly narrated the chronology of police actions. In one instance, she recalled, a number of boys were either picked up outside their homes, so that their families had no idea about the detentions, or picked up from home without disclosing the reason or the destination to their families.[38]

A prominent journalist involved in the *Mecca Masjid* case explained that youth were often detained in farmhouses, some Muslim owned, and Muslim police officers were sometimes asked to torture them.[39] The police would often pick up youth against whom they held grudges, he noted: "For them, easiest is to book someone."[40] The police might also add charges like sedition, which made bail difficult.[41] Lack of support for these charges typically became evident when the police offered no proof, and courts eventually had to recognize their falsity. As one journalist laughingly recounted, "But they [the police] ... they have committed so many mistakes that they ... they were caught in their own web.... You know, there was a standard FIR [first information report] for all the boys. They thought no one can challenge them."[42]

Here the scaffolding has several components: detaining the youth, focusing on preexisting grudges, failing to acknowledge their custody, and creating standard FIRs. Eventually, the youth in the *Mecca Masjid* case were acquitted, partly because even the actors involved in creating the scaffold began to dissociate themselves from the narrative. The commissioner of police in Hyderabad, for example, recognized the fabrications and lack of evidence against the boys. Right-wing Hindu activists from Abhinav Bharti made parallel confessions. Even the chief minister offered an apology if harassment could be proved. Activists, however, wanted more than the youths' release.[43] They demanded compensation and rehabilitation packages for torture in detention. These compensations were offered but then challenged by someone in the high court who deemed them beyond the state's prerogative, and the government was asked to take back the money.[44]

Lawyers and activists articulated implicit or explicit critiques of the courts, doctors, and magistrates,[45] whose inability to ascertain the volition of statements and confessions and ensure medical examinations as protection against torture made them liable. As one lawyer explained,

> And they [the youth] were all produced before magistrates at 11 in the night in a group. The judge doesn't even ask them, "Why are you producing these guys at 11 in the night?," doesn't even physically examine these people, and they just get remanded to judicial custody. Habeas contestations are dealt with mechanically.[46]

Another lawyer associated with the case similarly underscored the lack of court monitoring, noting that documented torture was completely absent from the magistrate's remand proceedings or jail records. "It means the magistrate, the judiciary has failed," he lamented. "So my question is, How come the judiciary, how come those magistrates who remanded these boys without complying with that mandatory requirement of the Supreme Court, how come disciplinary action was not taken against them?"[47] In the absence of action against judges who convict on flimsy evidence or magistrates who fail to follow safeguards against torture, this lawyer noted, "Otherwise, what is the message I get as a Muslim? They were able to play football with your life, your career, your human rights. And this—damn all that you can do it. And what's the message judges will get? Play whatever games you can; you're immune."[48]

At least six of the youth had been sent for narcoanalysis and charged on the basis of the results.[49] Lawyers and police, however, eventually shared their skepticism about the technique. By December 2007, as one journalist reported, the joint commissioner of police had sent a CD of confessions and narcoanalysis reports to the Central Bureau of Investigation but the CBI eventually found it to be fake evidence.[50] A lawyer involved in the case, whose interest in narcoanalysis predated its introduction in India, placed this discussion in a broader context, arguing that the dignity of the body was at stake.[51] Locating the origins of truth machines in fiction, he reflected,

> I have always been doing a fair amount of reading from my childhood days when I used to start reading Perry Mason and stuff like that. . . . I was aware of Sodium Pentothal as a drug and stuff like that. . . . I've been teaching law for quite some time, so I've many students in the police forces, and they discuss things with me. So I'm aware that when people were taken from here to Bangalore, I'm talking about these Muslim boys after the Mecca Masjid blasts.[52]

An advocate closely associated with the report noted, "And if you're saying the choice is between crude versus sophisticated torture and that is the choice we have to make, I'm not a part of that game."[53]

Another lawyer argued that, despite the Supreme Court's decision allowing the use of truth machines only with consent, a suspect's right to avoid self-incrimination was adequate protection in cases involving narcoanalysis.[54] A prominent journalist, also, explained that the argument about replacing third-degree interrogation with narcoanalysis failed to make sense: "But, but this is also third degree, na. In narcoanalysis what you are suggesting [is] certain things when that fellow is not in control of his senses. Given that it wasn't present in all police stations ... that it was really a culture of *danda* [beating with a stick] that he [police] also used to extract money for land grabbing, etc."⁵⁵

A number of lawyers in Andhra Pradesh reported narcoanalysis being used primarily for economic offenses. As one long associated with the human rights movement noted, Article 21, the legal procedure for expanded due process, is applied in economic offenses involving the rich: "They conduct investigation such as narcoanalysis or in a very scientific, in the sense, orally making them sit and have a lengthy question only for very economic offences cases only. They follow the law. . . . they follow a due process of law only in a rich people who are involved in a economic offences cases."⁵⁶ But he went on to explain that in Chhattisgarh, the state where most Maoists are active, no such rights are ensured. Narcoanalysis, he lamented, is "also against the right to life, and it violates the basic fundamental right."⁵⁷

Nonetheless, this lawyer added, very few cases involved truth machines, because, "most of the time, they wanted to have an illegal detention, torture, and get the extrajudicial confession."⁵⁸ Instead, his civil liberties group routinely dealt with three kinds of cases: special acts, used against Maoists; general IPC cases, used for robbery; and terrorism cases, In all three, "most of them were picked up and tortured and then kept [in] illegal detention for days together."⁵⁹ In Andhra Pradesh, skepticism about narcoanalysis existed alongside torture and illegal detention in both routine and extraordinary cases.

In the *Mecca Masjid* case, torture dominated the experience of the detained youth, and their lawyers opposed narcoanalysis on principle. But they were also troubled about the possibility of manipulated narcoanalysis results, and both detainees and lawyers explicitly described falsification. The lawyer for the Muslim youth elaborated:

> On the way, the gentleman of the police accompanying them handed them RDX [a type of high explosive] and said, "This is what it looks like, see" Throughout, "you handled RDX." "No, I didn't." "No, you did." "See, this is what it is like. You've handled, haven't you. You know what it is like." Now, when this guy is then taken there and put under sedation, he will describe RDX, won't he? Now, how does an ordinary citizen unconnected with terrorism know about RDX? Therefore, bang, this fellow is guilty. This is horrendous in the context of the fact that when you have reversed the law of evidence. Across all civilized ju-

risdictions, you will find that the law says, "Innocent until proved guilty." So you bring in TADA [Terrorism and Disruptive Activities (Prevention) Act] and POTA [Prevention of Terrorism Act] and organized control or organized crime rubbish, and then you say that this means that you have to prove your innocence, they pick up poor people who don't have logs about where they've gone or where they've been. You know, every city I go to, I use a debit card or a credit card. They don't have that, so their movements are difficult for them to establish. They don't keep a diary. Then they're sucked into false accusation situation[s] like this. And then they are downed, induced, misled into incriminating themselves and then "you prove your innocence."[60]

The emphasis on confession, this lawyer explained, occurred mostly in the absence of other evidence:

Narcoanalysis is not an answer, nor is any form of extraction of a confession. And the Supreme Court has had occasions to express surprise that in cases where there is evidence linking the accused with the crime, there are never any confessional statements. It is only when there is no evidence available that the accused conveniently comes and confesses before the police. Very cooperative criminals we have.[61]

A prominent journalist further noted occasions when an accused's narcoanalysis report had been supposedly shown to community journalists as evidence, it was instead a test of someone known to be a police informer.[62]

In the *Mecca Masjid* case, rejection of narcoanalysis as evidence by the CBI and National Investigative Agency (NIA) went a long way toward delegitimizing both the technique and the cases against the Muslim youth. All were acquitted. The reason, I suggest, is the inability of the system of policing to create scaffolding of a rule of law that could withstand the pressure from activists and human rights lawyers and the internal critique from police themselves. Active intervention by lawyers, activists, and the state, together with a lack of extraordinary laws (such as the UAPA), may have also helped in undermining the scaffolding in this case.

As the advocate noted, for him, narcoanalysis was a breach of "what you in America call the due process and what we in India call the rule of law; [it] is arguably the greatest contribution of a civilized society or the greatest characteristic of a civilized society, and any dent on that guarantee is likely to affect a much larger group than the victims of a known offence."[63] Narcoanalysis, he continued, violated human rights because instead of "abusing the body," the technique abused the suspect's mind, the subconscious, and slowly created cracks in that wall: "If social order justifies piercing into the privacy of an individual or begins to disrespect the halo of his self-respect," he reflected, "it's slowly heading towards a very fascist form of governance."[64] The system, he emphasized, asked the accused to cooperate in a process established by the prosecution.[65]

The *Mecca Masjid* case thus reflects principles opposed to a functioning rule of law, undermining the "greatest characteristic of a civilized society" through torture and narcoanalysis. As the Ravi Chander Commission report stated, "Custodial Violence strikes at the very roots of the rule of law."[66] In this case, the presumption of guilt and the procuring of evidence through framing and torturing suspects and through the application of truth machines rather than independent investigations became elements in policing. Undermining the scaffolding then led to the suspects' acquittal and the upholding of the "rule of law."

The Mumbai Blast Case

On July 11, 2006, seven bombings occurred on local trains in Mumbai. One hundred eighty-nine people were killed and over eight hundred injured. Once the Anti-Terrorism Squad (ATS), Mumbai, took over, thirteen men were charged with the crime either as members of the Students Islamic Movement of India (SIMI), or as Lashkar-e-Taiba. In 2015 twelve of them were convicted and one acquitted.[67] By the time of the trial, the accused had already spent seven years in jail, having been charged under the IPC as well as under two extraordinary laws, the 1967 Unlawful Activities Prevention Act and the 1999 Maharashtra Control of Organised Crime Act (MCOCA).

The investigation in this case shares features of the Hyderabad case—notably, Muslim men picked up for questioning because of long-standing enmity with the police. One of the accused mentioned a dispute with a police officer stemming from his complaint about the officer's role in removing a slum area and a subsequent incident in which this officer had fired his weapon and a relative had died.[68] Some were also suspected members of SIMI, with travel to Iran and Pakistan a cause for suspicion.[69] As a policeman explained to one of the accused, "If they catch a cycle thief, they foist all such unsolved cases on him."[70]

Observers challenged aspects of the trial court judgment, and some concerns of torture were raised in courts along the way.[71]

All the accused were reportedly tortured, and twelve of them confessed.[72] The accused reported torture with methods—most commonly electric shocks and beatings with a flour mill belt—that appeared to be more systematic than in the *Mecca Masjid* case. As one recounted, the police "started beating me by flour mill belt and sticks on my palm[s] and soles. I was tied by rope and given electric shocks to my private parts."[73] Other methods included stripping men naked, putting them in stress positions, beating the palms of their hands and feet, and forcing them to sit with their feet at 180 degrees. One detainee mentioned the injecting of liquid chemicals through the anus.[74] A torture room used by the ATS figures in these narratives. Methods for instilling fear were threats of torture, detention, and extrajudicial killing, together with the targeting of family members, including the threat of rape for women. Family members might be brought to the station to be harassed and insulted and occasionally also subjected to stripping and beating.[75]

As in the *Mecca Masjid* case, the magistrates in front of whom these men were produced rarely inquired closely into their cases. Rather, before each hearing, the accused were threatened not to reveal their experiences. As one detainee noted, the police "threatened that if we complain about beating and torture, they would involve our family members in the case and would torture us more. Therefore, I did not say anything before the judge because of the fear."[76] Another of the accused explained that he was produced in front of both doctors and magistrates, none of whom intervened in his situation.[77]

All suspects were taken to Bangalore Hospital for narcoanalysis, where they were interrogated by forensic psychologists. At least one was at first, apparently, relieved to be facing a person wearing a laboratory coat rather than a police uniform and reported feeling relaxed about the test:

> The narco-test, he believed, would clear the "misunderstanding" and he would be spared the ordeal of being further tortured. It would prove him to be innocent, he was convinced. He, in fact, greeted Dr. Malini in Bangalore and blurted out, "I am innocent, Ma'am." But, the doctor ignored him and did not seem to have taken any notice of what he had said. That was when he began worrying.[78]

The accused also insisted that they were forcibly asked to consent to narcoanalysis.[79] Consent in custody thus becomes a charged concept, as the following account demonstrates:

> Dr. Malini misbehaved and slapped me twice before the test. They asked me to say some things before a video camera and beat me before asking me to say the sentences. She threatened that if I do not give correct answers, she would give me [an] AIDS injection. I became semiconscious after the injection of [the] narco test was given. She asked illogical questions to me during this condition. The camera was switched on, and first she asked how many bombs were prepared. I answered that I am not concerned and I am falsely involved. She slapped me strongly and started pinching my left ear with pliers, because of which I suffered much. She then asked me what comes after six and I answered "seven." She asked me on what TV operates and I answered that it operates on electricity. She again slapped me strongly and caught my ear with pliers and told me to say "by remote." She asked me many such illogical questions and used to ask me to repeat the answers if I did not give the expected answers. Both tortured me badly during the narco test.[80]

Human rights activists have criticized narcoanalysis as a violation of the self-incrimination clause of the Indian Constitution, and with questions asked of someone not fully conscious, and the entire process also violates human dignity (see chapter 5). This instance, however, appeared to violate even the self-proclaimed standards for narcoanalysis as conducted in a hospital or forensic laboratory away from police custody. Pliers were reportedly used during the procedure, illogical questions were asked, and specified answers were demanded. Each test concluded with an interrogator's insistence on a signature on a tailored confession. The depositions in these cases thus undermine even any claim to replacing torture with narcoanalysis and police with forensic psychologists.

The simultaneity of torture and truth machines is important here. Torture leads to a confession that must be recreated through a "nonphysical," scientific technique. According to both the accused and their lawyers, CDs from narcoanalysis sessions were edited to suit the police narrative. As a lawyer described the account of one of the accused, "They played the CD of the narco test to me, and I was shocked to see that in place of my reply to the question as to how many bombs were prepared, the reply was 'seven.' Anyone could see that the CD was edited, because the words were not in sync with the video."[81]

Another of the accused, who had undergone narcoanalysis three times, explained that he had been asked to repeat things he had not done, and his responses were then edited to appear as if he had confessed to committing them.[82] As Shaikh warns in *Begunah Qaidi*, suspects should never answer in the negative, because their responses could be manipulated to appear as if they were answering other questions.[83] The video camera thus becomes a means for generating public confessions. Nonetheless, a video that is awkward or out of sync might also serve as evidence for the failure of narcoanalysis except that, as noted in the previous chapter, the forensic psychologist's report creases out any inconsistencies and the public versions of videos edited.

If they protested, the accused were tortured again. One had an infected ear from the use of pliers, but he was warned not to complain or the torture would be even more brutal. Another detainee described waterboarding: "A wet cloth was put on my face, because of which I was not able to breathe. They had an apparatus with them, by which probably they were measuring my blood pressure[,] and after a certain level was reached, they used to remove the cloth."[84] Only when he agreed to confess did the torture stop. He was then given some ointments or taken to the hospital, where he was warned not to complain to the doctor. When a higher officer asked him to repeat the confession, he was tortured again.[85] Only occasionally, he recalled, would a magistrate ask for a medical examination, but doctors mostly overlooked his injuries,[86] even when they were aware of severe torture. Officials, citing national security concerns, told detainees not to report evidence. As another recounted, "If sometimes the medical officer asked us, the officer or constable used to reply that there is no problem. It usually happened that the doctor did not ask us anything, but obtained our thumb impression."[87]

Before a court hearing, suspects might be allowed to sleep so that they did not appear tortured in front of the magistrate. As one accused explained, "I was taken for medical checkup many times during police custody, but was not physically checked by the doctors, not allowed to speak with the doctors; the veil was not removed at any time, but only my thumb impressions were taken."[88] After his brother was also tortured, another of the accused realized that the *panchnamas* (record of investigation) he was forced to sign involved recovery of admissible evidence. Physicality thus remains central to the IEA. The body must provide proof. Doctors and magistrates, charged with ensuring the veracity of procedures, thus fail to challenge physicality.

Rather than replacing torture, therefore, truth machines merely change interrogation procedures so that suspects are taken to different settings and face different actors. For example, one detainee cited illegal narcoanalysis conducted at ATS headquarters:

> A person wearing an apron and having white spots on his face was with them. Deshmukh told me to repeat what they tell me and if I do not do as they say, they would give me more dose, because of which I may die. I refused and did not follow their instructions. Deshmukh tortured me there itself, made me half unconscious and did my narco test.[89]

Another had undergone narcoanalysis at the *chowki* (police station), a setting also noted by a forensic psychologist.

In convicting twelve of the accused, the trial court spent some of its eighteen-hundred-page judgment considering allegations of torture and forced confessions (which were mostly retracted). In their depositions, the accused had to reaffirm that their allegations had not been prompted by the al Qaeda manual urging them to allege torture by the police investigating agency.[90] Ultimately, however, the judge explained away their allegations by citing scant medical evidence and injuries that could be attributed to a variety of factors. Their lack of complaints when in front of magistrates was also a consistently cited reason for disbelief. Doctors and magistrates thus became central to the process and central as well to the scaffolding of the rule of law.

Reports of cases from Maharashtra (where Mumbai is located) acknowledge the highest number of custodial death cases there, including those due to torture. This finding led the high court to attempt a reduction in custodial deaths, with a determination that closed-circuit television (CCTV) should be installed in all jails and lockups.[91] Suspects' experiences, however, suggest that cameras can be manipulated and videos edited, so CCTV is likely an uncritical means of ensuring accountability especially if magistrates and doctors are unwilling to scrutinize the process closely. Keeping these high-profile cases in mind, then, how do we contextualize the apparatus of policing, the rule of law, and the techniques of interrogation?

POLICING APPARATUS

The *Mecca Masjid* and Mumbai blast cases exemplify a pattern visible in numerous terror cases: they focus on specific communities and bypass the usual safeguards.[92] In his insights into police functioning, as well as the steps in the legal process, Shaikh uses the example of murder, with the police failing to find the killer, to identify three options. First, the police may close the file. Second, they may accept failure and ask the public and the government for more time. With both of these options, Shaikh notes, the police experience disrepute,[93] and they would also experience criticism and risk the possibility of transfer or an inquiry into their conduct (as chapter 2 elaborated). As Shaikh explains, however, they have a third option:

> *woh teesra kaam yeh haih ki police kisi nirdosh ko bali ka bakra banakar us case mein hatyare ke roop mein giraftar kar leti hain aur media ke samne prastut kar bade bade daawe karti hain ki humne badi mehnat aur lagan se ise giraftar kiya hai aur hamare paas iske khilaf suboot hain. Phir jhuthe gawahon ki sahayata se aarop patra adalat mein daakhil kiya jata haih.*

> The third thing they do is to catch hold of a sacrificial lamb and arrest him in that case and then produce him in front of the media and claim that they arrested him after much hard work and effort and that they have evidence against him. Then[,] using false witnesses, they enter the charge sheet into the court.[94]

In the chapter titled "Police *ki kahaani*" (Police Story), Shaikh systematically links across all aspects of the trial process, through which the police create a web. He cites stock witnesses and routine informers who appear both in the identification parade and in the trial process. Detainees may be tortured or pressured to provide false statements, although some refuse despite the threat or experience of torture. In the Mumbai blast case, Shaikh disbelieves the witnesses who provided testimonies in the case because basic questions were never asked about the absence of papers for taxi drivers or railway passes for those traveling by train.

Shaikh also refers to the difficulties of proving innocence when the police control the process. Even when the accused can access alternative witnesses or records, he says, these are ignored and the police believed. Shaikh even includes a commonly used sample confession covering all aspects of the Mumbai blast case and identifies similarities in the formats of the confessions, despite the detainees being taken to different police stations.[95] The testimonies and memoirs of detainees, especially in the *Mecca Masjid* and Mumbai blast cases, thus illustrate the political imperatives of terrorism trials. These accounts also document procedures that I term "scaffolding" of the rule of law.

Documentation of procedures is important to scaffolding. In terrorism cases, media trials need nationalist discourses.[96] But the government also needs to demonstrate a constantly evolving and efficient system—similar to the system Laleh Khalili describes for the Abu Ghraib prison in Iraq—detailed and meticulous.[97] As Beatrice Jauregui explains, even when ease in proving the crime allows police to use a different provision of law, they are careful to complete all paperwork systematically.[98] Following procedures based in the rule of law thus maintains the scaffold. Even when most crudely visible, it is held together by police, doctors, and magistrates and supported by compliant witnesses.

Criminal Racialization and Feminization of Detainees

Rather than limited to terrorism cases, torture and state violence manifest also in routine criminal cases and in conflict areas. Yet Islamophobia—and the targeting of Muslims—renders some Indian antiterror cases distinct. Often targeted are members of SIMI and men from particular Muslim-dominated areas, such as old Delhi, Jamia or the walled city in Hyderabad.[99] Although terrorism charges affect more than Muslim men, the predominant nationalist narrative links Muslims to Pakistan and the disputed territories of Kashmir.[100] In custody, the racialization and feminization of Muslims become central processes in this targeting.

Singh considers the focus on Muslim men under the antiterrorism laws TADA and POTA a process of creating a suspect community. Analyzing the application of such laws across a range of cases, he writes, "The experience with anti-terror laws has shown that more often than not they are directed primarily at one section of the public in a way that it becomes a suspect community."[101] As a category, the notion of a suspect community has existed in India since colonial times and elsewhere as well. The police have targeted tribes in colonial India,[102] Blacks, and Native Americans in the United States, women who have been deemed criminal,[103] and others defined as unproductive segments of society.[104] In Argentina, *delincuente* (young poor men), are treated distinctly from *gente*, or the elite.[105] Police in the United States have historically treated black and brown bodies as disposable in prisons or in everyday encounters.[106]

Terrorism cases in India focus on the precarity of young men, boys of the Muslim community (their ages vary, but still they are often termed boys, or *ladke*).[107] Hence I apply the term "criminal racialization," the construction of these young men as suspicious and dangerous criminals on the basis of shared characteristics, in this case, religion and masculinity.[108] The methods used to torture them reflect these assumptions. Shaikh notes in his chapter on police torture that two common techniques were "stripping" and religious "abuses," both noteworthy in a chapter that lists techniques like electric shock, rectal assault, water torture, solitary confinement, mock executions, and sleep deprivation.

Of eleven available depositions related to the Mumbai blast case, ten mention nakedness as a form of abuse, sometimes in conjunction with other techniques of physical torture.[109] As Mohd. Ansari stated, "I was stripped naked and many shocks were given to my private parts."[110] Nakedness, however, was meant to induce a particular reaction. As Shaikh notes, the accused would often be stripped and paraded in front of relatives and family members. Sometimes even the family members would be stripped and paraded in front of the accused, as he elaborates:

> *Torture se abhiyukta tadapkar cheekhne lagta haih aur 'allah' ko yaad karta haih tou ATS wale (allah ki panah) allah, rasul, aur islam ko gaaliyan bakte rahte hain. Ma- Behan ki gaali dena unke liye aam baat haih.*

> Affected by the torture, the accused remembers Allah, so in response the ATS officers end up abusing Allah, Rasul, and Islam. Swearing against mother/sister is of course a common occurrence.[111]

Like the U.S. soldiers in Iraq and Guantánamo, Cuba, the police targeted religious beliefs with practices assumed to be torturous to Muslims. As Cynthia Enloe argued about the United States, the attempt is also to feminize detainees, to impose on them "allegedly feminine characteristics—fear, sexual vulnerability, docility, subservience."[112] In India, stripping and parading are public spectacles also used to target *dalit* women.[113] Here humiliating Muslim detainees in front of their family members, either by stripping the accused or making them watch women stripped, is meant to lower their status. The intention is apparently to invoke shame as a form of mental torture and to violate the masculinity of the accused, as the testimony of one detainee exemplifies:

> Officers Phadke and Dalvi and constables forcefully removed his clothes and made him naked and paraded him. They were pressurizing accused no. 3 Faisal to accept the crime of the bomb blasts or all his family members will be similarly treated. They brought a veiled woman there, whose veil was forcefully removed in front of all.[114]

Or as Muzzammil Shaikh narrated, "My father was tortured and stripped naked before my co-accused."[115]

Suhail Shaikh elaborates on the combined impact of such techniques:

> I saw Tanveer, Faisal, Ehtesham and Muzzammil also handcuffed in the main hall and being beaten. This was going on till late night. The accused no. 3 and 9's father was brought there along with a veiled woman member of their family. We all were naked at that time and the officers and constables were using filthy and dirty language. They stripped accused no. 3's father's clothes, abused and misbehaved with him. Officer Dalvi scolded the woman and used bad language and took off her veil. The accused no. 3 and 9 were beaten heavily during this period. They were pleading and crying on seeing the misbehaviour with their father. When their father tried to hide his modesty, he was beaten on his hands and told to hold the hands high. The officers were threatening the accused no. 3 and 9 to tell what they did and even if they do not know they should take the responsibility of the blasts and that their father would take the responsibility. They also threatened me to take the responsibility of the blasts or else they would bring my women family members there and would strip them in our presence and the drug addicts would be asked to molest them.[116]

As Shaikh's affidavit indicates, these methods focus on the women of the family. Even in the *Mecca Masjid* case, the police used abusive language against women family members and forced the detainees to hail Hindu deities.

Patriarchal modes of shame and honor, together with threats of rape, are techniques of mental torture and those are repeatedly mentioned in depositions alongside the application of electric shocks to their private parts. Threatening to involve drug addicts to molest the women relatives of the accused is also to force other bodies (involving drugs in another way) to become live instruments of physical torture. Whereas stripping and parading are recognized crimes in other contexts, these techniques are deployed here to collect evidence and therefore remain unaddressed as means of abuse. Criminal racialization and feminization during torture and interrogation are thus engaged to humiliate an entire community.

The targeting of Muslims must also be situated in the marginalization and othering to which Muslims are subjected, together with the history of communal conflicts in India and the conflict in Kashmir. As Mohammad Aamir Khan recounts in his memoir, the police displayed torture equipment that had been used since the Mughal period, saying, "*tumhare zamane ka haih, Mughal zamane ka haih*" (These are from your time, Mughal times).[117] Chillingly, only the effort to avoid death limits torture, as Shaikh explains from a Muslim prisoner's perspective:

> *Muslim samaj ke ek aham sadasya ka, jo varshon se jhuthe case ke tehat jail mein band haih, yah sunehra kathan yaad rakhiye: "30 din ka torture bardasht kijiye ya tees saal ki saza. Faisla aap per haih."*

> Remember the words of an important member of the Muslim community who has been imprisoned for a number of years under a false case: "Tolerate thirty days of torture or thirty years imprisonment. The decision is yours."[118]

Fear of long term imprisonment may thus counter the humiliation and violence of racialization and feminization as those tortured endeavor to survive. As long as the accused is alive, and the violence in contained in custody, however, the scaffolding of the rule of law also survives. There is a deliberate targeting of detainees' masculinity and religious identity (although, of course, forced humiliation of men and women would also be a form of violence for other religions).[119] Physical and mental torture, together with narcoanalysis, thus become the apparatus of policing, with effects that we can identify by focusing on individual experience to understand the rule of law.

Experience as an Element of Analysis of the Rule of Law

The Supreme Court has consistently upheld the constitutionality of the extraordinary laws. The Court's decisions, therefore, are inadequate.[120] But occasional moments of introspection among Supreme Court justices are evident in the dissenting opinions on Kartar Singh's case regarding TADA, the acquittal of Syed Abdul Rahman Geelani in the Parliament attack case, and the Manipur encounter cases under the Armed Forces (Special Powers) Act (AFSPA).[121] And many terrorism cases do adhere to formal legality.[122] Legal rules often authorize government action, and independent courts determine its legality. Although the Supreme Court has upheld the extraordinary laws as a parallel system of governance, the police do not openly defend their actions as sovereign actors or use specific laws to defend torture or other constitutional violations. Rather, precisely because constitutional violations cannot be easily upheld, we find occasional respite in even terror-related cases.[123]

Since the state cannot explicitly uphold the violence, the police, along with doctors and magistrates, intentionally create a scaffolding of the rule of law. Rather than considering these actors incidental to the apparatus of policing, we must thus acknowledge their centrality in police procedure.[124] The actions of officials are more than just "rule by men," or "rule by law"; they are also not only representing the sovereign actions. Instead, breaking down the process of policing invites us to recognize the everyday acts not as moments of technical procedure but as roadblocks to the possibility of substantive justice. As Nandita Haksar, who helped write Khan's memoir, notes, "None of the magistrates ever asked him when he had been arrested; whether he had been tortured and how to ensure his safety."[125] This process is Kafkaesque, as Sethi powerfully characterized the terror trials,[126] yet the legal process is also a rational set of procedures requiring the police to create alternative stories, thereby building the scaffolding that supports the existing apparatus.

The scaffolding relies on confessions, on an extended remand, and, with the help of doctors and magistrates, on a distinct conception of temporality. Urgent situations—like the ticking bomb scenario that is a basis for upholding antiterror legislation and extraordinary laws—is here replaced by a delay before presenting a suspect to a magistrate so that the marks of interrogation disappear.[127] Shaikh's book reveals the actors involved, the testimonies of torture, and the violence in the procedures. The suspect's family is threatened, witnesses are targeted, the accused are tortured, inculpatory evidence is created, and evidence of innocence is obscured.

To ensure coherence and consistency, the police and ATS are sometimes especially strategic about the number of witnesses they produce, and in these cases, paperwork and documentation become crucial. As Khan writes, "My tormentors threatened to pull out the [finger]nails one by one till I signed all the papers. I would still hear the screams from the other room. . . . I signed and signed and signed. There must have been at least 100 to 150 blank pages."[128] Unlike the paperwork in forensic psychologists' laboratories, which remains in the shadow of law, the scaffolding of the rule of law requires detailed public documentation.[129]

Manisha Sethi captures this dynamic in *Kafkaland*: "Such is the machinery of our criminal justice system: investigators who torture; doctors who comply; pseudo-scientists with dubious truth serums; judges who ignore signs of torture; and a media which carries the burden of national security on its frail shoulders."[130] Sethi correctly defines this process that I argue remains apparently rational. Each step in the procedure must be technically followed, even as it is substantively undermined. For instance, even under MCOCA, applied in the Mumbai blast case, a confession must be voluntary.[131] The accused must be warned by the deputy commissioner of police, without police pressure, about the right to silence and then asked to repeat the confession in front of a magistrate, who ensures a medical examination outside police custody. All of these measures ostensibly ensure the accused's volition, but in practice, each step becomes little more than a bureaucratic check mark, indicative more of scaffolding than the rights of the accused. Notably, the police, even in the higher ranks, are charged with ensuring detainees' protection, despite their role in conducting torture.

The activists and human rights lawyers, the memoirs and testimonies that detail these processes can help, however, to dismantle the scaffolding and contribute to a resistance that emerges from and contributes toward human rights discourse. Shaikh's primer about avoiding torture, for example, offers revelations about scaffolding that chillingly yet effectively challenge scaffolding by warning others who might become trapped in a web of terrorism trials. In "Confession Is Conviction," he asserts, "*aapko police ka torture bardasht karna haih. yaad rakhiye 'tees din ka torture ya tees saal kis qaid.'*" (To survive police torture, you must remember: "thirty days of torture or thirty years in prison").[132]

Shaikh also urges the accused either to refuse to sign their statements or to keep changing them in court in order to force judges to acknowledge inconsistencies: "*apna angutha tod lijiye, lekin kisi kagaz par dastakhat mat kijiye.*" (Just break your thumb but don't sign any paper.)[133] No one, he says, should ever confess in front of a camera:

chunache vah torture se bachne ke liye police ke ishare par chalta rehta haih. Us samay abhiyukta ki halat hum samajhte hain. Lekin yaad rakhiye, police aapko torture se maar nahin dalegi. Wah tou keval itna maregi ki aap dar kar uska kaam kar de. Vah is tarah nahin maregi jisse gahri zakhm ho. Isliye puri koshish karein ki camera ke samne koi bayaan na de.

Because suspects want to protect themselves from torture, they follow the police directions. We can understand the situation that the accused are in. But you should remember that the police *will not kill you* with the torture. They will only beat you to the extent that you agree to do their work. The police won't beat you in such a way that there are physical wounds. So try your best not to give a statement in front of a camera.[134]

Each of Shaikh's instructions is meant to hold the rationality of the procedures accountable, and, curiously, as chapter 2 explains, these measures do contribute to the police's pastoral function, as they avoid severe wounds and custodial deaths. Indeed, this was a key reason for the ostensible move to truth machines.

Resistance is evident in prisoners' speech. With pain a constant feature of life in custody or in prison, detainees devise colloquial names for the experience. As Arun Ferreira writes, "During his [Taksande] reign, the assaults had become such a frequent practice that inmates began to refer to them as *shyam ka bhajan* [hymns for a Hindu God Krishna]."[135] The new young jailor soon acquired a reputation as a *Dabangg* who, like his Bollywood version, would swing his baton in a way to impress the women watching him.[136] Another detainee, Mohammad Aamir, recounts beatings when tied to a pole. A "kind of beating leaves no marks," he explains, "but it is very painful. In jail parlance it is called *Lakshman Jhoola*" (a suspension bridge linked to crossing the Ganges near Rishikesh).[137] As Marguerite Feitlowitz notes in *Lexicon of Terror*, torture techniques and instruments often acquire new names intended either to deny the pain or to break the silence.[138] She cites, for instance, the term *parilla*, a grill for meat, applied to a torture apparatus.

This renaming challenges the rationality of procedures that mask custodial violence. Because violence occurs despite formal legality and review, the scaffolding of the rule of law exists based on these procedural safeguards. In India a parallel system for addressing terrorism and organized crime is supported not only by the extraordinary laws but also by the scaffolding that appears to support legal procedures. However, theorizing in light of the experiences of those involved reveals this scaffolding and the violence it obscures. Once revealed, violence can be resisted, its logic leading to possibilities for relief, as in the *Mecca Masjid* case and the one acquittal in the Mumbai blast case.

Beneath the scaffolding is the apparatus of policing—the police, doctors, magistrates, and forensic psychologists—that maintain a foundation of violence. Ultimately, the scaffolding keeps these elements of the system in place, providing a rational bureaucratic system. The security state is not the only source of this scaffolding of the rule of law. Rather, the rights-based liberal state promotes a logic of enforcement through violence. The police, doctors, and magistrates are aware of the purpose of the scaffold, but a higher purpose and a commitment to the procedural system—that upholds the liberal and the security state—maintain their participation.

CONCLUSION

Interviews with lawyers and activists and the testimonies and memoirs of the accused trace the mechanisms for managing the everyday violence of state agents. Whereas a focus on the jurisprudence and actions of police agents is crucial, the focus here is on, first, the role of doctors, magistrates, and forensic psychologists in enabling violence and, second, the procedural safeguards that become the mechanisms through which this enabling takes place. Procedural safeguards not only provide the scaffolding of the rule of law but also allow counteragents engaging with state actors to challenge both the extraordinary laws and the scaffold. Theorizing about the rule of law, therefore, must account for the experience of violence, both to reveal and to challenge the scaffold.

As Foucault explains in *Discipline and Punish*, the spectacle of the scaffold was abandoned because it tended to undermine the purpose it was supposed to fulfill. Applied to uphold the absolute power of the sovereign, the spectacle was subverted by the last words of the condemned, the acknowledgment of the crime, and the truth of the punishment. In India after the Emergency period (from 1977 onward), the emergence of movements for democratic rights and the consolidation of the civil liberties led to some recognition of rights. Perhaps the testimonies that belie the scaffold of the rule of law can reveal its violent foundations and make way for transformation to a more substantive conception of the rule of law.[139]

Chapter 7

CONCLUSION

The Contingent State

Abdul Wahid Shaikh reminds prisoners to remember the purpose of torture in investigations:

> *Lekin yaad rakhiye, police aapko torture se maar nahin dalegi. Wah tou keval itna maregi ki aap dar kar uska kaam kar de. Vah is tarah nahin maregi jisse gahri zakhm ho. Isliye puri koshish karein ki camera ke samne koi bayaan na de.*

> But you should remember that the police will not kill you with the torture. They will beat you only to the extent that you agree to do their work. The police won't beat you in such a way that there are physical wounds. So try your best not to give a statement in front of a camera.[1]

The Truth Machines proposes a disaggregated conception of the state, or what I term a "contingent state." Two prominent frameworks theorize the relationship between state power and legal violence in liberal democracies. One is rational bureaucracy, which assumes a near monopoly of the state over routine violence. The other is a state of exception, which explains state violence in conflict areas and crisis situations. In contrast to the monolithic conception of the state assumed in both of these frameworks, this book reveals multiple sites of interaction—and thus multiple contingencies—among law, science, and policing.

This study points to a more disaggregated conception of the state to highlight possible sites of critique and limits on legal violence. The term "contingent state" indicates a state that may at times emerge as unitary and at other times reveal its contingencies. A continuous process of negotiation between the unitary and the contingent, then, affects people's experience of the state. Hence, *The Truth Machines* calls attention to possibilities not only for accessing the materiality of everyday experiences of the state but also for resisting state power. The contingent state is, above all, a reminder that even the police, with their proximity to violence, reflect possibilities for shifts from within.

THE POLICE IN A CONTINGENT STATE

Scholars of policing have focused primarily on an ideological understanding of the police. Here, however, I reveal tension between the ideological imperatives of the police and the structural contingencies that render the police unable to operate in a unitary way, even when using violence. Whereas discretion has been important to studying policing, *The Truth Machines* points to contingency as a structural element of police action. Police discretion allows officials to use power at the micro level. Contingency, in contrast, is much more structural and counters the notion of unified, rule-based policing (see chapter 2).

The Indian state's apparent embrace of truth machines in the 1990s and 2000s coincides with a period of consolidation in the wake of human rights movements and establishment of the National Human Rights Commission. With concern for human rights, the police negotiate two roles—the pastoral and the repressive—even in the dark recesses of custody, and they seek to avoid custodial deaths or bodies with marks. The police explain their pragmatic logic for using third-degree interrogation to counter public distrust, limited time in custody, and the need to recover materials, but their performance as police in a *liberal democracy* creates the basis for interventions by courts and human rights activists.

The Indian courts uphold the rule of law by subjecting all state actions to constitutional interpretation (see chapter 5). While condemning torture and custodial deaths, however, the Indian Supreme Court has rarely addressed the conditions that allow torture to persist. This flaw in the art of governing represents a peculiarly postcolonial legacy, as modernization and science frame a system that accommodates a colonial legal framework associated with the most brutal forms of violence. As chapter 6 reveals, the police, alongside magistrates and medical professionals, create a scaffold of the rule of law to hide or erase the experiences of violence in terrorism cases. Unlike the Foucaldian spectacle of the scaffold, which relied on terror, the scaffold of the rule of law hides violence in its procedures.

The study of both the unitary representation of the state, together with the rule of law, and the contingencies of the everyday policing exposes the scaffold. For terror suspects experiencing state violence, its contingencies may mean life or death. As chapter 6 explains, official critiques and the voices of those targeted may reveal the scaffolding to be inadequate for hiding the violence. Understanding the rule of law, therefore, requires attention to the experience of those affected. Those subject to the everyday behavior of state actors are thus well positioned both to reveal the scaffolding of the rule of law and to actively resist it.

THE STATE, INFRASTRUCTURE, AND STATE VIOLENCE STUDIES

The Truth Machines analyzes the relationship between state power and legal violence through a study of forensic techniques. Since my research began, scholars in social sciences and humanities have focused on the phenomenon of infrastructure, drawing upon disciplines such as planning, architecture, physical sciences, planning, and information science.[2] As Cymene Howe and colleagues explain:

> While the popular imagination might recognize infrastructure as the mundane mechanisms within, beneath, and supporting the maintenance of quotidian life, many scholars have foregrounded the agency, performativity, and dynamism of infrastructure. Infrastructure is not inert but rather infused with social meanings and reflective of larger priorities and attentions.[3]

In chapter 4, I discuss the creation of a state forensic architecture akin to an infrastructure of interrogations in forensic laboratories and forensic psychology. As Howe and her coauthors further note, "Infrastructure is material (roads, pipes, sewers, and grids); it is social (institutions, economic systems, and media forms); and it is philosophical (intellectual trajectories: dreamt up by human ingenuity and nailed down in concrete forms)."[4]

Forensic psychology—the polygraph machines, the laboratories, and the BEOS and brain fingerprinting machines—represent the conditions that make possible the ingenuity and philosophical innovation of forensic psychologists. These conditions include structural support from the Ministry of Home Affairs, which made these techniques a priority for police reform, and the economic interests in their success, which led to patents, private companies, and private laboratories maintaining and expanding their use despite legal and ethical challenges. As Brian Larkin notes, "The act of defining an infrastructure is a categorizing moment."[5]

This scholarship focuses attention not only on infrastructure but also on the ruins associated with projects of modernity. The state forensic architecture—a futile attempt to draw upon science, technology, and expertise for policing in postcolonial India—thrives among these ruins. The origins of the state forensic architecture reveal, in turn, the infrastructure of interrogation, together with the risks and dangers of ruin. Despite the significance of "infrastructure", nonetheless, in *The Truth Machines* I retain the concept of state. Here, the notion of a contingent state focuses on the material and ideological conditions that both maintain state power and legal violence and allow state and non-state actors to innovate.

Scientific techniques—brain scans, lie detectors, and narcoanalysis—are seemingly innocuous developments at the margins of police practice, emerging to replace physical torture, the absence of which is central to a self-defined liberal democracy. My interviews with police, lawyers, and forensic psychologists, however, reveal the need for the state to create constantly new confessional sites. The investment in truth machines as part of a forensic architecture requires constant innovation at all costs (see chapter 4). Rather than scientific validity or legal admissibility as the foundation for innovation, experts and media become central in the cultural construction of truth (see chapter 3).

Of course, even if the confessional site is just reconstructed in forensic science laboratories, it offers a space away from police custody where science and art converge in the cyborg-like forensic psychologist. In chapter 4 I focus on the ways state actors constantly seek to create a unitary structure from the disparate attempts of innovative experts and to portray an overall shift in the forms used for police interrogation. Bolstering forensic psychologists' claims to expertise are both their therapeutic skills and the scientifically grounded knowledge that truth machines promise to provide.

The states' forensic architecture must conform to a narrative of science and modernization in which the postcolonial system accommodates human rights to make the regime less brutal (even if it fails). The scaffolding of the rule of law therefore includes police, lawyers, and forensic psychologists to keep the rational bureaucracy in place and functioning. Despite the difficulties of definitions, the state (as opposed to infrastructure), then, persists in the popular imagination as an important conception, and the police and prisons remain its most visible sites of coercion. Furthermore, the state maintains a deep relationship to violence, with its agents still enjoying the most legitimacy (and impunity) for violence in its name.

The complex but integral relationship between state power and legal violence suggests a focus on state violence studies (SVS). Whereas violence has been richly theorized and the state much studied,[6] SVS specifies the bodies targeted at sites of state power and the need to understand mechanisms of state violence in liberal democracies. SVS highlights the constantly negotiated relationship of the state to violence. Police proximity to the means for violence requires scrutiny of the police and their everyday interactions with subjects. Considering human rights reports and testimonials documenting everyday practices, SVS can conceptualize state violence through attention to concerns like impunity or custody.[7] Identifying the mechanisms through which the state applies violence, SVS can also mediate theoretical assumptions about the police as either a bureaucratic body or a monolithically repressive institution. The notion of a contingent state thus accounts for the need to study the shifts, cracks, and possibilities of transformation.

NOTES

Chapter 1

1. The *Aarushi-Hemraj* double murder case became controversial for several reasons. First, the officers involved in the case itself went through different changes. The CBI officer who had taken over the case from the local police was later replaced by another officer, who eventually filed a closure notice citing a lack of adequate evidence. Second, despite the "lack of evidence," the judicial magistrate refused to allow the case to be closed, and eventually the case in the trial court appears to have been mostly decided on the basis of circumstantial evidence. See Jinee Lokaneeta, "Narco Videos, Forensic Psychologists, and the Truth-Telling Apparatus: Tracing Evidence, Law, and Media Trials," in *The Act of Media: Workshop on Law, Media, and Technology in South Asia*, Sarai Programme, Centre for the Study of Developing Societies, Delhi, January 8–10, 2016.

2. Two films have been made on the case and a book has been written, which is not necessarily unusual, but these attempts were meant to raise consciousness and in effect challenge the legitimacy of the trial court verdict against the parents. *Talvar* (English title of the film- Guilty) was released in September 2015 at the Toronto Film Festival. *Rahasya (mystry)* was directed by Manish Gupta and released in January 2015. The book was written by Avirook Sen, *Aarushi* (Gurgaon, India: Penguin, 2015). See Lokaneeta, "Narco Videos."

3. Petitions were created in support of the parents; a website (justiceforarushitalwar.com) and a Facebook page were also created. The film *Talvar*, Avirook Sen's book *Aarushi*, and two media articles by Shoma Chaudhury were explicitly mentioned in a petition, and Sen and the Talwars' lawyer attended events organized by the Justice for Talwar website. The Facebook page had sixty-two thousand "likes," and the *Times of India* had its own campaign with thirty-seven thousand supporters, while the film actors who were a part of the film *Talvar* also questioned the verdict, thereby feeding into one another's outrage. More recently, a podcast called *Trial by Error*, conceptually based on the extremely popular U.S. podcast *Serial* on the Adnan Syed case, has appeared in the *Aarushi* case. All of these popular campaigns emphasized the importance of the narcoanalysis tests, and the narco

videos are available on YouTube. I discuss this briefly in chapter 3. See Lokaneeta, "Narco Videos."

4. Jinee Lokaneeta, "Why Narco, Brain Scan & Lie Test Should Be Junked," *Times of India*, October 25, 2017, https://timesofindia.indiatimes.com/city/delhi/why-narco-brain-scan-lie-test-should-be-junked/articleshow/61211439.cms

5. Lie detectors have been used from the late 1960s, although the more official records are from 1973 onward. Brain electrical oscillation signature (BEOS) tests were first used in 2003, and narcoanalysis was first used in 1989 (I discuss details of these techniques in chapter 3), but they grew into prominence collectively in the early 2000s.

6. In the book I use the terms "third degree" and "torture" interchangeably because "third degree" has become synonymous with torture and the interviewees often used them interchangeably. The origin of the term (at least in the U.S. context) as explained in the 1931 Wickersham Commission on the third degree refers to third degree as interrogation; the first degree is arrest, and the second degree is confinement. Wickersham Commission Report; Zechariah Chafee Jr., Walter H. Pollak, and Carl Stern, *The Third Degree: Report to the National Commission on Law Observance and Enforcement (June 1931)* (New York: Arno Press, 1969). Richard A. Leo notes, "The term 'third degree' connotes, in American folklore, extreme interrogation." Richard A. Leo, *Police Interrogation and American Justice* (Cambridge, MA: Harvard University Press, 2008). Interviews conducted for another project in India suggest that "normally, they [the police and elite classes] talk of the 'third degree' rather than 'torture' because the term is less offensive; but they accept it because they think it is the only method that an inefficient system is equipped to employ." Jinee Lokaneeta and Amar Jesani, "India," in *Does Torture Prevention Work?*, ed. Richard Carver and Lisa Handley, 501–47 (Liverpool: Liverpool University Press, 2016), 544. Thus, it is true that the interviewees for this book on their own accord were much more likely to use the term "third degree" than "torture" unless pushed, although I tended to use the term "torture." Furthermore, such a distinction would sometimes break when interviewees used "third-degree torture" to emphasize the seriousness of the interrogation.

7. *Smt. Selvi & Others v. State of Karnataka* (2010). I discuss this case in chapter 5.

8. As I show in chapter 3, these techniques are considered as unreliable. That said, as science and technology scholars have noted, studies on the use of DNA suggest that such infallibility of the DNA itself should not be assumed. Instead, as Michael Lynch and his colleagues point out, there are always judgments and contingencies involved in the use of any forensic method. Michael Lynch, Simon A. Cole, Ruth McNally, and Kathleen Jordan, *Truth Machine: The Contentious History of DNA Fingerprinting* (Chicago: University of Chicago Press, 2012).

9. Mohammed Akhef, "To Avoid Custodial Deaths, Follow SOP, CIDs Instructions: DGP," *Times of India*, December 3, 2017.

10. *Ram Baran v. The State of NCT of Delhi* (W.P.[CRL] 3115/2018); Akanksha Jain, "Surprised at People Travelling to Gujarat for Narco Test, HC Orders Govt to Make Facility Available at Delhi FSL in 3 Months," Livelaw.in, January 11, 2019, https://www.livelaw.in/news-updates/surprised-people-travelling-gujarat-narco-test-hc-orders-facility-available-delhi-fsl-3-months-142051

11. I tend to use the term "legal violence" in the book. I do so in order to emphasize that the usual distinctions between illegal and legal (or legitimate/illegitimate) violence actually fail to recognize the continuum between the two. As I discussed in my previous book *Transnational Torture*, there is a "constant difficulty of defining and distinguishing among different forms of state violence: torture, cruel, inhuman, and degrading, humiliating treatment and coercion." Jinee Lokaneeta, *Transnational Torture: Law, Violence, and State Power in the United States and India* (New York: New York University Press, 2011), 32–33. Thus, in understanding torture, I suggested the term "excess violence" as a constantly negotiated category that exists on a continuum of coercion to torture where only when a particular threshold of violence is difficult to discursively uphold is it defined as a violation. While in a particular legal case, these distinctions might be important to determine punishment, analytically these distinctions provide the flexibility to a state to deny or accommodate its own violence.

12. As I argue in chapter 4, the state forensic architecture is constituted when forensic psychologists (experts) are inserted into the state planning priorities of expansion and development of the police (bureaucratic agents of state power) by creating material conditions (machines/drugs/labs/courses), changes in legal procedures, and legitimation through media and state initiatives.

13. Max Weber, "Bureaucracy," in *Economy and Society: An Outline of Interpretive Sociology*, ed. G. Roth and C. Wittich, reprinted in *Anthropology of the State: A Reader*, ed. Aradhana Sharma and Akhil Gupta, 211–42 (Malden, MA: Blackwell, 2006).

14. Giorgio Agamben, *State of Exception*, trans. K. Attell (Chicago: University of Chicago Press, 2005); Giorgio Agamben, *Homo Sacer: Sovereign Power and Bare Life*, trans. D. Heller-Roazen (Stanford, CA: Stanford University Press, 1998).

15. See Partha Chatterjee, "The State," in *The Oxford Companion to Politics in India*, ed. Niraja Gopal Jayal and Pratap Bhanu Mehta, 3–14 (Delhi: Oxford University Press, 2010); Ujjwal Kumar Singh, *The State, Democracy, and Anti-Terror Laws in India* (New Delhi: Sage, 2007).

16. The high courts had about 4.3 million and the Supreme Court had 57,000 in backlog. "CJI-Designate Ranjan Gogoi Says He Has a Plan to Tackle Judicial Backlog," *Hindustan Times*, September 30, 2018, https://www.hindustantimes.com/india-news/cji-designate-ranjan-gogoi-says-he-has-a-plan-to-tackle-judicial-backlog/story-PRqWd-4J7mxUjRbZ8BFFatI.html

17. Harish V. Nair, "3.3 Crore Backlog Cases in Courts, Pendency Figure at Highest: CJI Dipak Misra," *India Today*, June 28, 2018, https://www.indiatoday.in/india/story/3-3-crore-backlog-cases-in-courts-pendency-figure-at-highest-cji-dipak-misra-1271752-2018-06-28. Crore refers to 10 million.

18. David H. Bayley, "The Police and the Political Order in India," *Asian Survey* 23, no. 4 (1983): 492–93.

19. The structure of the Indian police is as follows. The top tier (about 1 percent) is the director general of police (DGP) in charge of a state/union territory; followed by the additional director general or inspector general of police in charge of a zone (formed of many ranges) or special department; followed by a deputy inspector general of police, head of a range (formed of districts); followed by the superintendent of police, head of a district (formed of many stations or subdivisions); followed by an assistant/deputy superintendent, heading a subdivision of a district. The next tier (14 percent) is formed of junior-ranking officers composed of inspector, head of a police station; followed by sub-inspector, heading a smaller police station or staff; followed by an assistant sub-inspector with some administrative and investigative authority. The majority (85 percent) of the police force is made up of a head constable and constables who are the staff. Human Rights Watch, *Broken System: Dysfunction, Abuse, and Impunity in the Indian Police* (New York: Human Rights Watch, 2009), 2. Policing in the union territories is managed by the Central Government. The state has armed police and civil police, and the center also has a number of armed forces to be sent out to the state when required.

20. Commonwealth Human Rights Initiative, *Rough Roads to Equality: Women Police in South Asia* (New Delhi: Commonwealth Human Rights Initiative, 2015), 46; Human Rights Watch, *Broken System*; Commonwealth Human Rights Initiative, *Police Organisation in India* (New Delhi: Commonwealth Human Rights Initiative, 2008). For comparison, it is one of the lowest police population ratios in the world (according to a report in 2010), with the United States having 1 officer for 436 people and South Africa 1 for 347. "India Is Short of 5 Lakh Policemen. Here's Why It Matters (And Why It Doesn't)," *Scroll*, July 29, 2016, https://scroll.in/article/812672/india-is-short-of-5-lakh-policemen-heres-why-it-matters-and-why-it-doesnt

21. Human Rights Watch, *Broken System*, 8. See the discussion in Guillermina Seri and Jinee Lokaneeta, "Police as State: Governing Citizenship through Violence," in *Police Abuse in Contemporary Democracies*, ed. Bonner et al. 55–80 (New York: Palgrave Macmillan, 2017).

22. A refusal to file First Information Reports, especially regarding the violence against *dalits*, tribals and women, is also mentioned in Human Rights Watch, *Broken System*. In addition, the participation of the police in both the 1984 violence against Sikhs and the 2002 violence against Muslims is also well documented. Bhajan Singh Bhinder and Patrick

J. Nevers, *Demons Within: The Systematic Practice of Torture by Indian Police*, Organization of Minorities in India (Lathrop, CA: Sovereign Star Publishing, 2011), http://www.sikhmail.org/ofmi/wp-content/uploads/2013/08/Demons-Within.pdf

23. National Human Rights Commission reports compiled by Asian Centre for Human Rights, *Torture in India 2011*, 2–5, http://www.indianet.nl/pdf/torture2011.pdf

24. "Torture Update India: Five Custodial Deaths per Day during 2017–2018," Asian Centre for Human Rights, June 26, 2018, http://www.achrweb.org/press-release/torture-update-india-five-custodial-deaths-per-day-during-2017-2018

25. In 2014–2015 there were about 353 cases of torture and cruel, inhuman, or degrading treatment in Manipur alone. Centre for Organisation Research and Education/Human to Humane Transcultural Centre for Torture and Trauma Victims (H2H), "Report of Torture in Manipur, 2014–2015" (Manipur: Centre for Organisation Research and Education, 2015). Jinee Lokaneeta, "Manipur Fake Encounters Case Could Highlight the Immense Power of the Judicial Word," *Wire*, July 27, 2018, https://thewire.in/law/manipur-fake-encounters-supreme-court-case. Similarly, Amnesty International alone pointed to the 800 cases of torture and deaths in Kashmir and many more extrajudicial killings from 1989 to 2013. Amnesty International India, *"Denied" Failures in Accountability for Human Rights Violations by Security Force Personnel in Jammu and Kashmir* (London: Amnesty International, 2015); Haley Duschinski. "Reproducing Regimes of Impunity: Fake Encounters and the Informalization of Violence in Kashmir Valley." *Cultural Studies* 24.1(2010): 110–32. One of the most comprehensive reports on torture is Kashmir has been released in Feb 2019. *Torture: Indian State's Instrument of Control in Indian administered Jammu and Kashmir*, Association of Parents of Disappeared Persons (APDP) and Jammu Kashmir Coalition of Civil Society (JKCCS), February 2019. The reports of torture have increased since August 2019 when the Indian state abrogated article 370 regarding the autonomy of Kashmir.

26. Neha Dixit, "A Chronicle of the Crime Fiction That Is Adityanath's Encounter Raj," *Wire*, February 24, 2018, https://thewire.in/rights/chronicle-crime-fiction-adityanaths-encounter-raj

27. See Lokaneeta and Jesani, "India," 501–47.

28. The term *dalits* refers to those who were discriminated the most in the caste hierarchy. While that is predominantly the case, it is also true that "the victims selected by Indian police for torture are diverse." Bhinder and Nevers, *Demons Within*, 7. See specific sections on how the marginalized may be targeted for their identity; for example, the *hijra* transgender community may be intentionally targeted. Along these lines, three directors general of police—Sanjeev Dayal (Maharashtra), Deoraj Nagar (Uttar Pradesh), and K. Ramanujam (Tamil Nadu)—admitted that minorities, in particular Muslims, have a "trust deficit" toward the police. Muslims, a newspaper report notes, "see them [the police] as 'com-

munal, biased and insensitive . . . ill-informed, corrupt and lacking professionalism.'" Smita Nair, "Muslims Think We Are Communal, Corrupt: Police," *Indian Express*, July 14, 2014.

29. "Opening Statement by Attorney General for India at the Third Universal Periodic Review of India (Geneva, May 04, 2017)," https://www.mea.gov.in/Speeches-Statements.htm?dtl/28437/Opening+Statement+by+Attorney+General+for+India+at+the+Third+Universal+Periodic+Review+of+India+Geneva+May+04+2017

30. A state of emergency was declared by the then prime minister Indira Gandhi between 1975 and 1977 declaring that "the Security of India is threatened by internal disturbances." See the discussions on human rights movements in Ajay Gudavarthy, "Human Rights Movement(s) in India: State, Civil Society, and Beyond," in *Human Rights and Peace: Ideas, Laws, Institutions, and Movement*, ed. Ujjwal Singh, 252–75 (New Delhi: Sage, 2009); G. Haragopal and K. Balagopal, "Civil Liberties Movement and the State in India," in *People's Rights: Social Movement, and the State in the Third World*, ed. Manoranjan Mohanty, Partha Nath Mukherji, and Olle Tornquist, 353–72 (New Delhi: Sage, 1998); and Upendra Baxi, *The Crisis of the Indian Legal System* (New Delhi: Vikas Publishing House, 1982).

31. *Nilabati Behera v. State of Orissa* (1993) 2 SCC 746; *D. K Basu v. State of W. B.* (1997) 1 SCC 416. There is, of course, a related debate on whether the courts have always been weak on civil liberties, as Pratap Bhanu Mehta puts it, or, as Uday Mehta explains, the emphasis on dangers of trying to deal with social questions leads to the lack of limits on political power—the sphere of liberty. P. B. Mehta. "The Inner Conflict of Constitutionalism: Judicial Review and the 'Basic Structure,'" in *India's Living Constitution: Ideas, Practices, Controversies*, ed. Zoya Hasan, E. Sridharan, and R. Sudarshan, 179–206 (London: Anthem Press, 2005); Uday S. Mehta, "Constitutionalism," in *The Oxford Companion to Politics in India*, ed. Niraja Gopal Jayal and Pratap Bhanu Mehta, 15–27 (Oxford: Oxford University Press, 2010). Anuj Bhuwania links that further to the question of the arbitrary actions of judges in Public Interest Litigations. Anuj Bhuwania, "Courting the People: The Rise of Public Interest Litigation in Post-Emergency India," *Comparative Studies of South Asia, Africa, and the Middle East* 34, no. 2 (2014): 314–35.

32. "India's Democracy at 70," *Journal of Democracy* 28, no. 3 (2017): 39.

33. Sumit Ganguly, "India's Democracy at 70: The Troublesome Security State," *Journal of Democracy* 28, no. 3 (2017): 125.

34. The voice analyzer is a new technology being used to determine deception. One of the reasons most forensic psychologists did not want their interviews to be recorded is because they were aware of this technology.

35. Vicky Nanjappa, "The Truth about Narcoanalysis," December 21, 2012, https://vickynanjappa.com/category/narco-analysis

36. My interviewees were often surprised to see that I am an "Indian" academic based in the United States.

37. I also tend to use the term "scientific techniques" in my description of polygraphs, brain scans, and narcoanalysis, since I am mostly interested in their discursive framing as scientific, which falls apart on closer scrutiny yet keeps reappearing as "scientific" based on expertise.

38. Akhil Gupta, *Red Tape: Bureaucracy, Structural Violence and Poverty in India* (New Delhi: Orient BlackSwan, 2012), 45.

39. See, for example, Elizabeth Mertz and Jothie Rajah, "Language-and-Law Scholarship: An Interdisciplinary Conversation and a Post-9/11 Example," *Annual Review of Law and Social Sciences* 10 (2014): 169–83.

40. Aradhana Sharma and Akhil Gupta, eds., *The Anthropology of the State: A Reader* (Malden, MA: Blackwell, 2006).

41. Akhil Gupta, "Blurred Boundaries: The Discourse of Corruption, the Culture of Politics, and the Imagined State," in *Anthropology of the State*, ed. Sharma and Gupta, 211–42, 212.

42. Wendy Brown, *Walled States, Waning Sovereignty* (Boston, MA: MIT Press, 2010).

43. Veena Das and Deborah Poole, eds., "State and Its Margins: Comparative Ethnographies," in *Anthropology in the Margins of the State*, ed. Das and Poole, 31–34 (Santa Fe, NM: School of American Research Press, 2004).

44. Ibid.

45. Ibid., 8.

46. Veena Das, "The Signature of the State: The Paradox of Illegibility," in *Anthropology in the Margins of the State*, ed. Das and Poole, 225–52, 225–26.

47. Timothy Mitchell, "Society, Economy, and the State Effect," in *Anthropology of the State*, ed. Sharma and Gupta, 169–86, 170.

48. Ibid., 174.

49. Timothy Mitchell, "The Limits of the State: Beyond Statist Approaches and Their Critics," *American Political Science Review* 85, no. 1 (1991): 77–96.

50. Ibid., 81.

51. Ibid., 91.

52. See also the discussion on a Weberian notion of state in Timothy Kaufman-Osborn, *From Noose to Needle: Capital Punishment and the Late Liberal State* (Ann Arbor: University of Michigan Press, 2002).

53. Aradhana Sharma and Akhil Gupta, "Introduction: Rethinking Theories of the State in an Age of Globalization," in *Anthropology of the State*, ed. Sharma and Gupta, 10.

54. Gupta, *Red Tape*, 47; emphasis added.

55. Nayanika Mathur, *Paper Tiger: Law, Bureaucracy, and the Developmental State in Himalayan India* (Cambridge: Cambridge University Press, 2015).

56. Ibid., 3.

57. See also Aradhana Sharma, *Logics of Empowerment: Development, Gender, and Governance in Neoliberal India* (Minneapolis: University of Minnesota Press, 2008).

58. Sudipta Kaviraj, "On the Enchantment of the State: Indian Thought on the Role of the State in Narrative of Modernity," in *The Trajectories of the Indian State*, 40–47 (New Delhi: Orient BlackSwan, 2010), 76. See also Manorajan Mohanty, "Indian State: The Emerging Trends," *Social Action* 40 (July–September 1990): 219–31, where he notes that the "state is coercive, responsive as well as a legitimative organisation" (220). While Mohanty focuses on the coercive and authoritarian aspects of the state in the post-Emergency period, especially pointing to extraordinary laws, the mechanisms and innovations of the state violence are not analyzed as such.

59. Kaviraj, "Enchantment of the State," 75.

60. Chatterjee, "The State."

61. In this essay, he notes the important scholars through the different phases, such as Rajni Kothari, Atul Kohli, Francine Frankel, James Manor, K. N. Raj, Pranab Bardhan, and Sudipta Kaviraj, among others.

62. The contradictory impulses of the 1990s and liberalization/globalization period in Kerala, and also more generally in India, are well explained in Ritty Lukose, *Liberalization's Children: Gender, Youth, and Consumer Citizenship in Globalizing India* (Durham: NC: Duke University Press, 2009).

63. Chatterjee, "The State," 8.

64. Kaviraj, "Enchantment of the State," 75. Or, in "standard academic discourse, the state comprises the army, the bureaucracy, and the government."

65. Chatterjee, "The State," 8.

66. In its most narrow conceptualization, the Marxist conception of the state views it as the instrument of the ruling class, its most expansive conceptualization coming from Antonio Gramsci (the state cannot be reduced to just the repressive state apparatus) and Louis Althusser (a combination of the Ideological State Apparatus and Repressive State Apparatus). But none of them really focused on the relationship between state, law, and violence and focused as much on the police as a distinct site of state power.

67. K. G. Kannabiran, *The Wages of Impunity: Power, Justice, and Human Rights* (New Delhi: Orient Longman, 2003); K. Balagopal, "Law Commission's View of Terrorism," *Economic and Political Weekly* 35 (2000): 2114–22; K. Balagopal, "In Defence of India: Supreme Court and Terrorism," *Economic and Political Weekly* 29 (1994): 2054–60; U. K. Singh, *State, Democracy, and Anti-Terror Laws*. See also Nandini Sundar and Sanjib Baruah who have also focused on the nature of the state and democracy in their work. Nandini Sundar, "Interning Insurgent Populations: The Buried Histories of Indian Democracy," *Economic and Political Weekly* 46, no. 6 (2011): 47–57; Sanjib Baruah, "Routine Emergencies: India's Armed Forces Special Powers Act," in *Civil War and Sovereignty in South Asia: Regional and Political Economy Perspectives*, ed. Aparna Sundar and Nandini Sundar, 190–211 (New Delhi: Sage, 2014). This integral relationship between law, state,

and violence has also been noted more generally by scholars such as Robert Cover and Austin Sarat. Robert Cover, "Violence and the Word," in *Narrative, Violence, and the Law: The Essays of Robert Cover*, ed. Austin Sarat, M. Ryan, and M. Minow, 203–38 (Ann Arbor: University of Michigan Press, 1992).

68. In that sense we see a much more robust work on the techniques of state violence in the U.S. context. Kaufman-Osborn, *From Noose to Needle*; Austin Sarat, *Gruesome Spectacles: Botched Executions and America's Death Penalty* (Stanford, CA: Stanford University Press, 2014) (writing in the context of the United States); D. Rejali, *Torture and Democracy* (Princeton, NJ: Princeton University Press, 2007).

69. Only human rights groups have systematically studied state violence in the routine context. And Santana Khanikar's important new work addresses many of the gaps in earlier work, such as a focus on everyday actions of the police in the routine and extraordinary contexts, although her focus is more on legitimacy than techniques per se. Santana Khanikar, *State, Violence, and Legitimacy in India* (Delhi: Oxford University Press, 2018). Nitya Ramakrishnan's book *In Custody* focuses on the routine experience of torture in custody. Nitya Ramakrishnan, *In Custody: Law, Impunity, and Prisoner Abuse in South Asia* (New Delhi: Sage, 2013).

70. Rejali, *Torture and Democracy*.

71. Jeffrey C. Isaac, "The American Politics of Policing and Incarceration," *Perspectives on Politics* 13, no. 3 (2015): 609–16.

72. Keally McBride, "Punitive Politics in the United States: The End of an Era?," *Perspectives on Politics* 13, no. 3 (2015): 749–53.

73. See Andrew Dilts, *Punishment and Inclusion: Race, Membership, and the Limits of American Liberalism* (New York: Fordham University Press, 2014); also more generally on critical carceral studies historically tracing this field, see Michelle Brown and Judah Schept, "New Abolition, Criminology, and a Critical Carceral Studies," *Punishment and Society* (September 7, 2016).

74. See, for example, Vesla M. Weaver, "Black Citizenship and Summary Punishment: A Brief History to the Present," *Theory and Event* 17, no. 3 (2014); Rosa Squillacote and Leonard Feldman, "Police Abuse and Democratic Accountability," in *Police Abuse in Contemporary Democracies*, ed. Bonner et al., 135–64.

75. Nicole Gonzalez Van Cleve, *Crook County: Racism and Injustice in America's Largest Criminal Court* (Stanford, CA: Stanford University Press, 2016).

76. Clearly these are overlapping categories, but the distinction is meant to indicate the specificity of a particular kind of literature. I should say that all of the examples I mention here are illustrative and not exhaustive.

77. Mohammad Aamir Khan with Nandita Haksar, *Framed as a Terrorist: My 14-Year Struggle to Prove My Innocence* (New Delhi: Speaking Tiger Publishing, 2016); Arun Fer-

reira, *Colours of the Cage: A Prison Memoir* (Delhi: Aleph Books, 2014); Abdul Wahid Shaikh, *Begunah Qaidi* (in Hindi) (New Delhi: Pharos Media and Publishing, 2017); Essar Batul et al., *Do You Remember Kunan Poshpora?* (New Delhi: Zubaan Books, 2016).

78. See "Death Penalty India Report," National Law University, Delhi, 2016, http://deathpenaltyindia.com/The-Death-Penalty-India-Report-2016.jsp; Lokaneeta and Jesani, "India."

79. Nivedita Menon's and Rajeswari Sunder Rajan's works on the relationship between feminist campaigns and the state on violence against women note the intractable relationship between the two. Nivedita Menon, *Recovering Subversion: Feminist Politics beyond the Law* (Urbana: University of Illinois Press, 2004); Rajeswari Sunder Rajan, *The Scandal of the State: Women, Law, and Citizenship in Postcolonial India* (Durham, NC: Duke University Press, 2003). Srimati Basu and Pratiksha Baxi more recently conducted ethnographic studies of the state's and the law's failure to represent the rights of women. Pratiksha Baxi, *Public Secrets of Law: Rape Trials in India* (Delhi: Oxford University Press, 2014); Srimati Basu, *The Trouble with Marriage: Feminists Confront Law and Violence in India* (Berkeley: University of California Press, 2015).

80. Women against Sexual Violence and State Repression, https://wssnet.org; Zubaan Books, http://zubaanbooks.com. Some of this work is inspired by the life and work of human rights activist Ram Narayan Kumar and the lifelong work of feminist/democratic rights activist Uma Chakravarti among others. Uma Chakravarti, "Archiving Disquiet: Feminist Praxis and the Nation-State, in *Human Rights and Peace: Ideas, Laws, Institutions, and Movement*, ed. Ujjwal Singh, 49–73 (New Delhi: Sage, 2009). In this reflective article, Chakravarti writes about the lack of focus by feminist groups on the repressive nature of the state, which is theorized more commonly by Pakistani and Sri Lankan feminists. This is particularly striking because, even though some early cases of sexual violence challenged by the women's movement since the 1970s were custodial rape cases (Mathura and Rameeza Bee), state violence hadn't necessarily become the primary arena of intervention. Thus, it was only due to critiques emerging from the Northeast and Kashmir about both the limits of nationalism and the rapes and sexual violence being a part of the political strategy enabled by extraordinary laws that feminists have more recently taken up state repression as an explicit point of focus. According to Chakravarti, it was only the protest of Manipuri women against the rape and murder of Manorama (who had been picked up as a suspected insurgent in 2004) and the fast of Irom Sharmila since 2000 against the Armed Forces Special Powers Act that "have all shaken the women's movement in India" or at least a section of it.

81. Navsharan Singh and Patrick Hoenig, eds., *Landscapes of Fear: Understanding Impunity in India* (New Delhi: Zubaan Books, 2014). Uma Chakravarti, ed., *Fault Lines of History* (Delhi: Zubaan Books, 2016). Batul et al.'s *Do You Remember Kunan Poshpora?* connects the narratives to sexual impunity. V. Geetha, *Undoing Impunity: Speech after Sexual Violence* (Delhi: Zubaan Books, 2016).

82. Navsharan Singh and Patrick Hoenig, eds., *Landscapes of Fear: Understanding Impunity in India* (New Delhi: Zubaan Books, 2014), 1.

83. An important volume on violence studies also notes the different aspects of the violence ranging from the individual to the structural based on caste, gender, labor, and sexuality. In this narrative, state and law play a role in the forms of violence embedded in society. Kalpana Kannabiran, ed., *Violence Studies* (Delhi: Oxford University Press, 2016).

84. Beatrice Jauregui, *Provisional Authority: Police, Order, and Security in India* (Chicago: University of Chicago Press, 2016); Rachel Wahl, *Just Violence: Torture and Human Rights in the Eyes of the Police* (Stanford, CA: Stanford University Press, 2017); Khanikar, *State, Violence, and Legitimacy*.

85. Charles Tilly, "War Making and State Making as Organized Crime," in *Bringing the State Back In*, ed. Peter Evans, Dietrich Rueschemeyer, and Theda Skocpol, 169–87 (Cambridge: Cambridge University Press, 1985), 171; emphasis added.

86. Weber, "Bureaucracy," 57.

87. Ibid., 58.

88. Ibid.

89. Agamben, *State of Exception*, 4; Agamben, *Homo Sacer*.

90. Gupta, *Red Tape*, 17.

91. M. Dubber and M. Valverde, "Policing the Rechtsstaat," in *Police and the Liberal State* (Stanford, CA: Stanford University Press, 2008), 5; Mark Neocleous, "Theoretical Foundations of the 'New Police Science,'" in *The New Police Science: The Police Power in Domestic and International Governance*, ed. Markus D. Dubber and Mariana Valverde, 17–41 (Stanford, CA: Stanford University Press, 2006).

Chapter 2

1. M. S. Gore, *Committee on Police Training*, Ministry of Home Affairs, Government of India, 1971, 26 (henceforth Gore Committee Report).

2. Interview with police official, Bangalore, 2014.

3. I am referring to the police as state actors and the forensic psychologists as semi-state actors partly because the latter are not directly part of the police and are sometimes formally independent.

4. Here, of course, I am using the term "violence" in a very specific sense—namely, in the context of investigations in custody. Police violence in India ranges from extrajudicial killings, to participation in riots, to torture in custody. This conception of violence is epistemologically different from a very broad conception of violence that includes the use of language, which may in turn represent or deny the experience of violence. On this point, see Cover, "Violence and the Word." Also see the discussion in Lokaneeta, introduction to *Transnational Torture*.

5. Max Weber, "The Economic System and the Normative Orders," in *Law in Economy and Society*, ed. Max Rheinstein (Cambridge, MA: Harvard University Press, 1966), 14.

6. M. S. Gore, Committee on Police Training, Ministry of Home Affairs, Government of India, 1971, 26 (henceforth Gore Committee Report).

7. Weber, "Bureaucracy," 49.

8. Seri, *Seguridad*, 133.

9. In previous work, I have suggested that law itself can accommodate excess violence. Lokaneeta, *Transnational Torture*.

10. Dubber and Valverde, "Policing the Rechtsstaat," 5.

11. Neocleous. "Theoretical Foundations," 21.

12. Markus Dubber and Mariana Valverde, "Perspective on the Power and Science of Police," in *New Police Science*, ed. Dubber and Valverde, 4–5.

13. Ibid.

14. Mariana Valverde, "Police, Sovereignty, and Law: Foucaultian Reflections," in Dubber and Valverde, *Police and the Liberal State*, 17–18.

15. Interview with police official, Bangalore, 2014.

16. Interview with forensic psychologist, Mumbai, 2013.

17. I thank Bhavani Raman for this important insight.

18. Mitchell, "Society, Economy, and the State Effect," 170.

19. In fact, the police official credits a British lord for giving Coorgis the right to carry weapons without requiring a license.

20. Interview with police official, Bangalore, 2014.

21. Ibid.

22. See chapter 5 for details of critiques by human rights activists.

23. Ferreira, *Colours of the Cage*, 96–97.

24. Interview with another police official, Bangalore, 2014. The use of biryani is significant because it also came up in the context of Ajmal Kasab (convicted and hanged in the Mumbai attacks case in 2008). Reports that he had demanded mutton biryani in jail made him a major target of criticism. Later, however, the public prosecutor in the case agreed that this report was just a rumor to quash any sympathy for the terrorist. "Kasab Never Asked for Biryani, We Fabricated It, Public Prosecutor Ujjwal Nikam Says," *Times of India*, March 20, 2015, http://timesofindia.indiatimes.com/india/Kasab-never-asked-for-biryani-we-fabricated-it-public-prosecutor-Ujjwal-Nikam-says/articleshow/46639254.cms

25. Interview with another police official, Bangalore, 2014.

26. Ibid.; emphasis added.

27. I thank Pratiksha Baxi and Bhavani Raman for this insight.

28. Austin Sarat, *When the State Kills: Capital Punishment and the American Condition* (Princeton, NJ: Princeton University Press, 2001); Rejali, *Torture and Democracy*.

29. Ibid.

30. See chapter 5 for detailed critiques by human rights activists.
31. Interviews with forensic psychologists, 2013, 2014, 2016.
32. Weber, "Bureaucracy," 57.
33. Laleh Khalili, *Time in the Shadows: Confinement in Counterinsurgencies* (Stanford, CA: Stanford University Press, 2012).
34. Gupta, *Red Tape*, 13. See also the discussion on contingency and discretion in Leonard C. Feldman, "The Banality of Emergency: On the Time and Space of Political Necessity," in *Sovereignty, Emergency, Legality*, ed. Austin Sarat, 136–64 (Cambridge: Cambridge University Press, 2006).
35. Seri, *Seguridad*, 110. See discussion on police discretion in creating complaints in Pooja Satyogi. "Law, police and domestic cruelty: Assembling written complaints from oral narratives." *Contributions to Indian Sociology*, February 25, 2019. https://doi.org/10.1177/0069966718812522
36. Michel Foucault, *Security, Territory, Population: Lectures at the College de France, 1977–78*, ed. Michel Senellart (London: Palgrave-Macmillan, 2007), 327.
37. Valverde, "Police, Sovereignty, and Law," 27.
38. Louis Althusser, "Ideology and Ideological State Apparatuses (Notes towards an Investigation)," reprinted in *Anthropology of the State*, ed. Sharma and Gupta, 86–111.
39. Markus Dirk Dubber, *The Police Power: Patriarchy and the Foundations of American Government* (New York: Columbia University Press, 2005).
40. Julia Eckert, "The Trimurti of the State: State Violence and the Promises of Order and Destruction," *Max Planck Institute for Social Anthropology Working Papers*, 2005, 15; emphasis added.
41. Jyoti Belur, *Permission to Shoot? Police Use of Deadly Force in Democracies* (New York: Springer, 2010), 188; emphasis added.
42. Rachel Wahl, "Justice, Context, and Violence: Law Enforcement Officers on Why They Torture," *Law and Society Review* 48, no. 4 (2014): 807–36.
43. Wahl, *Just Violence*.
44. Jauregui, *Provisional Authority*, 98
45. Feldman, "The Banality of Emergency," 157.
46. U. Baxi, *Crisis of the Indian Legal System*.
47. The Police Act of 1861. In article 246, the Indian Constitution "assigns the responsibility of policing" to the twenty-nine states. Each state can set its own rules for police recruitment and governance. In turn, a central police unit governs seven additional union territories, while the central, federal government can send other armed guards to the states. With no national or federal police, the upper ranks of the states' forces come from the central government. Once recruited through the Indian Police Service examinations, new members of the police are sent to the states. Commonwealth Human Rights Initiative—

Rough Roads to Equality: Women Police in South Asia (Delhi: Commonwealth Human Rights Initiative, 2015); Commonwealth Human Rights Initiative, *Police Organisation in India*.

48. Kannabiran, *Wages of Impunity*; Haragopal and Balagopal, "Civil Liberties Movement."

49. U. Baxi, *Crisis of the Indian Legal System*, 85.

50. K. S. Subramanian, *Political Violence and the Police in India* (New Delhi: Sage, 2007).

51. Interview with police official, Delhi, 2013.

52. Kalpana Kannabiran, "The Contexts of Criminology: A Brief Restatement," in *Challenging the Rule(s) of Law: Colonialism, Criminology, and Human Rights in India*, ed. Kalpana Kannabiran and Ranbir Singh, 461–62 (New Delhi: Sage 2008).

53. Nair, "Muslims Think We Are Communal, Corrupt"; "Death Penalty India Report," National Law University, Delhi, 2016.

54. The practical implication of police power representing the household is, of course, that the status of some individuals—for example, vagrants, immigrants, and dangerous classes—can be subject to police actions without necessarily having even the intent of committing a criminal act. Dubber, *The Police Power*.

55. As I discuss in chapter 4, lie detectors were used in the 1960s and 1970s, but the combination I term "truth machines" comprises lie detectors, brain scans, and narcoanalysis for policing.

56. Gore Committee Report.

57. Ibid., 9. This is particularly significant because policing is a state subject.

58. Ibid.

59. Ibid., 22

60. Ibid., 31.

61. The committee is remarkable in defining the police as representing the legal and constitutional values. The role of the police in promoting the welfare state and the people's expectations was put squarely on the syllabus of the National Police Academy. Gore Committee Report, 49. It may also be because Professor M. S. Gore, a famous Indian social scientist and former director of the Tata Institute of Social Sciences in Bombay, was its chairperson.

62. Gore Committee Report, 19.

63. Ibid., 121. Five-Year Plans were reflections of planning priorities of the nation.

64. Ibid., 28; emphasis added.

65. Interview with police official, Delhi, 2013.

66. Weber, "Bureaucracy," 59.

67. Srirupa Roy, *Beyond Belief: India and the Politics of Postcolonial Nationalism* (Durham, NC: Duke University Press, 2007).

68. Gore Committee Report, 63.

69. Ibid., 41; emphasis added.

70. House of Commons, *Report of the Commission for the Investigation of Alleged Cases of Torture in Madras* Britain, July 1855.

71. Gore Committee Report, 19.

72. National Police Commission, Fourth Report (henceforth NPC IV).

73. The Shah Commission of Inquiry, Interim Report I, March 11, 1978, 4. The Shah Commission was instituted after the emergency declared between 1975 and 1977 by Prime Minister Indira Gandhi under Article 352 of the Indian Constitution. The commission was charged with inquiring into the very declaration of the emergency as well as the excesses that had taken place during this time. The first interim report was released on March 11, 1978; the second on April 26, 1978; and the third on August 6, 1978. There is now an emerging literature on the Indian emergency that provides insights into the legal and political framework of Indian democracy that gave rise to the emergency. Gyan Prakash. *Emergency Chronicles: Indira Gandhi and Democracy's Turning Point* (Princeton, NJ: Princeton University Press, 2019).

74. I thank Vrinda Grover for pointing me to this distinction between the demand for freedom from political control, often initiated by the police themselves, and the demand for police accountability by human rights activists and lawyers.

75. On human rights initiatives, see http://www.humanrightsinitiative.org/index.php?option=com_content&view=article&catid=91%3Ashiva&id=746%3Apolice-reforms-indiathe-national-police-commission-npc&Itemid=98.

76. The Supreme Court in the 2006 *Prakash Singh* case acknowledged that the recommendations of the NPC had been ignored for twenty-five years, thus requiring the Court to intervene. *Prakash Singh & Ors. vs. Union of India & Ors* 2006 (8) S.C.C.1.

77. This part about the third degree and torture is related to the Criminal Procedure Code, which was introduced in 1861 after the Madras Commission report on torture and later modified in 1973.

78. NPC IV, 13.

79. Ibid.

80. Ibid.

81. Some of these suggestions have subsequently been reasserted by the courts and also included in the Criminal Procedure Code.

82. *Committee on Reforms of Criminal Justice System*, Government of India, Ministry of Home Affairs (henceforth Malimath Committee Report), vol. 1, March 2003, 6. The committee was led by Justice V. S. Malimath.

83. Ibid.

84. Ibid., 10.

85. Ibid., 269–70.

86. For a more stringent critique of the Malimath Committee, see U. K. Singh, *State, Democracy, and Anti-Terror Laws*. After 9/11 a worldwide effort to dilute safeguards against torture and detention may have played a role, but India had a longer history of antiterror and preventive detention that the Malimath recommendations clearly echoed. I thank the anonymous reviewer for suggesting this point. Kim Lane Scheppele, "Law in a Time of Emergency: States of Exception and the Temptations of 9/11," *University of Pennsylvania Journal of Constitutional Law* 6 (2004): 1001–83; Kim Lane Scheppele, "Other People's Patriot Acts: Europe's Response to September 11," *Loyola Law Review* 50 (2004): 89–148; Jayanth K. Krishnan, "India's 'Patriot Act': POTA and the Impact on Civil Liberties in the World's Largest Democracy," *Law and Inequality* 22, no. 2 (2004): 265–300.

87. Malimath Committee Report, 34.

88. *Kashmiri Devi v. Delhi Administration and Others*. This is an important case of custodial death in which the death was a result of torture. Malimath Committee Report, 33–34.

89. Malimath Committee Report, 87.

90. Ibid.

91. Ibid., 104. Several police officials also mentioned forensic science laboratories at the district level as a priority.

92. Ibid.

93. Ibid. Rachel Wahl mentions a high-ranking officer explicitly stating that "technology can be a substitute for the third degree if police are equipped properly. Today, to get a lie detector test we have to go to the lab. Why can't there be a lie detector in a police station?" Wahl, *Just Violence*, 80.

94. *Prakash Singh & Ors. vs. Union of India & Ors* 2006 (8) S.C.C. 1. The Court reiterated a recommendation of a public complaints authority at the local and state levels, where people could complain about the police in instances of custodial violence, arbitrary arrests and detentions, and police excesses. The state-level complaints authority would then look into serious cases, such as deaths, grievous hurt (in the absence of a specific law on torture), and rape in custody. In the Ribeiro Committee (1998 and 1999), a police complaints committee was suggested at the district level to deal with police excesses, custodial violence, detention, and other concerns.

95. Jinee Lokaneeta, "Defining an Absence: Torture 'Debate' in India," *Economic and Political Weekly* 49, nos. 26–27 (2014): 69–76.

96. Ramakrishnan, *In Custody*; Lokaneeta, *Transnational Torture*.

97. National Crimes Research Bureau reports compiled in Lokaneeta and Jesani, "India," 501–47.

98. National Crimes Research Bureau, 2015.

99. "India Is a Secular State with No State Religion, Citizens' Freedoms Are Well-Protected: AG Mukul Rohatgi Tells UNHRC," May 5, 2017, Live Law.in, https://www.livelaw.in/india-secular-state-no-state-religion-citizens-freedoms-well-protected-ag-mukul-rohatgi-tells-unhrc.

100. For example, a police official affiliated with the NHRC was very hesitant to meet my colleague and me, and when he finally did, he met with us only briefly and kept looking at the door.

101. Michael Taussig, *Defacement: Public Secrecy and the Labor of the Negative* (Stanford, CA: Stanford University Press, 1999), 5.

102. Ramakrishnan, *In Custody*, 3. See also Anupama Rao, "Torture, the Public Secret," *Economic and Political Weekly*, June 5, 2004.

103. See Wahl, *Just Violence*; Jauregui, *Provisional Authority*; and Khanikar, *State, Violence, and Legitimacy*.

104. See Section 57 of CrPC (1973).

105. Interview with police official, Ahmedabad, 2013.

106. NPC IV.

107. Interview with senior police official, Delhi, 2013.

108. Google alerts related to requests for lie detectors, brain scans, and narcoanalysis suggest that they are made quite often even if the requests are not necessarily followed up.

109. Interview with police official, Hyderabad, 2013.

110. Interview with police official, Mumbai, 2013.

111. U. Baxi, *Crisis of the Indian Legal System*, 135.

112. See the discussion in Lokaneeta, "Defining an Absence."

113. Interview with police official, Bangalore, 2014.

114. Ibid.

115. Interview with police official, Delhi, 2013.

116. See, for instance, "Woman Police Officer in U.P. Who Arrested BJP Leaders, Transferred," Hindu.com, July 2, 2017, https://www.thehindu.com/news/national/up-woman-police-officer-who-arrested-bjp-leaders-transferred/article19198171.ece.

117. With respect to confessions, the key provisions are Section 164 of the 1973 Code of Criminal Procedure, which describes the procedure for recording confessions by the magistrate, and Sections 24–27 of the 1872 Indian Evidence Act. Section 24 disallows any confession that appears to be based on "any inducement, threat or promise." Section 25 specifies that confessions recorded by the police are inadmissible as evidence, while Section 26 recognizes that confessions may be used as evidence in routine cases only if they have been recorded before a judicial or metropolitan magistrate. A loophole under Section 27, however, allows items that are "recovered" as a result of confessions to be admitted as evi-

dence, creating an incentive to torture. Most extraordinary laws on terrorism bypass these procedural safeguards altogether.

118. Interview with senior police official, Mumbai, 2013.
119. Interview with police official, Hyderabad, 2013.
120. Interview with police official, Bangalore, 2014.
121. Interview with police official, Hyderabad, 2013.
122. Interview with police official in Bangalore, 2014.
123. "Tamil Nadu Ranks First in Recovery of Stolen Goods: NCRB," *Times of India*, July 2, 2014.
124. Interview with police officials, Hyderabad, 2013.
125. Interview with police official, Delhi 2013.
126. This recommendation is consistent from the 1979–81 National Police Commission Report, to the 2000 Padmanabhaiah Committee on Police Reforms, to the 2003 Malimath Committee Report.
127. NPC IV, 17–18. This change also arises in the context of the Gore Committee Report in 1971; see 118–19.
128. Malimath Committee Report, 27.
129. See Ramakrishnan, *In Custody*.
130. A number of studies point to ways in which torture is allowed to continue despite certain checks by magistrates and others. See Ramakrishnan, *In Custody*.
131. P. Baxi, *Public Secrets of Law*, 324.
132. Ibid. See also Wahl on this point of remand. Her interviewee states that if remand is legal, torture is implicitly acceptable, because judges know that remand allows for torture. Wahl, *Just Violence*, 16–17.
133. Beatrice Jauregui, "Beatings, Beacons, and Big Men: Police Disempowerment and Delegitimation in India," *Law and Social Inquiry* 38, no. 3 (2013): 643–69. Khanikar, *State, Violence, and Legitimacy in India*.
134. Jauregui, *Provisional Authority*.
135. Jauregui, "Beatings, Beacons, and Big Men," 657.
136. Ibid., 665–66. See the discussion on Jauregui and the question of the police officer as sovereign in Nick Cheesman, *Opposing the Rule of Law: How Myanmar's Courts Make Law and Order* (Cambridge: Cambridge University Press, 2015), chapter 5. In *Provisional Authority* Jauregui mostly characterizes the lower echelons of the police as similar to subalterns and points to the lack of complete authority even for higher-level police officials who are controlled by political leaders.
137. Khanikar, *State, Violence, and Legitimacy in India*.
138. U. Baxi, *Crisis of the Indian Legal System*, 86.
139. Ibid.

140. See Lokaneeta and Jesani, "India," on this point.
141. This point is reiterated in interviews with a government doctor in Bangalore, 2014.
142. Interview with senior police official, Hyderabad, 2013.
143. Markus D. Dubber, "The New Police Science and the Police Power Model of the Criminal Process," in *New Police Science*, ed. Dubber and Valverde, 107–44.
144. Dubber, *Police Power*, 40.
145. Ibid., 185.

Chapter 3

1. Alan M. Dershowitz, "Is There a Torturous Road to Justice?," *Los Angeles Times*, November 8, 2001; Jonathan Alter, "Time to Think about Torture," *Newsweek*, November 5, 2001.
2. Kenneth Lasson, "Torture, Truth Serum, and Ticking Bombs: Toward a Pragmatic Perspective on Coercive Interrogation," *Loyola University Chicago Law Journal* 39 (2008): 329–60. Also see Linda Keller, "Is Truth Serum Torture?," *American University International Law Review* 20, no. 3 (2005): 521–612.
3. In response to a Freedom of Information Act request, a report was released stating that drugs were not used to facilitate interrogations. However, there was recognition that at times drugs used for treating detainees could have the impact of impairing their ability to give information and were used at times during the interrogations (although not for that purpose). *Investigation of Allegations of the Use of Mind-Altering Drugs to Facilitate Interrogations of Detainees*, U.S. Department of Defense Inspector General, September 2009.
4. Summary and Reflections of Chief of Medical Services on OMS Participation in the RDI Program, Released in November 2018, ACLU.org, https://www.aclu.org/report/summary-and-reflections-chief-medical-services-oms-participation-rdi-program (henceforth OMS Report). I am very grateful to the Torture Listserv, where discussions on torture take place routinely; while I am not a very active member, the generosity of the members is in their replies to this random question on truth serums.
5. *State of Wisconsin v. Steven Avery* (affidavit of Lawrence Farwell), http://www.stevenaverycase.org/wp-content/uploads/2017/06/100-Affidavit-of-Dr-Farwell.pdf.
6. The researchers I interviewed mentioned that the BFP helped them in solving an old murder case involving a missing woman in Dubai. "2005 Missing Woman Case: Suspects Taken to Gujarat for Brain Fingerprint," *Indian Express*, Ahmedabad, June 23, 2016. The clinical psychologist I interviewed sent me newspaper cuttings from November 2016 of a murder case in Bhilai, Madhya Pradesh, that has been solved with the help of the Brain Electrical Oscillation Signature test. "Blind Murder Mystery Solved after Ten Years," *Central Chronicle*, November 26, 2016.

7. "1984 Riots Case: Conclude Verma's Lie-Detector Test by Nov-end," *Press Trust of India*, November 1, 2017, http://www.india.com/news/agencies/1984-riots-caseconclude-vermas-lie-detector-test-by-nov-end-2589231. In the United States, despite the long history of the unreliability of the polygraph, its use continues in key cases—for example, in the *Adnan Syed* case. Justin George, "State: 'Serial' Murder Case Should Not Be Reopened," *Baltimore Sun*, January 14, 2015, https://www.baltimoresun.com/news/maryland/crime/bs-md-adnan-syed-serial-20150114-story.html. In the Senate hearings for Brett Kavanaugh in 2018, Christine Blasey Ford's polygraph test was prominently discussed. Christal Hayes, "Here's the Polygraph Test Christine Blasey Ford Took on Her Allegations against Kavanaugh," *USA Today*, https://www.usatoday.com/story/news/politics/2018/09/26/christine-blasey-fords-polygraph-test-brett-kavanaugh-sexual-assault-allegations/1434270002.

8. As Geoffrey Bunn puts it, "Spectacular science is a mode of scientific inquiry that is created and sustained by popular culture." Geoffrey C. Bunn, "Spectacular Science: The Lie Detector's Ambivalent Powers, *History of Psychology* 10, no. 2 (2007): 156.

9. Page duBois, *Torture and Truth* (New York: Routledge, 1991), 64.

10. Ibid.

11. Michel Foucault, *Discipline and Punish: The Birth of the Prison*, trans. Alan Sheridan (New York: Vintage Books, 1977).

12. Ibid., 41.

13. Lynn Hunt, *Inventing Human Rights: A History* (New York: W. W. Norton, 2007).

14. Lisa Silverman, *Tortured Subjects: Pain, Truth, and the Body in Early Modern France* (Chicago: University of Chicago Press, 2001); Karl Shoemaker, "The Problem of Pain in Punishment: Historical Perspectives," in *Pain, Law, and Death*, ed. Austin Sarat, 15–42 (Ann Arbor: University of Michigan Press, 2001).

15. John Langbein, *Torture and the Law of Proof: Europe and England in the Ancient Regime* (Chicago: University of Chicago Press, 1997); Edward Peters, *Torture* Expanded edition (Philadelphia: University of Pennsylvania Press, 1996). For an overview of the history of torture and the debates surrounding it, see Lisa Hajjar, *Torture: A Sociology of Violence and Human Rights* (New York: Routledge, 2012).

16. Rejali, *Torture and Democracy*.

17. See, for instance, the excerpts in chapter 5 of William F. Schultz, ed., *The Phenomenon of Torture: Readings and Commentary* (Philadelphia: University of Pennsylvania Press, 2007). Chapter 5 points to the social dynamics of torture. Drawing from Hannah Arendt's *Origins of Totalitarianism* to Kanan Makiya's *Republic of Fear*, the chapter points to the role that power structures and hierarchies play in the practices of torture and the support in society for the practice.

18. Schultz, *Phenomenon of Torture*.

19. Elaine Scarry, *The Body in Pain: The Making and Unmaking of the World* (New York: Oxford University Press, 1985).

20. See, for example, Anand A. Yang, "Disciplining 'Natives': Prisons and Prisoners in Early Nineteenth-Century India," *South Asia: Journal of South Asian Studies* 10, no. 2 (1987): 29–46.

21. Partha Chatterjee, "The Nation and Its Fragments," in *The Partha Chatterjee Omnibus* (New Delhi: Oxford University Press, 1999). Nasser Hussain, *The Jurisprudence of Emergency* (Ann Arbor: University of Michigan Press, 2003).

22. Elizabeth Kolsky, *Colonial Justice in British India: White Violence and the Rule of Law* (Cambridge: Cambridge University Press, 2010); see chapter 3, "'Indian Human Nature': Evidence, Experts, and the Elusive Pursuit of Truth," 108–41.

23. Elizabeth Kolsky, "'The Body Evidencing the Crime': Rape on Trial in Colonial India, 1860–1947," *Gender & History* 22, no. 1 (2010): 109–30, 113.

24. Kolsky, *Colonial Justice*, 141.

25. P. Baxi, *Public Secrets of Law*, 67.

26. Kolsky, "'Body Evidencing the Crime,'" 120.

27. P. Baxi, *Public Secrets of Law*, 62–63. See more generally on colonial torture, Anupama Rao, "Problems of Violence, States of Terror: Torture in Colonial India," in *Discipline and the Other Body: Correction, Corporeality, Colonialism*, ed. Steven Pierce and Anupama Rao (Durham, NC: Duke University Press, 2006); Anupama Rao and Steven Pierce, "Discipline and the Other Body: Humanitarianism, Violence, and the Colonial Exception," in *Discipline and the Other Body*, ed. Pierce and Rao; Anuj Bhuwania, "'Very Wicked Children': 'Indian Torture' and the Madras Commission Report of 1855," *Sur International Journal of Human Rights* (2009): 7–27; Radhika Singha, *A Despotism of Law: Crime and Justice in Early Colonial India* (Delhi: Oxford University Press, 1998). On torture, bureaucracy, and colonial police, also see Deana Heath, "Bureaucracy, Power, and Violence in Colonial India: The Role of Indian Subalterns," in *Empires and Bureaucracy in World History*, ed. Peter Crooks and Timothy H. Parsons, 364–90 (Cambridge: Cambridge University Press, 2016).

28. P. Baxi, *Public Secrets of Law*; and Kolsky, "'Body Evidencing the Crime.'"

29. Simon Cole, *Suspect Identities: A History of Fingerprinting and Criminal Identification* (Cambridge, MA: Harvard University Press, 2001); Ken Alder, *The Lie Detectors: The History of an American Obsession* (New York: Free Press, 2007); Geoffrey Bunn, *The Truth Machine: A Social History of the Lie Detector* (Baltimore: Johns Hopkins University Press, 2012).

30. Bunn, *Truth Machine*, 61.

31. Alder, *Lie Detectors*, 67.

32. Cole, *Suspect Identities*, 120. Cole writes about how the Chinese Exclusion Act (1882) had a provision under which Chinese who had been living in the United States could visit China and return to the United States with the help of return certifications that were being misused.

33. Melissa Littlefield, *The Lying Brain: Lie Detection in Science and Science Fiction* (Ann Arbor: University of Michigan Press, 2011), 19.

34. Darius Rejali traces the drug to the 1890s when German doctors first started experimenting with scopolamine on pregnant women. Rejali, *Torture and Democracy*, chapter 19. As the chapter indicates, it is not just the United States where the drugs were used or pharmacological torture occurs, but shared more wide appeal.

35. Robert E. House, "The Use of Scopolamine in Criminology," *American Journal of Police Science* 2 (1931): 328–36.

36. Ibid., 332.

37. House quoted in Alison Winter, "The Making of 'Truth Serum,'" *Bulletin of the History of Medicine* 79, no. 3 (2005): 520.

38. Ibid., 514.

39. Ibid.

40. Ibid.

41. "Scientists Astounded: Use New Serum on Criminals; Discovery of Texas Doctors Forces," *Los Angeles Times*, February 14, 1922; emphasis mine.

42. Ibid.

43. "Truth Serum Test Proves Its Power: Dr. House of Texas Tells Anesthetists It Makes Convicts Confess Their Deeds," *New York Times*, October 22, 1924; Edward H. Smith, "Chemistry Furnishes Clues to Detectives: The Laboratory Plays a Large Part in Modern Crime Detection," *New York Times*, December 19, 1926.

44. While the impulse behind the Wickersham report was to enforce Prohibition and curb organized crime, it also included an attempt to study police interrogation practices. Chafee, Pollak, and Stern, *The Third Degree*. See Lokaneeta, *Transnational Torture*, chapter 1; Samuel Walker, *The Police in America: An Introduction* (Boston: McGraw Hill College, 1999).

45. "Getting Confession by New Truth Serum," *Sun*, August 12, 1923.

46. Winter, "Making of 'Truth Serum,'" 525; Smith, "Chemistry Furnishes Clues." An article in 1923 on the use of science in criminal justice discussed truth serums in relation to lie detectors and suggests that these methods are merely meant to replace the third degree.

47. *Brown v. Mississippi*, 297 U.S. 278 (1936).

48. The ten problems of the criminal justice system to be solved that House listed were as follows: persons can acquit or convict themselves, there was no question of immunity since it was done without their consent, no perjury, force spies to speak, increase the rates

of conviction, stop false convictions, find gang members, free the innocents, and deal with criminality in society. "Getting Confession by New Truth Serum."

49. "Truth Serum Test Proves Its Power."
50. "Getting Confession by New Truth Serum."
51. Ibid.
52. As Winter notes, House conducted these tests on at least eighty-six cases of prisoners, and the new information led to the release of at least twenty-six of them. Winter, "Making of 'Truth Serum'"
53. "Crime Secrets Revealed by Truth Serum Tests: Convicts Under Drug's Influence," *Los Angeles Times*, June 27, 1923; "Getting Confession by New Truth Serum."
54. This happened, for example, in the *Wilkins* murder case in San Quentin. "Crime Secrets Revealed." See "Getting Confession by New Truth Serum" and "Reiterates Innocence Under Truth Serum," *Washington Post*, January 1, 1926.
55. "Reiterates Innocence." Reports of how a robbery suspect also confessed under scopolamine kept appearing in newspapers. See "Shreveport Cops Force Confession by Truth Shot," *Atlanta Constitution*, September 14, 1923.
56. National Research Council (NRC), *The Polygraph and Lie Detection* (Washington, DC: National Academies Press, 2003).
57. For example, a relevant question might ask whether a suspect was involved in a robbery, while an irrelevant question may just have to do with any random question unrelated to the crime. The NRC report states that this is commonly used in criminal investigations as well as in National Security Administration preemployment screenings. NRC, *Polygraph and Lie Detection*.
58. Paul Root Wolpe, Kenneth Foster, and Daniel D. Langleben, "Emerging Neurotechnologies for Lie-Detection: Promises and Perils," *Scholarly Commons*, Center for Neuroscience & Society, University of Pennsylvania, March 1, 2005, http://repository.upenn.edu/neuroethics_pubs/7
59. The precursors to the lie detector are the galvanometer, electric psychometer, and other such instruments. See Bunn, *Truth Machine*, chapter 5.
60. Ibid., 117.
61. Alder, *Lie Detectors*, 22–23.
62. Ibid., 67.
63. Ibid., 109.
64. Bunn, *Truth Machine*, 173.
65. Ibid., 115.
66. Ibid.
67. Jane Campbell Moriarty, "Visions of Deception: Neuroimaging and the Search for Evidential Truth," *Akron Law Review* (2009): 745.
68. Wolpe, Foster, and Langleben, "Emerging Neurotechnologies." See also Jordan

T. Cohen, "Merchants of Deception: The Deceptive Advertising of fMRI Lie Detection Technology," *Seton Hall Legislative Journal* 35, no. 1 (2010): 158–67.

69. Lawrence A. Farwell, Drew C. Richardson, and Graham M. Richardson, "Brain Fingerprinting Field Studies Comparing P300-MERMER and P300 Brainwave Responses in the Detection of Concealed Information," *Cognitive Neurodynamics* 7 (2013): 266. See critique in J. Peter Rosenfeld, "'Brain Fingerprinting': A Critical Analysis," *Scientific Review of Mental Health Practice* 4, no. 1 (2005): 20–37, http://groups.psych.northwestern.edu/rosenfeld/NewFiles/BFcritiquerevsub3-6.pdf

70. As an Indian researcher explained the method to me, there appears to be an additional step of pressing a button on the left or the right depending on whether a figure is familiar or not when the stimuli are shown.

71. "Brain Fingerprinting," marketing material for Brainwave Science, UC Global Security Consulting, https://www.uc-global.com/wp-content/uploads/2019/01/brain_eng.pdf

72. Farwell, Richardson, and Richardson, "Brain Fingerprinting Field Studies," 271.

73. S. L. Vaya, *Normative Data for Brain Electrical Activation Profiling*, research project (Gujarat: Directorate of Forensic Science, March 2006–March 2008), Executive Summary, 1.

74. Mukundan quoted in D. A. Puranik et al., "Brain Signature Profiling in India. Its Status as an Aid in Investigation and as Corroborative Evidence—as Seen from Judgments," paper presented at Proceedings of XX All India Forensic Science Conference, Jaipur, November 15–17, 2, https://www.axxonet.com/pdfs/beos_in_india.pdf

75. Interview with Clinical Psychologist, December 2016.

76. Champadi R. Mukundan, Nilesh B. Wagh, Gunjan Khera, Shraddha U. Khandwala, Tara L. Asawa, Namrata M. Khopkar, and Dharmistha D. Parekh, "Brain Electrical Oscillations Signature Profile of Experiential Knowledge," https://pdfs.semanticscholar.org/e25a/ea0629da7eb73b7ebcf7d07f6dbc6adb387b.pdf?_ga=2.81619351.1486569554.1563302300-723783808.1563302300

77. C. R. Mukundan, "Scientific Methods of Extraction of Information from Suspects: An Analysis of Current Trends," *Indian Journal of Clinical Psychology* 38, no. 2 (2011): 129–40. Mukundan also claims that, unlike manual calculation of polygraph results, in BEOS one can't change the data.

78. "Condemned Slayer of Dr. Eason to Take Truth Serum Test," *Pittsburgh Courier*, December 1, 1923.

79. "Truth Serum Called Clap Trap by High Court," *Washington Post*, December 21, 1926.

80. *State v. Hudson* (1926), quoted in Gilbert Geis, "In Scopolamine Veritas: The Early History of Drug-Induced Statements," *Journal of Criminal Law* 50 (1959–60): 355.

81. "Jury Gives Death to 'Axman,'" *Chicago Defender*, March 22, 1924.

82. "Hold 5 for Alabama Crimes: 5 Held for Ax Murders," *Chicago Defender*, January 19, 1924; "Jury Gives Death to 'Axman.'"

83. Roscoe Simmons, "'Old Guard' Precedents Thank Ransdell 'Wingo' Mr. Frank's Figures Is This Heflin?," *Chicago Defender*, March 29, 1924.

84. House, "Use of Scopolamine in Criminology," 334.

85. House, "Use of Scopolamine in Criminology."

86. J. F. Wilde, "Narco-Analysis in the Treatment of War Neuroses," *British Medical Journal*, July 4, 1942, 4.

87. Ibid., 6.

88. "Truth Serum Expert Conquers Subjects Determined to Lie," *Atlanta Constitution*, September 1, 1925.

89. "Truth Serum Is All Bunk, Trial Shows: Texas Doctor Flunks in Experiment," *Chicago Defender*, June 21, 1924.

90. Alison Winter, "The Making of 'Truth Serum,'" *Bulletin of the History of Medicine* 79, no. 3 (2005): 500–533.

91. Philip Kinsley, "Crime Fighters Unite in Battle to Uphold Law . . . ," *Chicago Daily Tribune*, November 21, 1930.

92. "Test Truth Drug to Obtain Facts from Criminals: 'Twilight Sleep' May Bare Underworld," *Chicago Daily Tribune*, April 5, 1931.

93. Kinsley, "Crime Fighters Unite."

94. "Police Seek Cause of Death of Boy: Chicago Officials Hope to Find If Child, 4, Drowned," *Sun*, April 30, 1935.

95. "'Truth Serum' Given Amnesia Victim Here in Effort to Restore Memory," *Hartford Courant*, January 3, 1935.

96. "'Truth Serum' Frees Two," *New York Times*, March 10, 1935; "Cleared by Truth Serum: Suspects in Oklahoma Slaying Freed by 'Spite' Admission," *New York Times*, November 29, 1935.

97. "Death Suspect Admits Truth Serum Confession," *Los Angeles Times*, November 4, 1935.

98. "'Truth Serum' Frees Robbery Suspect; Shows 'Almost Unbelievable' Tale True," *Hartford Courant*, June 18, 1935.

99. See Rejali, *Torture and Democracy*, 388.

100. Dorothy Dix, "The Truth Serum," *Boston Daily Globe*, April 12, 1922; "Dorothy Dix Talks to Girls: 'Would Women Really Want Men to Take the Truth Serum?'" *Sun*, August 30, 1924.

101. Dix, "Truth Serum."

102. Will Rogers, "A Few Shots of Scopolamin," *Washington Post*, July 15, 1923.

103. Ibid.

104. Ibid.

105. Ibid.

106. NRC, *Polygraph and Lie Detection*.

107. In the 2003 report, about thirteen federal agencies appeared to be using the polygraph for employee screening, NRC, 108.

108. Alder notes three major developments in the context of the polygraph after the *Frye* case. First, in 1988 the Congress passed the Polygraph Protection Act, which prohibited private employers from using polygraphs widely, thus leading to a decline in the use of polygraphs. In *Daubert v. Merrell* (1993), once standards of scientific evidence to be heard by juries were set up, polygraphers considered that as a moment to introduce evidence. Finally, the Supreme Court, in *Scheffer v. United States* (1998), intervened by a narrow ruling that allowed the polygraph evidence to be banned by a rule maker if some rationalization could be given. Alder, *Lie Detectors*, chapter 19.

109. Alder, *Lie Detectors*, 251.

110. NRC, *Polygraph and Lie Detection*, 20. Reports often refer to both reliability and validity of a method. Reliability refers to repeatability across times, places, subjects, and conditions, and validity refers to a process that measures what it is meant to measure.

111. Bennett L. Gershman, "Lie Detection: The Supreme Court's Polygraph Decision," *New York State Bar Journal* (September–October 1998): 34–37.

112. NRC, *Polygraph and Lie Detection*, 98.

113. Ibid., 18.

114. Littlefield, *Lying Brain*, 9.

115. Bunn, "Spectacular Science," 156.

116. Farwell's affidavit, http://www.larryfarwell.com/Harrington-Summary-dr-larry-farwell brain-fingerprinting-dr-lawrence-farwell.html.

117. Russell Brandom, "Is 'Brain Fingerprinting' a Breakthrough or a Sham?," *Verge*, February 2, 2015, https://www.theverge.com/2015/2/2/7951549/brain-fingerprinting-technology-unproven-courtroom-science-farwell-p300.

118. *Slaughter v. Oklahoma* 105 P.3d 832 (2005).

119. *Terry J. Harrington v. Iowa* No. 122/01–0653 (2003).

120. Ibid. An affidavit filed by Farwell mentions that the district court did admit the case as evidence, although he felt that it would not lead to a change in the decision, http://www.cognitiveliberty.org/neuro/harrington_amicus.html. He also mentions it in the *Avery* case affidavit, further claiming that such an admissibility of evidence is not seen in polygraphy cases. *State of Wisconsin v. Steven Avery* (Affidavit of Lawrence Farwell, PhD), http://www.stevenaverycase.org/wp-content/uploads/2017/06/100-Affidavit-of-Dr-Farwell.pdf.

121. *Terry J. Harrington v. Iowa.*
122. Puranik et al., "Brain Signature Profiling in India."
123. Ibid. The first case is most likely a reference to the *Aditi Sharma* case mentioned in chapter 5, and the second one is most likely referring to the infamous *Nithari* case. "Nithari Killings: A Timeline of the Case So Far," July 25, 2017, https://www.livemint.com.
124. Puranik et al., "Brain Signature Profiling in India," 7.
125. With S. Malini's use of the BFP, the success with brain fingerprinting wasn't separately focused as much. As I discuss in the next chapter, the three techniques were often used together.
126. Technically, these are research cases that are meant to test the validity of the technique, but it is being done in relation to solving cases.
127. Interview with researcher, Raksha Shakti University, Gandhinagar, Gujarat, December 2016.
128. Ibid.
129. Ibid.
130. S. L. Vaya, *National Resource Center for Forensic Psychology*, 2nd ed. (Gandhinagar, Gujarat: Directorate of Forensic Science, 2013), 1. Earlier Vaya was at the Forensic Science Lab, Gandhinagar, and mostly defended BEOS, but she started promoting research on BFP once she moved to Raksha Shakti University, from where she retired.
131. "Brain Fingerprinting," marketing material for Brainwave Science.
132. See Rosenfeld, "'Brain Fingerprinting;'" Ewout H. Meijer, Gershon Ben-Shakhar, Bruno Verschuere, and Emanuel Donchin, "A Comment on Farwell (2012): Brain Fingerprinting: A Comprehensive Tutorial Review of Detection of Concealed Information with Event-Related Brain Potentials," *Cognitive Neurodynamics* 7, no. 2 (2013): 155–58; *Investigative Techniques: Federal Agency Views on the Potential Application of "Brain Fingerprinting,"* United States General Accounting Office (GAO), Report to the Honorable Charles E. Grassley, U.S. Senate, 2001, Dr. Donchin, Appendix.
133. Rosenfeld, "'Brain Fingerprinting.'"
134. Ibid. See the discussion on the work by Elizabeth Loftus discussed here on the imperfect nature of memory. Moheb Costandi, "Evidence-Based Justice: Corrupted Memory," *Nature* 500 (2013): 268–70.
135. Rosenfeld, "'Brain Fingerprinting.'"
136. Wolpe, Foster, and Langleben, "Emerging Neurotechnologies."
137. U.S. experts have also widely discredited BEOS. See Moriarty, "Visions of Deception"; Anand Giridhardas, "India's Novel Use of Brain Scans in Courts Is Debated," *New York Times*, September 15, 2008. See a comprehensive discussion of the neurotechnologies in relation to the U.S. Constitutional provisions and the problems raised by these techniques. Amanda L. Pustilnik. "Neurotechnologies at the Intersection of Criminal Proce-

dure and Constitutional Law." eds John T. Parry and L. Song Richardson. *The Constitution and the Future of Criminal Justice in America*, 109–33. (Cambridge University Press, 2013).

138. Littlefield, *Lying Brain*. For Littlefield, the origin and philosophy behind the brain-imaging technologies arise from the fictions written in the 1930s–1950s. See chapter 6.

139. Ibid., 125.

140. Marketing materials for Brainwave Science; on file with author. Also available at http://www.kwicksoft.co.in/assets/files/Brain%20Fingerprinting.pdf.

141. Ibid., 2. As the CEO Krishna Ika said, "Brain Fingerprinting is a scientific and patented technology and does not have any competition worldwide. In other words, there is no equivalent product/forensic tool with similar technique and technology that gives such highly accurate and reliable results as given by Brain Fingerprinting." "Humane Interrogation through Scientific Technology for the Law Enforcement and Intelligence Industry: Interview with Krishna Ika," https://www.ceocfointerviews.com/interviews/BrainwaveScience14-CEOCFO-Article.pdf. One of the reasons why the current CEO may be emphasizing the role in Homeland Security Law Enforcement is because he was founder of a company called Government Works, which provided products to various government agencies.

142. Brandom, "Is 'Brain Fingerprinting' a Breakthrough?" The Brainwave Science CEO, Krishna Ika, in an interview, explains the brain fingerprinting method using exactly the same language of success without referring to Farwell. Their global program was launched in 2014, and apparently since then Florida police and Singapore have signed on and a former deputy director of Shin Bet has recently joined the board. Additionally, officials in Saudi Arabia, India, and Australia have offered testimonials about the utility of the techniques. https://brainwavescience.com.

143. Farwell (2012) mentions studies for validation of the P-300 MERMER. Farwell, "Brain Fingerprinting: A Comprehensive Tutorial Review of Detection of Concealed Information with Event-Related Brain Potentials," *Cognitive Neurodynamics* 6 (2012): 115–54. However, this article, too, was criticized, and a demand for retraction was made by a response. See Meijer et al., "A Comment on Farwell (2012)": "We argue in this comment that Farwell . . . is misleading and misrepresents the scientific status of brain fingerprinting technology" (155). "By selectively dismissing relevant data, presenting conference abstracts as published data, and most worrisome, deliberately duplicating participants and studies[,] he misrepresents the scientific status of brain fingerprinting. Thus, the review violates some of the cherished canons of science and if Dr. Farwell is, as he claims to be, a 'brain fingerprinting scientist' he should feel obligated to retract the article" (158).

144. Farwell, Richardson, and Richardson, "Brain Fingerprinting Field Studies," 292.

145. Even as the techniques were being used in these cases and promoted more widely, the U.S. General Accounting Office submitted a report on fingerprinting in 2001 to Senator Charles Grassley's office. The report very clearly stated that the relevant

federal agencies, such as the CIA, Department of Defense, Secret Service, and FBI, did not think this technique was useful because of its limited application. *Investigative Techniques*.

146. *State of Wisconsin v. Steven Avery* (Affidavit of Lawrence Farwell), http://www.stevenaverycase.org/wp-content/uploads/2017/06/100-Affidavit-of-Dr-Farwell.pdf. Here Farwell also explains that the test begins only after the investigative part is over and that further information is needed.

147. "Avery's Attorney Wants Brain Fingerprint Test Included in New Evidence," Ben Krumholz, FOX 11 News, June 7, 2017, http://fox11online.com/news/local/lakeshore/averys-attorney-wants-brain-fingerprint-test-included-in-new-evidence

See also http://www.larryfarwell.com/steven-avery-making-a-murderer-dr-larry-farwell-brain-fingerprinting-dr-lawrence-farwell.html. While critics of the techniques do see Brainwave Science as a company associated with Farwell, Farwell himself claimed on his website that he has nothing to do with Brainwave Science, which may be a more recent development since 2012. See Brandom, "Is 'Brain Fingerprinting' a Breakthrough?"; Rosenfeld, "'Brain Fingerprinting'"; and Wolpe, Foster, and Langleben, "Emerging Neurotechnologies," which connects both. Furthermore, even a 2012 article by Farwell (see n. 144) has a number of links to articles on the Brainwave Science website, none of which are active now, and the Farwell website address mentioned in the article is Brainwave Science. See http://www.larryfarwell.com

148. Wolpe, Foster, and Langleben, "Emerging Neurotechnologies."

149. Ibid.; http://www.larryfarwell.com

150. Alder, *Lie Detectors*, 251.

151. In season 2, episode 2, of the Netflix show *Making a Murderer*, Kathleen Zellner, the lawyer for Steven Avery, says, "I told Steven that the CIA, FBI, and navy were using a very sophisticated test to detect if someone was telling the truth or not about being innocent and would he do the test. Regardless of whether it would come to court or not, I convinced Steven Avery that it was 100 percent reliable, and then if he flunked it, we would have a big problem. He very enthusiastically agreed to subject himself to this testing. He was thrilled that something like that existed." Two days and thirteen hours of testing took place, and Dr. Farwell found that there was no response to the particular details of the crime. Dr. Farwell said to Avery, "You are innocent of the crime. . . . Anyone who understands the science will know it as well."

152. There are also continued attempts to validate the claims of BEOS. For instance, in an article coauthored by forensic scientists in the *Indian Police Journal*, the claim is that individuals who participated in an act could be differentiated from those who witnessed it. Yadav et al., "Differentiating between the Profiles of Participants vs Witness of an Event Using BEOS Test," *Indian Police Journal* (July–September 2012): 115–29. All of them are connected to the Forensic Science Labs or Forensic Science University.

153. The Axxonet website mentioned this. http://www.axxonet.com/forensics/11-forensics/20-nss-in-courts

154. As noted earlier, the 2003 NRC report was about using polygraphs for security purposes. On the Brainwave Science website, the emphasis is its use for national security, especially terrorism-related investigations. The site notes, "It can determine all levels of individuals involved in a terrorist organization from the foot soldier to the communicators and planners to the mastermind." These claims persist even though previous research suggested such a result required links to specific information, which is seldom available in these tests. http://brainwavescience.com/faq

155. Winter, "Making of 'Truth Serum,'" 533–34.

156. "Project MKUltra, the CIA's Program of Research in Behavioral Modification, Joint Hearing before the Select Committee on Intelligence and the Subcommittee on Health and Scientific Research of the Committee on Human Resources United States Senate," August 8, 1977; "Human Drug Testing by the CIA, Hearings before the Subcommittee on Health and Scientific Research of the Committee on Human Resources United States Senate, September 20 and 21, 1977." For a more detailed discussion on the different experiments and research, see Rejali, *Torture and Democracy*, 388–90.

157. Rejali, *Torture and Democracy*; "Project Mkultra."

158. "Project Mkultra." The Office of Medical Services (OMS) report released in 2018 regarding the post-9/11 discussions on the use of drugs mentions that the original source of this article is George Bimmerle, "'Truth' Drugs in Interrogation," *Studies in Intelligence* 5, no. 2 (Spring 1961): Al–A19. OMS Report.

159. "Project Mkultra," 27.

160. When injected, scopolamine, or Sodium Pentothal, sodium amytal, and Seconal led to four stages: (1) sedative stage; (2) unconsciousness, with exaggerated reflexes (hyperactive stage); (3) unconsciousness, without reflex even to painful stimuli; and, finally, (4) death. "Project Mkultra," 27, 30.

161. Ibid., 31.

162. Ibid., 32.

163. Ibid., 35.

164. Ibid.

165. See Alder, *Lie Detectors*, 216–17. Also see Alfred McCoy on why the methods in the war on terror were used by the CIA during the Cold War. Alfred McCoy, *A Question of Torture: CIA Interrogation, from the Cold War to the War on Terror* (New York: Metropolitan Books, 2006).

166. "Project MKUltra," 28.

167. The OMS report, for instance, mentions that despite the congressional hearings

in 1977, it remained a part of the experiments and was also mentioned in the KUBARK manual (1963 CIA Manual for Torture and Counterintelligence) as a possibility, even if as a placebo. OMS Report.

168. Ibid.

169. See discussions in McCoy, *Question of Torture*.

170. See See Introduction for an overview of these debates in Lokaneeta, *Transnational Torture*.. John T. Parry, *Understanding Torture: Law, Violence, and Political Identity* (Ann Arbor: University of Michigan Press, 2010). See Jared Del Rosso, "The Toxicity of Torture: The Cultural Structure of US Political Discourse of Waterboarding," *Social Forces* 93, no. 1 (2014): 383–404, on the importance of discourses while opposing or advocating torture in congressional debates.

171. On these particular aspects, see Lokaneeta, *Transnational Torture*, chapters 2 and 3.

172. Alter, "Time to Think about Torture."

173. Johanna McGeary, "Confessions of a Terrorist: Author Gerald Posner Claims an al-Qaeda Leader Made Explosive Allegations While Under Interrogation," *Time*, August 31, 2003.

174. Rebecca Leung, "Truth Serum: A Possible Weapon but Will It Work in the War on Terror?," cbs.com, April 23, 2003. Quoted in this article was Jed Babbin, who was deputy undersecretary of defense during the first Bush administration. In the OMS report released in 2018, there is a strong denial of this claim of the truth serum being used on Abu Zubaydah, though it had been considered. In a separate footnote, there is a mention that Versed—the drug that was being actively considered as a truth serum—was used on Abu Zubaydah along with morphine in order to ease his transfer, although not for interrogation purposes, thereby muddying the waters about its actual use. See OMS Report, 9n17.

175. The rationale for the drug mentioned –Versed- was that it appeared to be safer and more easily reversible in terms of its effects. OMS Report.

176. Articles such as the one mentioned here and in the 2018 OMS report suggest that more investigations and revelations remain to be seen. Jeff Kaye, "CIA Investigation Minimizes Use of Drugs on Rendition and Black Site Detainees," May 11, 2015, https://shadowproof.com/2015/05/11/cia-investigation-minimizes-use-of-drugs-on-black-site-detainees

177. *Townsend v. Sain, Sheriff et al.* 372 U.S. 293(1963).

178. Ibid.

179. Ibid., 307.

180. Ibid., 307–8.

181. Ibid., 309.

182. Lasson, "Torture, Truth Serum, and Ticking Bombs," 337.

183. See Keller, "Is Truth Serum Torture?" Within case law, *Chavez v. Martinez* (2003) is now often cited to support this understanding. The case involved the police questioning of Martinez without Miranda warnings while he was writhing in pain after being shot multiple times by the police during a narcotics-related shooting. In a civil case, the police officer claimed that it was not a violation of the self-incrimination clause, since a criminal case was not filed against Martinez in which the evidence was introduced. A plurality opinion of the Court agreed with this understanding. See Parry, *Understanding Torture*.

184. In *Schmerber v. California* (1966) the Supreme Court allowed the use of nonconsensual drawing of blood for alcohol testing, and in *Breithaupt v. Abram* (1957) the Court allowed drawing blood from an unconscious driver in a hospital, arguing that these cases did not fulfill the "shocking the conscience" test. Lasson, "Torture, Truth Serum, and Ticking Bombs."

185. Dershowitz, "Is There a Torturous Road to Justice?"

186. Ibid.

187. Even though one of the predicate acts for mental pain or suffering clarified by the United States in its ratification of the UN Convention specifies "the administration or application, or threatened administration or application, of mind altering substances or other procedures calculated to disrupt profoundly the senses or the personality," Lasson does not consider it mental torture, because it may or may not lead to prolonged mental harm. See Lasson, "Torture, Truth Serum, and Ticking Bombs." In contrast to this understanding of the UN Convention, Linda Keller argues in "Is Truth Serum Torture?" that "the administration or threatened administration of truth serum should be considered torture" (4) as it creates "a sense of personal invasion and helplessness so vast that it results in prolonged mental harm such as PTSD" (49), but she is unsure whether it fulfills the specific intent aspects of the provisions and whether the threat is adequate to fulfill the requirement.

188. OMS Report, 25.

189. Here I draw from Nasser Hussain's use of the term "hyperlegality" for understanding Guantánamo Bay, Cuba in relation to the torture debate. Nasser Hussain, "Beyond Norm and Exception: Guantanamo," *Critical Inquiry* (Summer 2007): 734–53; Jinee Lokaneeta, "Torture Debates in the Post-9/11 United States: Law, Violence, and Governmentality," *Theory and Event* 13, no. 1 (2010).

190. OMS Report, 25.

191. *Meet the Parents* (2000) and *Meet the Fockers* (2004).

192. Drugs were used in the post-9/11 context to induce "learned helplessness" using medical professionals. "Learned helplessness" in this context was the theory that detainees might become passive and depressed in response to adverse or uncontrollable events and

would thus cooperate and provide information. Senate Select Committee on Intelligence, "Committee Study of the Central Intelligence Agency's Detention and Interrogation Program," Executive Summary, 2014, 32n32. Although an inspector general's report ruled out the idea that drugs were used for interrogation, they were used in different ways to control the detainees, including learned helplessness. *Investigation of Allegations of the Use of Mind Altering Drugs to Facilitate Interrogations of Detainees*, Department of Defense Inspector General, September 2009. https://truthout.org/articles/new-revelations-suggest-dod-cover-up-over-detainee-drugging-charges/

193. Wigmore quoted in Geis, "In Scopolamine Veritas," 357.

Chapter 4

1. Here my usage of the term "forensic architecture" is different from the powerful work by Eyal Weisman, *Forensic Architecture: Violence at the Threshold of Detectability* (New York: Zone Books, 2017), since here it is primarily a state forensic architecture that represents an effort on the part of the state to use contingent efforts in a centralized manner to innovate its forms of violence.

2. My use of the term cyborg is simply a combination of human and machine. As Donna Haraway has argued in a very different context, "A cyborg is a cybernetic organism, a hybrid of machine and organism, a creature of social reality as well as a creature of fiction." Donna Haraway, "A Manifesto for Cyborgs: Science, Technology, and Socialist Feminism in the 1980s," *Socialist Review* 80 (1985), https://sites.evergreen.edu/politicalshakespeares/wp-content/uploads/sites/226/2015/12/Haraway-Cyborg-Manifesto-2.pdf

3. While there are many other figures in this arena, including Dr. Amita Shukla and Dr. Deepti Puranik, I choose to focus on these three as prominent figures to illustrate their role.

4. "Meet the Woman Who Bonds with Hardened Criminals," *DNA*, February 3, 2012.

5. Interview with forensic psychologist, Gandhinagar, November 2013.

6. Timothy Mitchell, *Rule of Experts: Egypt, Techno-Politics, Modernity* (Berkeley: University of California Press, 2002).

7. Ibid., 15–16.

8. Sameena Mulla, *The Violence of Care: Rape Victims, Forensic Nurses, and Sexual Assault Intervention* (New York: New York University Press, 2014).

9. Ibid. 217. I do not suggest a complete synonymity between the forensic nurses and forensic psychologists, especially since the subjects of interaction are often different. The women interacting with forensic nurses are primarily victims, not suspects, although it is important to recall that rape victims have a history of being subjected to the lie detector.

Similarly, all suspects are innocent until proven guilty and could then be victims of the techniques being used in custody. Another major distinction is that forensic labs in India are often under the control of the state government or Home Ministry, thereby making them state or semi-state actors in a very direct sense, which doesn't appear to be the case for the forensic nurses. Forensic nurses do end up working in particular hospitals and are a part of the designated state system of dealing with rape victims. But at least in Mulla's narrative, they do not appear to be influenced directly by the police as much as being institutionally determined by the needs of the legal system.

10. Mulla notes that nurses are 93 percent female and local police departments are 88 percent male. Mulla, *Violence of Care*, 14–15.

11. Mitchell, *Rule of Experts*, 20.

12. There is a long history of forensic science in India going back at least to 1849, when the first "chemical examiners lab" was set up in Madras. Later the name changed to "forensic science laboratories." In one of the few books that trace forensic science techniques in India, Chandak Sengoopta writes about the history of fingerprinting in the British colonial period. Chandak Sengoopta, *Imprint of the Raj: How Fingerprinting Was Born in Colonial India* (London: Macmillan, 2003). More recently, Mitra Sharafi's work describes the history of forensic science in India focusing on particular techniques. Mitra Sharafi, "The Imperial Serologist and Punitive Self-Harm: Bloodstains and Legal Pluralism in British India," in *Global Forensic Cultures: Making Fact and Justice in the Modern Era*, ed. Ian Burney and Christopher Hamlin, 60–85 (Baltimore: Johns Hopkins University Press, 2019).

13. Interview with forensic scientist, Hyderabad, November 2013. In another account, senior forensic scientist claimed that the first machine was only for teaching purposes and may have been in Chennai.

14. Interview with forensic scientist, Hyderabad, November 2013.

15. Ibid.

16. A loophole under Section 27 allows items that are "recovered" as a result of confessions to be admitted as evidence, creating an incentive to torture, while most extraordinary laws on terrorism bypass procedural safeguards altogether. See chapter 2 for details.

17. Ministry of Home Affairs, Government of India, *Annual Report*, 2013–2014.

18. The skepticism that had emerged vis-à-vis the lie detector in other parts of the world has seldom had much impact on the Indian discourses. See, for instance, Srujan Prakash Das, "Can Polygraph Be Deceived?," *CBI Bulletin* (August 1999): 31–32. Das, who worked at the State Forensic Science Laboratory in Bhubaneswar, Orissa, said, "It is next to impossible that one can deceive the polygraph" (32). As indicated in chapter 3, the polygraph continues to be used despite skepticism about its value.

19. A. K. Ganguly and S. K. Lahiri, "Application of the Polygraph in the Investigation of Crime in India," *Polygraph* 5, no. 3 (1976): 245.

20. Ibid., 248.
21. Gujarat Forensic Sciences University website, https://www.gfsu.edu.in
22. Another state that started the lie detector division at the Forensic Science Laboratory was Haryana in Madhuban, Karnal. Dr. Bibha Rani and Dr. V. K. Gupta, "Polygraph: An Alternative to Third Degree Method," *Social Defense* 1 (July 1988): 27–31. In Hyderabad the lie detector started being used in 1997 and the records existed from 1999.
23. Vaya, *National Resource Center*, 46.
24. On this point, see P. Baxi, *Public Secrets of Law*, 107n10.
25. Rani and Gupta, "Polygraph: An Alternative," 31.
26. Rani and Gupta, "Polygraph: An Alternative. See also Dr. Bibha Rani Ray and Dr. S. R. Singh, "Polygraph Examination: Indian Experience," *CBI Bulletin* (June–December 2006): 29–39. Ray was principal scientific officer in the Lie Detection Division, CFSL (CBI), in New Delhi, and S. R. Singh was the director of the CFSL (CBI), in New Delhi. In addition to replacing third degree, the overall emphasis of the polygraph was to ascertain the veracity of statements of the suspects, complainants, and the witnesses, in order to distinguish between those who were guilty from those who were innocent. Confessions and recovery of evidence are also mentioned in that context.
27. The assumption is that the "fear of detection is psychologically a stressful condition (for a person who deliberately attempts to conceal a fact) and consequently it produced changes in the various psychological parameters." Rani and Gupta, "Polygraph: An Alternative," 28.
28. Dr. (Mrs.) S. L. Vaya and J. M. Vyas, "The Polygraph (Lie Detector) Technique," *CBI Bulletin* (December 1998): 24.
29. Shyamal Kumar Sinha Ray, "Introduction of Polygraph in Criminal Investigation in India: A New but Cautious Stride," *Criminal Law Journal* (1988): 117–19. Indeed Ray writes about an explicit effort to amend the criminal procedure code to allow polygraph by medical practitioners as opposed to the police.
30. Ray and Singh, "Polygraph Examination."
31. Ibid., 29–39. In India police cannot record confessions, which can only be recorded in front of a magistrate.
32. Ibid., 29.
33. Interview with forensic psychologist, Hyderabad, 2013.
34. While in general polygraphs don't seem to have an adverse effect on a person's health, the psychologist did claim that they would use the polygraph only if the person wasn't insane, pregnant, or asthmatic. Ibid.
35. The complainant was Inder P. Choudhurie, who had been picked up in relation to a murder while he had gone to Shimla for another case. He was in police custody for several days and subjected to a test at that time.

36. "Guidelines on Administration of Lie Detector Test," National Human Rights Commission, 1999, http://nhrc.nic.in/disparchive.asp?fno=167. The nature of the drug is unclear, but if one considers the timing of this complaint, it could be either "official narcoanalysis" or "unofficial narcoanalysis," which police officers have mentioned in other contexts. Official narcoanalysis is the use of a particular drug (Sodium Pentothal) that was started by the forensic labs, as I discuss below, in the late 1990s and early 2000s, and unofficial narcoanalysis was the use of other methods that police used to lower inhibitions with the aid of drugs or alcohol while questioning. In chapter 2 I discuss what a police officer calls "unofficial narco," although it hasn't been verified by any other police officers. However, more recently, terror suspects in the Mumbai blast case in 2006 have spoken of the same (see chapter 6), and narco videos of Ajmal Kasab—arrested for his part in the Mumbai attacks in 2008—appear to have been done outside of a hospital or forensic lab. A prominent forensic psychologist in Gandhinagar also confirms the practice as a reason why they started using official narco.

37. "Guidelines on Administration of Lie Detector Test."

38. Ibid.

39. Ibid.

40. Vaya, *National Resource Center*. When you compare that with Hyderabad, where there was only polygraph, the numbers are much less. The figures available were from 1999 to 2013, and between 2003 and 2010 there was a total of 1,563 cases, with the maximum ones—between 100 and 250—interestingly, when the techniques seem most in demand elsewhere as well. There are also private labs where polygraphs are conducted, such as Truth Labs in Hyderabad and Delhi. Arun Ram, "Couples Take Lie-Detector Test to Save Their Marriage," *Times of India*, July 8, 2010, https://timesofindia.indiatimes.com/city/chennai/Couples-take-lie-detector-test-to-save-their-marriage/articleshow/6141239.cms. I Iclilt Labs, a private lab in Mumbai, which I visited, also uses BEOS and polygraphs.

41. Ministry of Home Affairs, Government of India, *Annual Report*, 2013–2014, 197.

42. For instance, courts often didn't know what to do with the information, because under Section 45 of the Indian Evidence Act, regarding the opinion of experts, there wasn't much clarity about what could be used and what the status of the experts was. Supposedly, the courts or the police would use the information but the police removed the actual one-hundred-page report. Interview with prominent forensic psychologist, Gandhinagar, November 2013.

43. According to the Directorate of Forensic Science website, there are thirty-two state forensic science labs. Six central forensic science labs operate directly under the DFS—in Chandigarh, Bhopal, Chennai, Hyderabad, Pune, and Guwahati—none of which appear to have a forensic psychology division, although one is mentioned on the Pune website.

The Delhi CFSL is under the CBI directly and has a forensic psychology division where voice stress analysis and brain testing are mentioned. Central Forensic Science Laboratory, http://www.cbi.gov.in/cfsl/cfsldivision.htm#liehttp://dfs.nic.in/aboutCfsl.html

44. The Ministry of Home Affairs Annual Report in 2004–2005 mentions that the Gujarat FSL would be adding narcoanalysis and brain mapping as a part of their FSL. Ministry of Home Affairs, Government of India, https://mha.gov.in/sites/default/files/ar0405-Eng.pdf. Even in its previous report of 2003–2004, there is a mention of a "state-of-the-art" forensic lab: "The state government of Gujarat has been able to develop the State Forensic Science Laboratories as one of the best equipped laboratories in the country that have been able to take important cases not only from the State but also from outside the State. They have state-of-the-art lie detection facilities, brain finger printing and narco analysis, DNA finger printing, speaker identification[,] etc.," http://mha.nic.in/sites/upload_files/mha/files/pdf/ar0304-Eng.pdf, 70. In subsequent reports (2005–2007), training, research and development, and reporting of evidence manuals are mentioned, especially for brain fingerprinting.

45. B. M. Mohan, "Is Narcoanalysis a Pseudo-Science?," *Hindu* (May 8, 2007). http://www.thehindu.com/2007/05/08/stories/2007050803500900.htm.

46. S. Malini and B. M. Mohan were associated with the Forensic Science Laboratory in Bangalore. Bannur Muthai Mohan, "Misconceptions about Narcoanalysis," *Indian Journal of Medical Ethics* 4, no. 1 (2007): 8.

47. Parth Shastri, "Decoding the Mind of a Killer," *Times of India*, January 11, 2011.

48. "New Bill to Admit Scientific Proof in Courts," *Times of India*, November 9, 2006.

49. Interview with senior police official, Mumbai, December 2013.

50. "CBI Plans to Set Up Narcoanalysis Centre in Delhi," *Times of India*, August 7, 2010.

51. Doctors, both anesthetists and psychiatrists, played an important role in the use of narcoanalysis. When asked whether psychiatrists felt a particularly difficult dilemma in their participation in the context of forensic science, a psychiatrist (who was involved for more than a decade in Gandhinagar) explained that they had been used to interview/question the patient using a "Pentothal interview or dizeapam interview.... So, as a psychiatrist, we're used to do[ing] this. We had experience. The only part is, it is used in a forensic aspect.... So it is nothing but a more deep interview with some psychological meaning and background to correlate the events." Interview with psychiatrist, December 2016.

52. Interview with doctor at government hospital, Bangalore, January 2014.

53. Divyani Rattanpal, "The Curious Case of Narco Tests in Aarushi-Hemraj Murder Mystery," *Quint*, December 10, 2017, https://www.thequint.com/news/india/the-curious-case-of-narco-tests-in-aarushi-hemraj-murder-mystery; Sheela Raval, "Fake

Stamp Paper Scam: Telgi's Narco Test Faces Legality Issues," *India Today*, February 23, 2004, https://www.indiatoday.in/magazine/states/story/20040223-narco-analysis-test-on-stamp-scam-accused-abdul-karim-telgi-790573-2004-02-23; "Mumbai Blasts 2 Accused Undergo Narco Test," Rediff.com, September 6, 2007, https://www.rediff.com/news/2006/sep/07blasts.htm; Anupam Dasgupta, "Narco Tests on Alleged Naxal Turns Out to Be Flop," May 28, 2007, DNA India, https://www.dnaindia.com/mumbai/report-narco-tests-on-alleged-naxal-turns-out-to-be-flop-1099527

54. Vaya, *National Resource Center*.

55. Ibid., 47. The training was for techniques to be used for criminal cases but also for noncriminal cases, civil cases, and rehabilitation of the victims of crime and the accused. Gradually, however, due to pressure resulting from criminal justice caseloads, the techniques became mostly restricted to scientific methods of interrogation in criminal cases.

56. Interview with forensic psychologist, Gandhinagar, November 2013.

57. Interview with clinical psychologist, Gandhinagar, December 2016.

58. The clinical psychologist I interviewed used the term "boys from IBM." Ibid.

59. Ibid.

60. Interview with clinical psychologist, Gandhinagar, November 2013.

61. Interview with clinical psychologist, Gandhinagar, December 2016.

62. Research associate, forensic science university, Gandhinagar, December 2016.

63. The committee was composed of five members, with then director/vice chancellor of NIMHANS, D. Nagaraja. Two other members were from NIMHANS, and a professor from the University of Allahabad and the Indian Institute of Science Bangalore. It was constituted by M. S. Rao, then director and chief forensic scientist for the Ministry of Home Affairs. "A Report on Brain Electro Physiology Based Technologies for Forensic Interrogation in India," Peer Review Committee headed by Prof. D. Nagaraja, Director, National Institute of Mental Health and Neuroscience (NIMHANS, Bangalore), 2007. A copy of the report was available in *Parliamentary Proceedings*, Appendix XVI, on file with author.

64. Nagaraja Committee, *Parliamentary Proceedings*, Appendix XVI, 462, letter from M. S. Rao, May 26, 2007.

65. While the Nagaraja Committee mentions the relationship between C. R. Mukundan and Axxonet more explicitly, the current website of Axxonet makes no mention of this connection. Perhaps doing so would create a conflict of interest, as Mukundan is associated with the DFS and Gujarat as the director of the Institute of Behavorial Science, GFSU.

66. Nagaraja Committee, *Parliamentary Proceedings*, 460.

67. Memo by Directorate of Forensic Science (DFS), Ministry of Home Affairs, "Technical Peer Review of Brain Electro Physiology Based Technique Used for Forensic

Interrogation in India," October 2008, on file with author (henceforth Memo by DFS).

68. There is some uncertainty about whether an MOU was signed with NIMHANS. That said, it appears clear that both Mukundan and Nagaraja were involved with the project, and an ethics committee had been set up where Nagaraja was involved.

69. Memo by DFS, 1.

70. Interviews with NIMHANS scholars and practitioners suggested they had serious concerns about using the techniques for legal purposes.

71. In 2003 the chief forensic scientist, M. S. Rao, had also become the head of the Directorate of Forensic Science, independent from the Bureau of Police Research and Development, based on the recommendations of the Padmanabhaiah Committee on Police Reforms. Thus, the development of forensic science was closely related to police reforms.

72. Memo by DFS, 3.

73. Ibid., 4.

74. Interview with forensic scientist, Bangalore, January 2014; see also Suresh Bada Math, "Supreme Court Judgment on Polygraph, Narco-Analysis & Brain-Mapping: A Boom or a Bane," *Indian Journal of Medical Research* 134 (July 2011): 4–7.

75. In response to a Delhi High Court order to set up a narco test facility in Delhi, the lab has apparently set up a brain fingerprinting machine. Akanksha Jain, "HC Direct Delhi Govt to Renovate Room for Brain Fingerprinting Facility in FSL, Rohini, within Six Months," Live Law.in, March 30, 2019, https://www.livelaw.in/news-updates/hc-delhi-govt-renovate-room-brain-fingerprinting-facility-fsl-rohini-six-months-143939

76. Raksha Shakti and its research projects were being run by former Gujarat FSL official Dr. Vaya, who ran them until she retired in 2018.

77. There is an MOU/arrangement between Brainwave Science and Raksha Shakti University headed by Dr. Vaya. Kaushik Joshi, "Picking a Criminal's Brain," India Legal Live, November 14, 2015, http://www.indialegallive.com/cover-story-articles/focus/picking-a-criminals-brain-7683

78. Vaya, *National Resource Center*; see also Dr. S. L. Vaya and Dr. Vinod Goyal, "Narcoanalysis in Crime Investigation: A Human Approach," *CBI Bulletin* (September 2003): 35–37. This article specifically mentions where the test led to an acquittal in the first and third case.

79. Interview with forensic psychologist, Gandhinagar, December 2016.

80. Ibid.

81. Vaya and Goyal, "Narcoanalysis in Crime Investigation."

82. When I had visited the Gandhinagar lab in 2013, they the forensic psychologists said that narcoanalysis had been declining since the Supreme Court judgment in 2010, although some requests continue. We don't have figures from July 2007–2010 until the Court's judgment was proclaimed in the Selvi case in May 2010.

83. Sourav Mukherjee, "Police Agencies Put 70 through Narco in 2013," *Times of India*, February 19, 2014, http://timesofindia.indiatimes.com/city/ahmedabad/Police-agencies-put-70-through-narco-in-2013/articleshow/30640013.cms

84. Parth Shastri, "Directorate of Forensic Sciences Does Record Number of Narco Analyses in Two Months," *Times of India*, July 12, 2017, http://timesofindia.indiatimes.com/city/ahmedabad/dfs-does-record-number-of-narco-analyses-in-two-months/articleshow/59551701.cms. While I was able to gain access to the Gandhinagar lab in 2013, by 2016 they administrators were more unwilling to talk about the use of narcoanalysis.

85. See P. Baxi, *Public Secrets of Law*; Ramakrishnan, *In Custody*; Lokaneeta and Jesani, "India."

86. Interview with forensic psychologist, Gandhinagar, December 2016.

87. "Withdraw Manual on Narco Analysis, Home Ministry Urged," *Hindu*, August 14, 2006.

88. In 2010 the Supreme Court in Selvi rejected the understanding that Section 53 could be used to justify the use of these techniques.

89. Annual Report, 2008–2014, Ministry of Home Affairs, Government of India.

90. Annual Report, 2013–2014, Ministry of Home Affairs, Government of India, 197.

91. Mitchell, *Rule of Experts*, 66.

92. Annual Report, 2013–2014, Ministry of Home Affairs, Government of India, 197.

93. Vaya, *National Resource Center*.

94. See *Townsend v. Sain, Sheriff, et al.* 372 U.S. 293 (1963), discussed in chapter 3.

95. Currently, of course, only the Gandhinagar laboratory is reportedly conducting the narco test.

96. *Ram Baran v. The State of NCT of Delhi* (W.P.(CRL) 3115/2018); Akanksha Jain, "Surprised at People Travelling to Gujarat for Narco Test, HC Orders Govt to Make Facility Available at Delhi FSL in 3 Months," January 11, 2019, https://www.livelaw.in/news-updates/surprised-people-travelling-gujarat-narco-test-hc-orders-facility-available-delhi-fsl-3-months-142051

97. Vaya, *National Resource Center*, 14.

98. Ibid., 49. See also Vaya and Goyal, "Narcoanalysis in Crime Investigation."

99. See Ferreira, *Colours of the Cage*.

100. Research associate, Forensic Science University, Gandhinagar, December 2016.

101. Ibid.

102. Interview with one of the senior-most forensic scientists in the country, based in Bangalore, January 2014.

103. S. Vijay Kumar, "Parliament Must Be Persuaded to Permit Polygraph, Brain Mapping," *Hindu*, May 30, 2010.

104. P. Chandrasekharan, An Open Letter to Ashwani Kumar, Director CBI, http://anopenlettertoashwanikumardirectorcbi.blogspot.com

105. Interview with one of the senior-most forensic scientists in the country, based in Bangalore, January 2014.

106. Dr. Gopal Ji Misra and Dr. C. Damodaran, *Perspective Plan for Indian Forensics: Final Report Presented to the Ministry of Home Affairs Government of India*, New Delhi, July 2010, 136.

107. See Ferreira, *Colours of the Cage*.

108. *Telgi* case, https://www.youtube.com/watch?v=PVZGv94klM4; narco of Krishna Thadarai in the *Aarushi-Hemraj* murder case, https://www.youtube.com/watch?v=6ka9V6wx2SI; narco of Sister Sefi in the *Sister Abhaya* murder case, https://www.youtube.com/watch?v=HcSZc4h-8YU

109. See Ferreira, *Colours of the Cage*.

110. Out of all the forensic psychologists (and forensic scientists) I interviewed, no one supported Malini.

111. *Dr. Malini vs The State of Karnataka*, April 15, 2013. The court notes: "She has done her yeoman service to the country and she has received [a] number of awards, appreciations and recommendations, including recommendations from [the] Maharashtra Government for solving the sensational Stamp Paper case[,] where she had conducted Narco Analysis test on Sri. Abdul Karim Telgi and for [the] Bombay Blast case, Malegoan Blast Case, wherein, because of her Narco Analysis Report, the Maharashtra Government was able to secure 38 live bombs. Further, she had also received recommendations from the Andhra Pradesh Government for helping to solv[e] the sensational Hyderabad Mecca Masjid Bomb Blast and also helped to solve the sensational Arushi case. In the Sister Abhaya murder case[,] which has been pending for nearly 17 years, [the] Kerala High Court gave their appreciation for the work the petitioner has performed." Indian Kanoon, http://indiankanoon.org/doc/167420402

112. Narco of Krishna in *Aarushi-Hemraj* murder case, https://www.youtube.com/watch?v=6ka9V6wx2SI

113. Axxonet website, http://www.axxonet.com/forensics/11-forensics/20-nss-in-courts. Page downloaded and on file with author

114. As one research associate described their frustrations: "Even judges are not aware that there is a difference between brain fingerprinting and BEOS. In their judgment they're using this term—brain mapping, which is [an] incorrect term." Research associate, Forensic Science University, Gandhinagar,, December 2016.

115. In a November 16, 2016, newspaper report titled "Blind Murder Mystery Solved after Ten Years: Brain Mapping Provided Missing Links of the Conspiracy," additional murder suspects apparently emerged in the course of the brain mapping of suspects and, when they were "thoroughly interrogated," confessed to the murder of a builder in Bhilai,

Madhya Pradesh. "Blind Murder Mystery Solved after Ten Years: Brain Mapping Provided Missing Links of the Conspiracy," *Central Chronicle*, November 26, 2016. Meanwhile, Raksha Shakti University continues to defend the Farewell P-300 technique to solve CBI cases as a research project with practical implications. For instance, in a highly publicized case, brain fingerprinting was used to solve the murder of a woman killed in Dubai in 2005. "2005 Missing Woman Case: Suspects Taken to Gujarat for Brain Fingerprint," *Indian Express*, June 23, 2016, https://indianexpress.com/article/india/india-news-india/2005-mssing-woman-kochi-smitha-george-suspect-brain-fingerprint-test-2870263

116. In Ram, "Couples Take Lie-Detector Test." According to this article, Truth Labs, a private firm, "offers a variety of other forensic services . . . [and] promises to deliver all kinds of test results within a week for fees of Rs 5,000."

117. Vikram Rautela, "For Outsiders, Services at Gujarat FSL Costlier by Rs 20,000," *Indian Express*, November 24, 2009, http://archive.indianexpress.com/news/for-outsiders-services-at-gujarat-fsl-costlier-by-rs-20000/545449

118. Ibid.

119. Gautam S. Mengle, "Nehru Nagar Murder: No Narco Analysis Yet," *Hindu*, July 13, 2016, https://www.thehindu.com/news/cities/mumbai/news/Nehru-Nagar-murder-no-narco-analysis-yet/article14485748.ece

120. *Ram Baran v. The State of NCT of Delhi* (W.P.(CRL) 3115/2018); Jain, "Surprised at People Travelling to Gujarat."

121. "HC Direct Delhi Govt to Renovate Room for Brain Fingerprinting Facility in FSL, Rohini, within Six Months," March 30, 2019, https://www.livelaw.in/news-updates/hc-delhi-govt-renovate-room-brain-fingerprinting-facility-fsl-rohini-six-months-143939

122. As Bunn notes, instruments replace the observer. Bunn, *Truth Machine*, 71. Here they don't replace the observer but there is a constant oscillation between the human and the nonhuman. The art of the human accompanies the machine.

123. *Ram Baran v. The State of NCT of Delhi* (W.P.(CRL) 3115/2018); Jain. "Surprised at People Travelling."

124. They used methods such as forensic psychological assessment and hypnosis, and all these techniques often required pre- and post-interviews, which were precisely the spaces where the forensic psychologists had to define their role. See the discussion on subjectivity and inconclusiveness in polygraphs and the desire to be read as more objective in Aruna Mishra, Devinder Singh, and Dr. Himakshi Bharadwaj, "Objectifying the Subjectivity in Polygraph Examination Procedure in Context of Personality Patterns," *Indian Police Journal* (October–December 2013): 236–42.

125. See Anand Mohan J., "New Forensic Science Technology Used Voice to Detect Lies," *Indian Express*, January 3, 2019, https://indianexpress.com/article/cities/delhi/new-forensic-science-technology-used-by-fbi-mossad-uses-voice-to-detect-lies-5520741

126. Interview with forensic psychologist, November 2013.

127. Forensic psychiatrist, Gandhinagar, December 2016. Pegs is a common measurement of alcohol similar to a shot. See the critique by N. Jagadeesh, "Narco Analysis Leads to More Questions Than Answers," *Indian Journal of Medical Ethics* 4, no. 1 (2016): 9, https://ijme.in/articles/narco-analysis-leads-to-more-questions-than-answers

128. Interview with forensic psychologist, Gandhinagar, November 2013.

129. Interview with clinical psychologist, Gandhinagar, December 2016.

130. Ibid. Even in a case where multiple murders were committed, it was insisted that traumatic subjects were avoided and words such as "cut" not "butchered," for instance, were used.

131. "Meet the Woman Who Bonds with Hardened Criminals."

132. Interview with clinical psychologist, Gandhinagar, December 2016.

133. Cole, *Suspect Identities*, 196.

134. Interview with research associate, Forensic Science University, Gandhinagar, Gujarat, December 2016.

135. See, for example, Vaya and Vyas, "Polygraph (Lie Detector) Technique"; Ray and Singh, "Polygraph Examination." Ray was principal scientific officer in the Lie Detection Division, CFSL (CBI), New Delhi, and Singh was the director of CFSL (CBI), New Delhi. Dr. Vaya, over time, did become established enough to get her own publications.

136. Interview with research associate, Forensic Science University, Gandhinagar, Gujarat, December 2016.

137. Ibid.

138. "Meet the Woman Who Bonds with Hardened Criminals."

139. Interview with forensic psychologist, Gandhinagar, December 2016. It's important to note that while I met a number of forensic psychologists during my research, not all of them were as willing to explain their role in these terms. But, considering that many of them had been trained by the same person, they seemed to share the dedication to these techniques.

140. This emphasis on extracting confessions at any cost emerges peculiarly in the Indian context in terms of the pretest and posttest interviews. A 1998 article by Dr. Vaya and then director of the FSL, Dr. Vyas, explains the pretest interview as "casual asking of a series of questions which are predesigned to elicit verbal and non-verbal responses without engaging in any accusatory interrogation." The authors suggest that the main purpose of the interview to prepare the questions and should be done in a "completely objective and non-committal" manner to avoid being an "interrogator rather than interviewer and examiner." Vaya and Vyas also note that a polygraph can replace the third degree, especially of innocent subjects. Vaya and Vyas, "Polygraph (Lie Detector) Technique," 24. Ray and Singh also added that this pretest interview allows them to inform the subjects about their legal rights, especially the voluntariness of the test, to establish a rapport with the suspects,

to familiarize oneself with their language and their medical background, any criminal background, and their mental capability. The authors also mention the need to extract the suspects' side of the story whether in narcoanalysis or even by actually testing their version of the story. Ray and Singh, "Polygraph Examination."

141. Interview with clinical psychologist, Gandhinagar, December 2016.

142. Interview with director of a facility and university, December 2016.

143. Interview with clinical psychologist, Gandhinagar, December 2016.

144. Interview with forensic psychologist, Mumbai, December 2016.

145. Interview with forensic psychiatrist, Gandhinagar, December 2016. Even the psychiatrist noted that while it was difficult to ensure effectiveness of the technique in the absence of proper feedback, and the need for data from one thousand cases for validation, and so on, he did think that it was effective in certain cases such as terrorism, but not burglary, theft, and other relatively minor crimes.

146. Interview with forensic psychologist, Gandhinagar, December 2016.

147. Ibid.

148. Geoffrey Bunn mentions the fear of the polygraph machines in *Truth Machine*.

149. Cole, *Suspect Identities*, 166.

150. Interview with research associate, Forensic University, December 2016.

151. Interview with clinical psychologist, Gandhinagar, December 2016.

152. Ibid.

153. It is more revealing to know that the BEOS is done only by the technicians, while the forensic psychologists focus on the overall cases, presumably the questioning.

154. Peter Brooks, *Troubling Confessions: Speaking Guilt in Law and Literature* (Chicago: University of Chicago Press, 2000).

155. See, for instance, in the *Aarushi* case, where the forensic psychologist's report doesn't mention the ambiguity in Krishna's (one of the suspect's) testimony. Sen, *Aarushi*.

156. New methods include the suspect detection system or voice layered analysis, which are also forms of truth machines where forensic psychologists play a major role.

157. At two labs, testers insisted on showing me how the lie detectors worked by asking for a couple of volunteers. At another lab, I witnessed a part of the test in a murder case where the forensic psychologist constantly asked the person being questioned to relax in order for the test to actually take place. The forensic psychologist did not know that I was watching from outside.

Chapter 5

1. Kannabiran, *Wages of Impunity*, 2.

2. Ibid., 3.

3. Andhra Pradesh Civil Liberties Committee and People's Union for Democratic Rights, "Position Paper on Encounters," XXIV Ramanadham Memorial Meeting, 2009.

4. Andhra Pradesh Civil Liberties Committee, *Life, Liberty, and Livelihood: Civil Liberties in Andhra Pradesh*, vol. 1 *(Fact Finding Committee Reports 1978–84)* (Hyderabad: APCLC, 1996); Kannabiran, *Wages of Impunity*, 9.

5. U. K. Singh, *State, Democracy, and Anti-Terror Laws*.

6. U. K. Singh, "State and Emerging Interlocking Legal Systems: 'Permanence of the Temporary,'" *Economic and Political Weekly* 39, no. 2 (2004): 149.

7. U. K. Singh, *State, Democracy, and Anti-Terror Laws*, 15.

8. Kannabiran, *Wages of Impunity*, 4.

9. Ibid.

10. Asian Centre for Human Rights, *Torture in India: A State of Denial* (Delhi: Asian Centre for Human Rights, 2008); National Human Rights Commission, *Annual Report* (New Delhi: NHRC, 2003–2004); *Custodial Deaths in Delhi, 2003* (Delhi: People's Union for Democratic Rights, 2004).

11. Lokaneeta, *Transnational Torture*, 131.

12. Lokaneeta, *Transnational Torture*.

13. *Third Periodic Report to the Human Rights Committee* (1996), http://www.unhchr.ch/tbs/doc.nsf/(Symbol)/CCPR.C.76.Add.6.En?Opendocument

14. See the debates on colonial and postcolonial continuity in, for example, Kalhan et al., "Colonial Continuities: Human Rights, Terrorism, and Security Laws in India," *Columbia Journal of Asian Law* 20, no. 1 (2006): 93–234; Arudra Burra, "What Is 'Colonial' about Colonial Laws?," *American University International Law Review* 31, no. 2 (2016): 137–67; and Jinee Lokaneeta, "Rule of Law, Violence, and Exception: Deciphering the Indian State in the Thangjam Manorama Inquiry Report," *Law, Culture, and the Humanities* (2018): 1–21, https://doi.org/10.1177/1743872118761349

15. There are also different versions of the lie detector test that I mention in chapter 3. Vaya, opcit.

16. See a discussion on how the different brain scan technologies have varied characteristics in Vaya, Op.cit.

17. "PUDR Paper," in *Twenty Second Dr Ramanadham Memorial Lecture* (Delhi: People's Union for Democratic Rights, 2008).

18. Dr. Amar Jesani, "Dr Ramanadham Memorial Lecture," in *Twenty Second Dr Ramanadham Memorial Lecture* (Delhi: People's Union for Democratic Rights, 2008), 26.

19. Jesani, "Dr Ramanadham Memorial Lecture."

20. Dr. B. M. Mohan, former director of the Forensic Science Laboratories, Karnataka, responded to this charge by Jesani and claimed that they have an accuracy of 96–97 percent to date for three hundred cases and that 20–25 percent were even found innocent.

This report was not released. Phone conversation with Jesani, 2009. See examples of lying under narcoanalysis in "PUDR Paper."

21. Giridhardas, "India's Novel Use of Brain Scans."

22. M. Raghava, "Narco-Analysis, Other Tests Are Psychological Third Degree Mode," *Hindu*, March 5, 2004, http://www.thehindu.com/2004/03/05/stories/2004030513850300.htm

23. Jesani, "Dr Ramanadham Memorial Lecture," 27.

24. "PUDR Paper," 7.

25. Ibid.

26. Ibid.

27. Giridhardas, "India's Novel Use of Brain Scans."

28. The reforms proposed in the Malimath Committee Report (2003) and the Madhava Menon Report (2007) have also been read as articulating a desire on the part of the state to encourage these "scientific modes of investigation" (see chapter 2). Indeed there was talk of a new bill that would allow for the admissibility of evidence from techniques such as narcoanalysis and brain mapping. "New Bill to Admit Scientific Proof in Courts," *Times News Network & Agencies*, November 9, 2006.

29. *Ramchandra Ram Reddy v. The State of Maharashtra* (2004) MANU/MH/0067/2004; *Smt. Selvi and Ors. v. State by Koramangala Police Station* (2004) MANU/KA/0588/2004; *Rojo George v. Deputy Superintendent of Police* (2006) MANU/KE/0084/2006; *Dinesh Dalmia v. State by SPE* (2006) MANU/TN/8154/2006; *Santokben Sharmanbhai Jadeja v. State of Gujarat* (2007) MANU/GJ/1365/2007; *State of Andhra Pradesh v. Smt. Inapuri Padma and Ors.* (2008) MANU/AP/0485/2008; *Sampatrao R. Arvellie and Anr. Etc. v. State of Maharashtra and Ors.* (2008) MANU/MH/1384/2008. One prominent exception was *Meera Walia v. State of Himachal Pradesh* (2008) MANU/HP/0213/2008, which considered these techniques unconstitutional.

30. *State of Andhra Pradesh v. Smt. Inapuri Padma and Ors.* (2008).

31. "CBI Plans to Set Up Narcoanalysis Centre."

32. Michel Foucault, "Governmentality," in *The Foucault Effect: Studies in Governmentality*, ed. Graham Burchell, Colin Gordon, and Peter Miller, 87–104 (Chicago: University of Chicago Press, 1991), 100.

33. Timothy Mitchell, *Rule of Experts*.

34. *Ramchandra Ram Reddy v. The State of Maharashtra* (2004).

35. *Smt. Selvi and Ors. v. State by Koramangala Police Station* (2004).

36. Ibid.

37. *Dinesh Dalmia v. State by SPE* (2006).

38. *Rojo George v. Deputy Superintendent of Police* (2006).

39. Ibid.

40. Ibid.; emphasis added.

41. *Santokben Sharmanbhai Jadeja v. State of Gujarat* (2007).

42. Ibid.

43. Ibid. Regardless of whether the Malimath Committee Report is implemented (chapter 2), the emphasis on truth and an adverse assumption of invoking a right to silence still informs the legal system.

44. S. Malini and B. M. Mohan were associated with the Forensic Science Laboratory, Bangalore. Mohan, "Misconceptions about Narcoanalysis."

45. It was only in 2017 that the Supreme Court actually disallowed the accused to use narcoanalysis for the purposes of exculpating oneself. Dhananjay Mahapatra, "Accused Can't Seek Narco Test to Prove Innocence: SC," *Times of India*, September 9, 2017, http://timesofindia.indiatimes.com/articleshow/60432928.cms?utm_source=content ofinterest&utm_medium=text&utm_campaign=cppst

46. *Smt. Selvi & Others v. State of Karnataka* (2010), http://www.indiankanoon.org/doc/338008

47. Ibid.

48. Ibid.

49. Interviews at Forensic Science Labs in Mumbai, Gandhi Nagar, and Bangalore.

50. Using all three techniques together is a specific feature of the Indian system. Lawrence Liang, ". . . And Nothing but the Truth, So Help Me Science," *Sarai Reader*, 2007.

51. See the following important works on colonial torture and violence: Rao, "Problems of Violence"; Kolsky, *Colonial Justice*; Bhavani Raman, *Document Raj: Writing and Scribes in Colonial India* (Chicago: University of Chicago Press, 2012). Chandak Sengoopta, in *Imprint on the Raj*, writes about the emergence and perfecting of the art of fingerprinting in colonial India precisely because the testing and use could be done without any concern for due process rights, which might have initially been an impediment in Britain.

52. Justice Markandey Katju, "Torture as a Challenge to Civil Society and the Administration to Justice," *Supreme Court Cases Journal* 2 (2000): 39.

53. *Smt. Selvi & Others v. State of Karnataka* (2010).

54. Ibid.

55. *Rojo George v. Deputy Superintendent of Police* (2006).

56. *State of Andhra Pradesh v. Smt. Inapuri Padma and Ors.* (2008).

57. Michel Foucault, *Foucault Live: Collected Interviews, 1961–1984*, ed. Sylvere Lotringer (New York: Semiotext, 1996), 197.

58. People's Union for Democratic Rights, *Capital Crimes: Deaths in Police Custody, 1980–1997* (Delhi: People's Union for Democratic Rights, 1998).

59. Arun Fereira, "My Tryst with Narcoanalysis," 2008, http://arunferreira.wordpress.com/torture/my-tryst-with-narco-analysis; Jinee Lokaneeta, "Truth-Telling Techniques in a Regime of Terror," *Canada Watch* (Winter 2012).

60. Physicians for Human Rights, *Broken Laws, Broken Lives*, 2008, http://brokenlives.info/?page_id=69

61. Lokaneeta, *Transnational Torture*.

62. Amar Jesani, "Editorial," *Indian Journal of Medical Ethics* 7, no. 3 (July–September 2010).

63. Dr. Gopal Ji Misra and Dr. C. Damodaran, *Perspective Plan for Indian Forensics: Final Report Presented to the Ministry of Home Affairs Government of India* (New Delhi, July 2010), 136.

64. *Bhagwan Singh and Another v. State of Punjab*, 1992 3 SCC 249.

65. *Shakila Abdul Gafar Khan v. Vasant Ranghunath Dhoble and Anr* (2003), http://indiankanoon.org/doc/1320561

66. The former law minister Ashwani Kumar had requested the Supreme Court to ensure that a law is passed against torture, which would be an important step for ratification of the UN Convention against Torture. The Supreme Court dismissed the plea stating that it could not direct the central government to pass an anti-torture law since it was a matter of policy and efforts were already underway to finalize a law. "SC Dismisses Plea To Direct Central Government To Enact Legislation Against Custodial Torture," Sep 5, 2019. https://www.livelaw.in/top-stories/plea-to-enact-legislation-against-custodial-torture-dismissed-147805

67. *State of Andhra Pradesh v. Smt. Inapuri Padma and Ors* (2008).

68. Ibid.

69. See Lokaneeta, *Transnational Torture*, 100–101. See Kevin Stenson's formulation that sovereignty, discipline, and governmentality work in synchronic ways in liberal democracies. Kevin Stenson, "Crime Control, Governmentality, and Sovereignty," in *Governable Places: Readings on Governmentality and Crime Control*, ed. Russell Smandych, 45–73 (Dartmouth: Ashgate, 1999).

70. Nawaz Kotwal, "A Landmark Judgment on Narcoanalysis," *CHRI, NIPSA Newsletter*, 2010; A. R. Lakshmanan, "Welcome Verdict but Questionable Rider," *Hindu*, July 9, 2010.

71. *State of Maharashtra v. Aditi Baldev Sharma and Pravin Premswarup Khandelwal*, Sessions Case No. 508/07, June 12, 2008, 60. See discussion in Jinee Lokaneeta, "Truth-Telling Techniques: The Aditi Sharma Case and the Implications for Human Rights in India," in *The State of Human Rights in Postcolonial India, 1947—2014*, ed. Om Dwivedi and V. G. Julie Rajan, 95–109 (New York: Routledge, 2016).

72. Shoma Chaudhury, "Framed? The Aarushi-Hemraj Murder Case—An Investigation," *Tehelka* 26, no. 10 (June 29, 2013), http://www.tehelka.com/2013/06/framed-the-aarushi-hemraj-murder-case-an-investigation/?singlepage=1

73. Ibid.

74. Ibid.

75. Sen, *Aarushi*, 284.

76. Ibid., 293.

77. Nishita Jha, *Trial by Error: The Aarushi Files*, podcast, 2016, http://www.arre.co.in/series/aarushi

78. While I am focusing on the role of media, cultural productions in the context of the challenge to the verdict, several commentators have also pointed to the media trial in the *Aarushi* case, especially against the mother, Nupur, on not showing emotion or the "immoral lifestyle" of the parents in terms of stories of wife swapping. See Shohini Ghosh, "The Talwars and Presumed Guilt," thehoot.org, http://www.thehoot.org/media-watch/media-practice/the-talwars-and-presumed-guilt-7127

79. Jha, *Trial by Error*.

80. Similarly, in episode 4 Nishita Jha goes back to the investigative process and points to the contrast between the polygraphs and psychological evaluation of the servants, especially Krishna, as being aggressive, hostile, and hiding something, while Nupur and Rajesh had no deception in both. While acknowledging that narcoanalysis is unethical because a person is under a drug and therefore not in full control, she still plays a sound bite from Krishna, barely clear, and suggests that under the Supreme Court decision, material evidence could be investigated. Soon after, she mentions the release of an edited video of Krishna after the publication of Sen's book, where she compares the procedure of narcoanalysis to MRI, requiring a forensic expert and doctor to interpret the results, once again giving it a more scientific basis in the process.

Chapter 6

1. Shaikh, *Begunah Qaidi*.

2. Narcoanalysis is the use of Sodium Pentothal to put a person in trance so that they can be asked questions. The Supreme Court made results of narco inadmissible in 2010, but it continues to be requested and used.

3. Hyderabad is the de jure capital city of Andhra Pradesh, and Mumbai (formerly Bombay) is the capital of Maharashtra. Here I acknowledge that in terms of scale, the two incidents are very different in terms of the number of people killed and the number of incidents that may have also led to the difference in the outcome of the two cases. I thank Biju Mathew for this point. But my point in comparing them is to illustrate a certain need to ensure a scaffolding of the rule of law in both these cases, even though in the latter case, one could have assumed that the police could have been more careless given the outrage.

4. It may be useful to mention that there are constitutional and statutory safeguards against the use of torture in Indian law, but some of those are bypassed in the context of

extraordinary laws. For instance, police are not allowed to record confessions, and only the magistrates can record confessions after ascertaining that the accused have not been tortured. In the two contexts that I draw upon—the Mecca Masjid blast and the July 11 blast cases—the laws used are MCOCA and the Unlawful Activities Prevention Act, though ultimately in the Hyderabad case, the Unlawful Activities Prevention Act was not used. And the interrogation rules in MCOCA, especially in terms of recording of confessions by the police, are already bypassed.

5. Brian Z. Tamanaha, "The History and the Elements of the Rule of Law," *Singapore Journal of Legal Studies* (2012): 232–47.

6. Ibid., 246.

7. Randall Peerenboom, "Varieties of Rule of Law," in *Asian Discourses of Rule of Law: Theories and Implementation of Rule of Law in Twelve Asian Countries, France and the U.S.* (London: Routledge, 2004).

8. Jothie Rajah, *Authoritarian Rule of Law: Legislation, Discourse, and Legitimacy in Singapore* (New York: Cambridge University Press, 2012); emphasis added.

9. Ibid., 4.

10. Cheesman, *Opposing the Rule of Law*, 25.

11. Hussain, *Jurisprudence of Emergency*; Keally McBride, *Mr. Mothercountry: The Man Who Made the Rule of Law* (New York: Oxford University Press, 2016).

12. McBride, *Mr. Mothercountry*, 154.

13. Singha, *A Despotism of Law*.

14. McBride, *Mr. Mothercountry*, 104.

15. Ibid., 108.

16. Kolsky, *Colonial Justice*.

17. Ranabir Samaddar, "Crimes, Passion, and Detachment: Colonial Foundations of Rule of Law," in *Challenging the Rules of Law: Colonialism, Criminology, and Human Rights in India*, ed. Kalpana Kannabiran and Ranbir Singh (New Delhi: Sage, 2008), 356.

18. Ibid., 366.

19. Upendra Baxi, *The Crisis of the Indian Legal System*. U. K. Singh, "State and Emerging Interlocking Legal Systems."

20. Sharib Ali, "Politics of Terror: The Mecca Masjid Blast Case," *Economic and Political Weekly* 48, no. 34 (August 24, 2013), 45.

21. For a more detailed discussion on the contradictory interventions of the Supreme Court, see Jinee Lokaneeta, "Debating the Indian Supreme Court: Equality, Liberty, and the Rule of Law," *Law, Culture, and the Humanities* (2015): 1–16.

22. Foucault, *Discipline and Punish*.

23. Ibid., 34–35.

24. Ibid., 35.

25. Ibid., 39.

26. Local community activist, Hyderabad, November 2013. Six people were killed and twenty-one were injured, including those who were transporting the injured to the hospital. According to activists, videos showed that the police deliberately pointed toward the chest of those in the crowds, even though the rules are that they should be shot either above the heads or below the knee.

27. A pattern is often created across all the blasts that took place before. Ali, "Politics of Terror."

28. The actual number of Muslims picked up is unclear, although clearly varying numbers were reported by activists and in the media. But if one considers the number of them who received compensations, the number mentioned is sixty-six, with sixteen youth charged. "Mecca Masjid Blast: Rs 3 Lakh Compensation for Acquitted Youths," Rediff.com, January 5, 2012, https://www.rediff.com/news/report/mecca-masjid-blast:-rs-3-lakh-compensation-for-acquitted-youths/20120105.htm

29. Local community activist, Hyderabad, November 2013.

30. Ali does point to the fact that many of the boys who were picked up ostensibly had ties to two men who had previously been picked up, charged, but acquitted in terror cases. "The rounding up and arrests were largely organised around two links: family, friends, and associates of Maulana Naseeruddin and Shahid Bilal." Ali, "Politics of Terror," 41. Nasseruddin is a cleric and Bilal is a part of his circle.

31. Local community activist, Hyderabad, November 2013.

32. *D. K. Basu v. State of W. B.* 1997 1 SCC 416.

33. Quoted in Ali, "Politics of Terror," 38.

34. Maoists/Naxalites have been active in certain parts of the country dominated by the most marginalized sections of India but have a particularly long history in Andhra Pradesh since the 1940s.

35. Prominent journalist for national paper, Hyderabad, November 2013.

36. See, for example, Andhra Pradesh Civil Liberties Committee, *Life, Liberty, and Livelihood*. Here too one observes the articulation of parallel modes of functioning with the preventive detention system being used for the Maoists and representing the "violence of jurisprudence."

37. An advocate closely associated with the report, Hyderabad, November 2013. This particular approach of picking up the youth is described in a number of journalistic and other reports.

38. Senior woman activist who had worked in the walled city Hyderabad for a number of years, November 2013.

39. Prominent local journalist, Hyderabad, November 2013.

40. Ibid.

41. See the history of sedition laws in India (and other liberal democracies) that are used against protesters and activists. Anuskha Singh, *Sedition in Liberal Democracies* (Delhi: Oxford University Press, 2018).

42. Prominent local journalist, Hyderabad, November 2013. First Information Report is a formal police complaint.

43. On December 31, 2009, the Court of the VII Additional Metropolitan Sessions judge cleared twenty-one people who had been accused of all charges. Vidya Subrahmaniam, "Accused without Any Evidence," *Hindu*, February 17, 2011 (updated October 13, 2016). As of 2018 all charges against the Hindu right-wing accused have been dropped, and the accused have been acquitted amid much criticism. Ajoy Ashirwad Mahaprashasta, "Explainer: Is No One Guilty in the Mecca Masjid Blast?," *Wire*, April 16, 2018.

44. "Mecca Masjid Blast."

45. There were four different cases by the Andhra Pradesh police and another one by the Central Bureau of Investigation.

46. An advocate closely associated with the report, Hyderabad, November 2013.

47. Lawyer representing the youth, Hyderabad, November 2013.

48. Ibid.

49. M. Srinivas, "Mecca Blast Case Casts Doubts on Narco," *Hindu*, February 22, 2013.

50. Ashish Khetan, "An Angry Hall of Fall Guys. And Unfair Arrests," *Tehelka* 2, no. 8 (2010).

51. Lawyer representing the youth, Hyderabad, November 2013.

52. Ibid.

53. An advocate closely associated with the report, Hyderabad, November 2013.

54. Prominent civil liberties lawyer, Hyderabad, November 2013.

55. Prominent journalist for national paper, Hyderabad, November, 2013.

56. Prominent civil liberties lawyer, Hyderabad, November 2013.

57. Ibid.

58. Ibid.

59. Ibid.

60. Lawyer representing the youth, Hyderabad, November 2013.

61. Ibid.

62. Prominent local journalist, Hyderabad, November 2013.

63. An advocate closely associated with the report, Hyderabad, November 2013.

64. Ibid.

65. In addition, a lawyer expressed surprise that in a context where "people are so hesitant to donate blood, how is narcoanalysis accepted by the majority?" Dershowitz had made a defense of truth serum at some point using a similar analogy about drawing blood for an alcohol test. Dershowitz, "Is There a Torturous Road to Justice?"

66. L. Ravi Chander Investigation Report, Advocate Commissioner for Minorities, on file with author.

67. The thirteen were Faisal Shaikh, Ali Bashir Khan, Mohammad Ali, Majid Shafi, Sajid Ansari, Kamal Ansari, Ethesham Siddiqui, Zameer Shaikh, Sohail Shaikh, Muzammil Shaikh, Tanvir Ansari, Naved Hussain, and Abdul Wahid Shaikh (the only one who got acquitted). They were charged with sections of the IPC, the Indian explosive acts, Prevention of Damage to Public Property Act, the offences under the Indian Railways Act, and two extraordinary laws—namely, the Unlawful Activities Prevention Act (UAPA, 1967) and the Maharashtra Control of Organised Crime Act (1999). MCOCA was initially enacted in the context of Maharashtra and then applied to Delhi as well, and versions of it were introduced in Karnataka and Andhra Pradesh. It is said to have extremely high conviction rates as compared to the Terrorism and Disruptive Activities (Prevention) Act (TADA). One of its most controversial provisions is allowing the use of intercepted communications—wire, oral, or electronic—in the case. It also allows for confessions to be recorded by senior police officials (above the rank of superintendent of police) and introduced against the co-accused, abettor, or conspirator. (On this point, see U. K. Singh, *State, Democracy, and Anti-Terror Laws*).

68. DW 49, or Asif Bashir Khan. Throughout the deposition, the name of the policeman keeps coming up as a consistent figure of intervention and torture. ("DW" refers to the deposition of witnesses for the defense, so accused). All depositions quoted in this section are on file with author.

69. DW 47, or Muzzammil Ataur Rehman Shaikh, and DW 44, or Suhail Mehmood Shaikh.

70. DW 49, or Asif Bashir Khan, 4.

71. For instance, one major issue that came up was the emergence of confessions by members of the Indian Mujhaheeden in the subsequent 2006 blast case that they were involved in. The lawyers for the accused wanted the confessions to be treated as evidence in the Mumbai blast case, but the trial court didn't allow that, and the motion went right up to the Supreme Court, which disagreed with the high court that those confessions could be brought in through the police officers who recorded them or that the confessions could be admitted despite the fact that they were not all about the same case and accused. *State of Maharashtra vs. Kamal Ahmed Mohammed Vakil Ansari & Ors.*, March 2013. CRIMINAL APPEAL NO.___445_____OF 2013 (Arising out of SLP (Crl.) No. 9707 of 2012)

72. Other depositions mention the names of other accused who were also tortured.

73. DW 46, or Mohd. Sajid Marghoob Ansari, 15.

74. DW 49, or Asif Bashir Khan.

75. DW 44, or Suhail Mehmood Shaikh, and DW 47, or Muzzammil Ataur Rehman Shaikh, who mentions his father being stripped and beaten and his sister-in-law's veil being removed.

76. DW 46, or Mohd. Sajid Marghoob Ansari, 23. DW 49, or Asif Bashir Khan, and DW 48, or Naveed Hussain Khan, described similar experiences.

77. DW 44, or Suhail Mehmood Shaikh.

78. Abdul Wahid Shaikh quoted in Vikrant Jha, "NH Conversation: A Case of Doctored Narco-Analysis," *National Herald*, May 12, 2017, https://www.nationalheraldindia.com/nh-conversation/2017/05/12/nh-conversation-a-case-of-doctored-narco-analysis-abdul-wahid-shaikh-mumbai-train-blast-case-begunah-qaidi

79. DW 46, or Mohd. Sajid Marghoob Ansari. This may be a little transformed post selvi in 2010 when the Supreme Court determined that consent had to be ensured voluntarily.

80. DW 46, or Mohd. Sajid Marghoob Ansari , 25.

81. Interview with lawyer, Mumbai, December 2013.

82. As DW 49, or Asif Bashir Khan, put it, "She told me to repeat what they say. She told me to say '*maine blasts nahi kiya*' [I did not do the blasts], '*maine bum nahi banaya*' [I did not make the bombs], '*maine conspiracy blasts karneki nahi ki*' [I did not do the conspiracy blasts][,] and '*main co-accused ko janata nahi hu*' [I don't know the co-accused] etc. [,] and they were doing the video shooting of the statements that I was making[,] and if I did not talk properly they used to torture me" (40).

83. Shaikh, *Begunah Qaidi*. All translations from Hindi to English are by the author.

84. DW 46, or Mohd. Sajid Marghoob Ansari, 29.

85. Confessions were either signed, or videos were recorded.

86. DW 46, or Mohd. Sajid Marghoob Ansari.

87. DW 44, or Suhail Mehmood Shaikh, 12.

88. DW 47, or Muzzammil Ataur Rehman Shaik, 9.

89. DW 49, or Asif Bashir Khan, 31.

90. DW 49, or Asif Bashir Khan (accused in two cases), Kalachowki ATS unit.

91. See the *Valdaris* case. Jayshree Bajoria, "When a Father Handed Over His Son to the Police in Mumbai and He Never Came Back," Scroll.in, December 19, 2016, https://scroll.in/article/824452/when-a-father-handed-over-his-son-to-the-police-in-mumbai-and-he-never-came-back

92. Manisha Sethi, *Kafkaland: Prejudice, Law, and Counterterrorism in India* (Gurgaon: Three Essays Collective, 2014); and U. K. Singh, *State, Democracy, and Anti-Terror Laws*. The Quill Foundation has also focused on wrongful prosecutions mentioning many Muslims who have been targeted in legal cases. Dipanjan Sinha, "Innocence Network: After Freedom, the Fight for Justice," February 27, 2017, https://www.hindustantimes.com/weekend/after-freedom-the-fight-for-justice/story-Gcg33k-19seHL5ksoc3w5VL.html?fbclid=IwAR3gNlqL-C68_FQJFzdDfDii9_TK7NanjmeRi94m6QKmD38QeMQbR4_w3wU

93. Shaikh, *Begunah Qaidi*, 19.

94. Ibid., 19–20.

95. See the sample confession in Shaikh, *Begunah Qaidi*.

96. Lawrence Liang and Smarika Kumar, "Terrorism, Media Trials, and the Right to Fair Trial," Academia; Sethi, *Kafkaland*.

97. Khalili, *Time in the Shadows*.

98. Jauregui, *Provisional Authority*.

99. While post-9/11 there remains an attempt to link terrorism-related incidents to non-Pakistani international terrorist groups, the dominant narrative is still linked to Kashmir and Pakistan. Khan with Haksar, *Framed as a Terrorist*.

100. For an informed analysis of the question of nationalism, the targeting of Muslims, and the Kashmir issue, see Hilal Ahmed, "What Muslims in India Say about Balakot, National Security, ISIS, and Kashmir," The print.in, May 13, 2019, https://theprint.in/opinion/muslim-vote/what-muslims-in-india-say-about-balakot-national-security-isis-and-kashmir/233649/

101. U. K. Singh, *State, Democracy, and Anti-Terror Laws*, 316. Also see response of courts more generally. Mayur Suresh "The social life of technicalities: 'Terrorist' lives in Delhi's courts." *Contributions to Indian Sociology*, February 25, 2019. https://doi.org/10.1177/0069966718812523

102. On criminal tribes, see Anand A. Yang, ed., *Crime and Criminality in British India* (Tucson: University of Arizona Press, 1985).

103. See Bunn, *Truth Machine*, discussed in chapter 3.

104. See Dubber, *Police Power*, discussed in chapter 2.

105. Seri, *Seguridad*, discussed in chapter 2.

106. See, for instance, how historically policing has focused on Native Americans and black and brown bodies, in Nikhil Pal Singh, "The Whiteness of Police," *American Quarterly* (2014): 1091–99.

107. One finds a targeting of young men and boys in Kashmir as well.

108. On racialization of Muslims in the post-9/11 context, see Sangay K. Mishra, *Desis Divided: The Political Lives of South Asian Americans* (Minneapolis: University of Minnesota Press, 2016). Also see Leti Volpp, "Citizens and Terrorists," *UCLA Law Review* 49 (2002): 1575–1600; and Muneer Ahmad, "Homeland Insecurities: Racial Violence the Day after September 11," *Social Text* 20, no. 3 (2002): 101–15. This phenomenon is integrally linked to the focus of policing on "borders" (territorial) and "boundaries" (of identities within) that Fassin writes about. Didier Fassin. "Policing Borders, Producing Boundaries: The Governmentality of Immigration in Dark Times." *Annual Review of Anthropology* 40 (2011): 213–26.

109. This happened with DW 49, or Asif Bashir Khan: "They handcuffed my brother to a hook on the wall and made him sit on the floor and stripped me naked, beat me and tortured me by flour mill belt for one hour" (34).

110. DW 46, or Mohd. Sajid Marghoob Ansari, 15.

111. Shaikh, *Begunah Qaidi*, 374.

112. Cynthia Enloe, "Wielding Masculinity Inside Abu Ghraib and Guantanamo: The Globalized Dynamics," in *Globalization and Militarism: Feminists Make the Link*, ed. Cynthia Enloe, 93–114 (New York: Rowman and Littlefield, 2007).

113. Pratiksha Baxi, "Impunity of Law and Custom: Stripping and Parading Women in India," in *Faultlines of History*, ed. Uma Chakravarti, 291–334 (Delhi: Zubaan Books, 2016).

114. DW 38, or Ehtesham Qutubuddin Siddiqui, 13.

115. DW 47, or Muzzammil Ataur Rehman Shaik, 8.

116. DW 44, or Suhail Mehmood Shaikh, 13.

117. Khan with Haksar, *Framed as a Terrorist*, 112–13.

118. Shaikh, *Begunah Qaidi*, 375.

119. See Basuli Deb, "Transnational Feminism and Women Who Torture: Re-imag(in)ing Abu Ghraib Prison Photography," *Postcolonial Text* 7, no. 1 (2012): 1–16.

120. See Bhuwania, "Courting the People"; U. S. Mehta, "Constitutionalism."

121. See the discussion in Lokaneeta, "Debating the Indian Supreme Court."

122. Brian Z. Tamanaha, "The History and the Elements of the Rule of Law," *Singapore Journal of Legal Studies* (2012): 246.

123. See the Anoop Bhuyan case for instance. The Court disallowed confession to be the sole piece of evidence even in a militancy case because of the alleged torture. *Arup Bhuyan v. State of Assam*, 2011 http://indiankanoon.org/doc/792920/

124. The 2016 Human Rights Watch Report, *Bound by Brotherhood: India's Failure to End Killings in Police Custody*, focuses on the lack of justice in custodial torture/death cases and does an excellent job of focusing on the doctors and magistrates in enabling the impunity.

125. Nandita Haksar, "The Context," in Khan with Haksar, *Framed as a Terrorist*, 33.

126. Sethi, *Kafkaland*.

127. On the point of temporality and the ticking bomb scenario, see Leonard C. Feldman, "Police Violence and the Legal Temporalities of Immunity," *Theory & Event* 20, no. 2 (2017): 329–50.

128. Khan with Haksar, *Framed as a Terrorist*, 100. Khan was framed in eighteen cases and spent fourteen years in jail.

129. On the significance of documents in the British colonial period in upholding bureaucracy, see Raman, *Document Raj*. On the workings of the contemporary Indian state taking the example of Indian legislation on rural employment—National Rural Employment Guarantee Act—see Mathur, *Paper Tiger*.

130. Sethi, *Kafkaland*, 24.

131. MCOCA, 1999.

132. Shaikh, *Begunah Qaidi*, 114.
133. Ibid., 117.
134. Ibid., 122.
135. Ferreira, *Colours of the Cage*, 97.
136. Ibid., 110.
137. Khan with Haksar, *Framed as a Terrorist*, 143.
138. Marguerite Feitlowitz, *Lexicon of Terror: Argentina and the Legacies of Torture* (Oxford: Oxford University Press, 2011).
139. After all, it is always those at the margins who are engaged in the transformation of the constitutional culture. See Rohit De. *A People's Constitution: An Everyday Life of Law in the Indian Republic* (Princeton: Princeton University Press, 2018). See also Kalpana Kannabiran's innovative discussion on "insurgent jurisprudence" (term from KG Kannabiran) as a way to remove the state as the main actor for defining the radical potential of constitutionalism. Kalpana Kannabiran, *Tools of Justice: Non-discrimination and the Indian Constitution* (New Delhi: Routledge, 2012).

Conclusion

1. Shaikh, *Begunah Qaidi*, 122.
2. Cymene Howe et al., "Paradoxical Infrastructures: Ruins, Retrofit, and Risk," *Science, Technology, and Human Values* (2015): 1–19, https://doi.org/10.1177/0162243 915620017
3. Ibid., 2.
4. Ibid., 3.
5. Brian Larkin, "The Politics and Poetics of Infrastructure," *Annual Review of Anthropology* 42 (2013): 330.
6. For instance, an important volume on violence studies also notes the different aspects of the violence ranging from the individual to the structural based on caste, gender, labor, and sexuality; state and law also play a role in the forms of violence embedded in society. Kannabiran, *Violence Studies*; Veena Das et al., *Violence and Subjectivity* (Berkeley: University of California Press, 2000); Nancy Scheper-Hughes and Philippe Bourgois, eds., *Violence in War and Peace: An Anthology* (Malden, MA: Blackwell, 2003).
7. Singh and Hoenig, eds., *Landscapes of Fear*; Uma Chakravarti, ed., *Faultlines of History* (Delhi: Zubaan Books, 2016); and Batul et al., *Do You Remember Kunan Pushpora?*

BIBLIOGRAPHY

Aamir Khan, Mohammad, with Nandita Haksar. *Framed as a Terrorist: My 14-Year Struggle to Prove My Innocence.* New Delhi: Speaking Tiger Publishing, 2016.

Agamben, Giorgio. *Homo Sacer: Sovereign Power and Bare Life.* Translated by Daniel Heller-Roazen. Stanford: Stanford University Press, 1995.

Agamben, Giorgio. *State of Exception.* Chicago: University of Chicago Press, 2005.

Ahmad, Muneer. "Homeland Insecurities: Racial Violence the Day after September 11." *Social Text* 20, no. 3 (2002): 101–15.

Alder, Ken. *The Lie Detector: The History of an American Obsession.* New York: Free Press, 2007.

Ali, Sharib. "Politics of Terror: The Mecca Masjid Blast Case." *Economic and Political Weekly* 48, no. 34 (August 24, 2013): 36–46.

Alter, Jonathan. "Time to Think about Torture." *Newsweek,* November 5, 2001.

Althusser, Louis. "Ideology and Ideological State Apparatuses (Notes towards an Investigation)." Reprinted in *Anthropology of the State,* edited by Sharma and Gupta, 86–111.

Amnesty International. *India: Torture, Rape & Deaths in Custody.* New York: Amnesty International, 1992.

Amnesty International. *Report on Torture.* New York: Farer, Straus, and Giroux, 1975.

Amnesty International. *Torture Worldwide: An Affront to Human Dignity.* New York: Amnesty International, 2000.

Amnesty International India. *"Denied" Failures in Accountability for Human Rights Violations by Security Force Personnel in Jammu and Kashmir.* Delhi: Amnesty International India, 2015.

Amnesty International USA. *Broken Bodies, Shattered Minds: Torture and Ill-Treatment of Women.* New York: Amnesty International USA, 2001.

Andhra Pradesh Civil Liberties Committee. *Life, Liberty, and Livelihood: Civil Liberties in Andhra Pradesh.* Vol. 1 *(Fact Finding Committee Reports 1978–84).* Hyderabad: APCLC, 1996.

Andhra Pradesh Civil Liberties Committee, and People's Union for Democratic Rights. "Position Paper on Encounters." XXIV Ramanadham Memorial Meeting, 2009.

Arnold, David. *Police Power and Colonial Rule: Madras, 1859–1947.* Delhi: Oxford University Press, 1986.
Asian Centre for Human Rights. *Torture in India: A State of Denial.* Delhi: Asian Centre for Human Rights, 2008.
Asian Centre for Human Rights. *Torture in India.* Delhi: Asian Centre for Human Rights, 2011.
Balagopal, K. "In Defence of India: Supreme Court and Terrorism." *Economic and Political Weekly* 29, no. 32 (1994): 2054–60.
Balagopal, K. "Law Commission's View of Terrorism." *Economic and Political Weekly* 35, no. 25 (2000): 2114–22.
Banerjee, Sumanta. "Torture in Custody: Method in Sadistic Madness." *Economic and Political Weekly* 36, no. 9 (2001): 723–24.
Baruah, Sanjib. "Routine Emergencies: India's Armed Forces Special Powers Act." In *Civil War and Sovereignty in South Asia: Regional and Political Economy Perspectives,* edited by Aparna Sundar and Nandini Sundar, 190–211. New Delhi: Sage, 2014.
Basu, Srimati. *The Trouble with Marriage: Feminists Confront Law and Violence in India.* Berkeley: University of California Press, 2015.
Batul, Essar, Ifrah Butt, Samreena Mushtaq, Munaza Rashid, and Natasha Rathe. *Do You Remember Kunan Pushpora?* New Delhi: Zubaan Books, 2016.
Baxi, Pratiksha. "Impunity of Law and Custom: Stripping and Parading Women in India." In *Fault Lines of History,* edited by Uma Chakravarti, 291–334. Delhi: Zubaan Books, 2016.
Baxi, Pratiksha. *Public Secrets of Law: Rape Trials in India.* Delhi: Oxford University Press, 2014.
Baxi, Upendra. *The Crisis of the Indian Legal System.* New Delhi: Vikas, 1982.
Baxi, Upendra. "An Honest Citizen's Guide to Criminal Justice System Reform: A Critique of the Malimath Report." In *The (Malimath) Committee on Reforms of Criminal Justice System: Premises, Politics, and Implications for Human Rights.* New Delhi: Amnesty International India, 2003.
Baxi, Upendra. "Post Colonial Legality." In *A Companion to Postcolonial Studies,* edited by Henry Swartz and Sangeeta Ray, 540–55. Oxford: Blackwell, 2000.
Baxi, Upendra. "Rule of Law in India: Theory and Practice." In *Asian Discourses of Rule of Law: Theories and Implementation of Rule of Law in Twelve Asian Countries, France and the U.S,* edited by Randall Peerenboom, 324–45. London: Routledge, 2004.
Beccaria, Cesare. *Of Crime and Punishment and Other Writings.* Edited by Richard Bellamy. Cambridge: Cambridge University Press, 1995.
Belur, Jyoti. *Permission to Shoot? Police Use of Deadly Force in Democracies.* New York: Springer, 2010.
Benjamin, Walter. "Critique of Violence." In *Reflections,* edited by Peter Dementz, 277–300. New York: Harcourt Brace, 1978.

Bhuwania, Anuj. "Courting the People: The Rise of Personal Interest Litigation in Post Emergency India." *Comparative Studies of South Asia, Africa, and the Middle East* 34, no. 2 (2014): 314–35.

Bhuwania, Anuj. "'Very Wicked Children': 'Indian Torture' and the Madras Commission Report of 1855." *Sur International Journal of Human Rights* (2009): 7–27.

Bloche, M. Gregg, and Jonathan H. Marks. "When Doctors Go to War." *New England Journal of Medicine* 352, no. 1 (2005): 3–6.

Brooks, Peter. *Troubling Confessions: Speaking Guilt in Law and Literature*. Chicago: University of Chicago Press, 2000.

Brown, Michelle, and Judah Schept. "New Abolition, Criminology and a Critical Carceral Studies." *Punishment and Society* (September 7, 2016).

Brown, Wendy. *Walled States, Waning Sovereignty*. Boston, MA: MIT Press, 2010.

Bunn, Geoffrey C. "Spectacular Science: The Lie Detector's Ambivalent Powers." *History of Psychology* 10, no. 2 (2007): 156–78.

Bunn, Geoffrey C. *The Truth Machine: A Social History of the Lie Detector*. Baltimore, MD: Johns Hopkins University Press, 2012.

Burra, Arudra. "What Is 'Colonial' about Colonial Laws?" *American University International Law Review* 31, no. 2 (2016): 137–67.

Centre for Organisation Research and Education/Human to Humane Transcultural Centre for Torture and Trauma Victims (H2H). "Report of Torture in Manipur, 2014–15." Manipur: Centre for Organisation Research and Education, 2015.

Chafee, Zechariah, Jr., Walter H. Pollak, and Carl Stern. *The Third Degree: Report to the National Commission on Law Observance and Enforcement (June 1931)*. New York: Arno Press, 1969.

Chakravarti, Uma. "Archiving Disquiet: Feminist Praxis and the Nation-State." In *Human Rights and Peace: Ideas, Laws, Institutions and Movement*, edited by Ujjwal Singh, 49–73. New Delhi: Sage, 2009.

Chakravarti, Uma, ed. *Faultlines of History*. Delhi: Zubaan Books, 2016.

Chatterjee, Partha. "The Nation and Its Fragments." In *The Partha Chatterjee Omnibus*. New Delhi: Oxford University Press, 1999.

Chatterjee, Partha. "The State." In *The Oxford Companion to Politics in India*, edited by Niraja Gopal Jayal and Pratap Bhanu Mehta, 3–14. Delhi: Oxford University Press, 2010.

Cheesman, Nick. *Opposing the Rule of Law: How Myanmar's Courts Make Law and Order*. New York: Cambridge University Press, 2015.

Cohen, Jordan T. "Merchants of Deception: The Deceptive Advertising of fMRI Lie Detection Technology." *Seton Hall Legislative Journal* 35, no. 1 (2010): 158–67.

Cole, Simon. *Suspect Identities: A History of Fingerprinting and Criminal Identification*. Cambridge, MA: Harvard University Press, 2001.

Committee on Reforms of Criminal Justice System. Vol. 1. Government of India, Ministry of Home Affairs, Delhi, March 2003.

Commonwealth Human Rights Initiative. *Police Organisation in India*. Delhi: Commonwealth Human Rights Initiative, 2008.

Commonwealth Human Rights Initiative. *Rough Roads to Equality: Women Police in South Asia*. Delhi: Commonwealth Human Rights Initiative, 2015.

Cover, Robert M. *Narrative, Violence, and the Law: The Essays of Robert Cover*. Edited by Martha Minow, Michael Ryan, and Austin Sarat. Ann Arbor: University of Michigan Press, 1992.

Cover, Robert M. "Violence and the Word." In *Narrative, Violence, and the Law: The Essays of Robert Cover*, edited by M. Minow, Michael Ryan, and Austin Sarat, 203–38. Ann Arbor: University of Michigan Press, 1992.

Das, Veena. "The Signature of the State: The Paradox of Illegibility." In *Anthropology in the Margins of the State*, edited by Das and Poole, 225–52.

Das, Veena, Arthur Kleinman, Mamphela Ramphele, and Pamela Reynolds, eds. *Violence and Subjectivity*. Berkeley: University of California Press, 2000.

Das, Veena, and Deborah Poole, eds. *Anthropology in the Margins of the State*. Santa Fe, NM: School of American Research Press, 2004.

Das, Veena, and Deborah Poole. "State and Its Margins: Comparative Ethnographies." In *Anthropology in the Margins of the State*, edited by Das and Poole, 3–34.

De, Rohit. *A People's Constitution: An Everyday Life of Law in the Indian Republic*. Princeton: Princeton University Press, 2018.

Deb, Basuli. "Transnational Feminism and Women Who Torture: Re-Imag(in)ing Abu Ghraib Prison Photography." *Postcolonial Text* 7, no. 1 (2012): 1–16.

Dershowitz, Alan M. "Is There a Torturous Road to Justice?" *Los Angeles Times*, November 8, 2001, B19.

Dhavan, Rajeev, Jasleen K. Oberoi, Niharika Bahl, and Dhruv Dhavan. "Step by Step: Fourth Annual Report of National Human Rights Commission: 1996–1997." *Journal of the Indian Law Institute* 41, no. 2 (1999): 160–200.

Dilts, Andrew. *Punishment and Inclusion: Race, Membership, and the Limits of American Liberalism*. New York: Fordham University Press, 2014.

Dubber, Markus Dirk. *The Police Power: Patriarchy and the Foundations of American Government*. New York: Columbia University Press, 2005.

Dubber, Markus D., and Mariana Valverde. "Introduction: Perspective on the Power and Science of Police." In *The New Police Science: The Police Power in Domestic and International Governance*, edited by Markus D. Dubber and Mariana Valverde, 1–15. Stanford, CA: Stanford University Press, 2006.

duBois, Page. *Torture and Truth*. New York: Routledge, 1991.

Duschinski, Haley. "Reproducing Regimes of Impunity: Fake Encounters and the Informalization of Violence in Kashmir Valley." *Cultural Studies* 24 no. 1 (2010): 110–32.

Eckert, Julia. "The Trimurti of the State: State Violence and the Promises of Order and Destruction." *Max Planck Institute for Social Anthropology Working Papers*, 2005.

Enloe, Cynthia. "Wielding Masculinity inside Abu Ghraib and Guantanamo: The Globalized Dynamics." In *Globalization and Militarism: Feminists Make the Link*, edited by Cynthia Enloe, 93–114. New York: Rowman and Littlefield, 2007.

Fassin, Didier. "Policing Borders, Producing Boundaries: The Governmentality of Immigration in Dark Times." *Annual Review of Anthropology.* 40 (2011): 213–26.

Farwell, Lawrence A., Drew C. Richardson, and Graham M. Richardson. "Brain Fingerprinting Field Studies Comparing P300-Mermer and P300 Brainwave Responses in the Detection of Concealed Information." *Cogn Neurodyn* 7 (2013): 263–99.

Farwell, Lawrence A. "Brain Fingerprinting: A Comprehensive Tutorial Review of Detection of Concealed Information with Event-Related Brain Potentials." *Cognitive Neurodynamics* 6 (2012): 115–54.

Feitlowitz, Marguerite. *Lexicon of Terror: Argentina and the Legacies of Torture.* Oxford: Oxford University Press, 2011.

Feldman, Leonard C. "The Banality of Emergency: On the Time and Space of Political Necessity." In *Sovereignty, Emergency, Legality*, edited by Austin Sarat, 136–64. Cambridge: Cambridge University Press, 2006.

Feldman, Leonard C. "Police Violence and the Legal Temporalities of Immunity." *Theory & Event* 20, no. 2 (April 2017): 329–50.

Ferreira, Arun. *Colours of the Cage: A Prison Memoir.* Delhi: Aleph Book, 2014.

Foucault, Michel. *Discipline and Punish: The Birth of the Prison.* Translated by Alan Sheridan. New York: Vintage Books, 1977.

Foucault, Michel. *Foucault Live: Collected Interviews, 1961–1984.* Edited by Sylvere Lotringer. New York: Semiotext, 1996.

Foucault, Michel. "Governmentality." In *The Foucault Effect: Studies in Governmentality*, edited by Graham Burchell, Colin Gordon, and Peter Miller, 87–104. Chicago: University of Chicago Press, 1991.

Foucault, Michel. *Security, Territory, Population: Lectures at the College De France, 1977–78.* Edited by Michel Senellart. London: Palgrave Macmillan, 2007.

Ganguly, A. K., and S. K. Lahiri. "Application of the Polygraph in the Investigation of Crime in India." *Polygraph* 5 no. 3 (September 1976): 244–49.

Ganguly, Sumit. "India's Democracy at 70: The Troublesome Security State." *Journal of Democracy* 28, no. 3 (July 2017): 117–26.

Geetha, V. *Undoing Impunity: Speech after Sexual Violence.* Delhi: Zubaan Books, 2016.

Geis, Gilbert. "In Scopolamine Veritas: The Early History of Drug-Induced Statements." *Journal of Criminal Law* 50 (1959–60): 347–57.

Gershman, Bennett L. "Lie Detection: The Supreme Court's Polygraph Decision." *New York State Bar Journal* (September–October 1998): 34–37.

Gonzalez Van Cleve, Nicole. *Crook County: Racism and Injustice in America's Largest Criminal Court*. Stanford, CA: Stanford University Press, 2016.

Gore, M. S. *Committee on Police Training*. Ministry of Home Affairs, Government of India, 1971.

Gossman, Patricia, and Vincent Iacopino. *The Crackdown in Kashmir: Torture of Detainees and Assault on the Medical Community*. Boston, MA: Physicians for Human Rights and Asia Watch, 1993.

Gudavarthy, Ajay. "Human Rights Movement(s) in India: State, Civil Society and Beyond." In *Human Rights and Peace: Ideas, Laws, Institutions and Movement*, edited by Ujjwal Singh, 252–75. New Delhi: Sage, 2009.

Guha, Ranajit. "Dominance without Hegemony and Its Historiography." In *Subaltern Studies VI: Writing on South Asian History and Society*, edited by Ranajit Guha, 210–309. Delhi: Oxford University Press, 1989.

Gupta, Akhil. "Blurred Boundaries: The Discourse of Corruption, the Culture of Politics, and the Imagined State." In *Anthropology of the State*, edited by Sharma and Gupta, 211–42.

Gupta, Akhil. *Red Tape: Bureaucracy, Structural Violence, and Poverty in India*. Delhi: Orient Blackswan, 2012.

Hajjar, Lisa. *Torture: A Sociology of Violence and Human Rights*. New York: Routledge, 2012.

Haragopal, G., and K. Balagopal. "Civil Liberties Movement and the State in India." In *People's Rights: Social Movement and the State in the Third World*, edited by Manoranjan Mohanty, Partha Nath Mukerji, and Olle Tornquist, 353–72. New Delhi: Sage Publications, 1998.

Heath, Deana. "Bureaucracy, Power, and Violence in Colonial India: The Role of Indian Subalterns." In *Empires and Bureaucracy in World History*, edited by Peter Crooks and Timothy H. Parsons, 364–90. Cambridge: Cambridge University Press, 2016.

House, Robert. "The Use of Scopolamine in Criminology." *American Journal of Police Science* 2 (1931): 328–36.

House of Commons. *Report of the Commission for the Investigation of Alleged Cases of Torture at Madras*. Britain, July 1855.

Howe, Cymene, Jessica Lockrem, Hannah Appel, Edward Hackett, Dominic Boyer, Randal Hall, Matthew Schneider-Mayerson, Albert Pope, Akhil Gupta, Elizabeth Rodwell, Andrea Ballestero, Trevor Durbin, Farès el-Dahdah, Elizabeth Long, and

Cyrus Mody. "Paradoxical Infrastructures: Ruins, Retrofit, and Risk." *Science, Technology, & Human Values* (2015): 1–19. https://doi.org/10.1177/0162243915620017

Human Rights Watch. *Broken System: Dysfunction, Abuse, and Impunity in the Indian Police*. New York: Human Rights Watch, 2009.

Human Rights Watch. *The Human Rights Crisis in Kashmir: A Pattern of Impunity*. New York: Human Rights Watch, 1993.

Human Rights Watch. *Punjab in Crisis: Human Rights in India*. New York: Human Rights Watch, 1991.

Human Rights Watch Asia, and Physicians for Human Rights. *Dead Silence: The Legacy of Human Rights Abuses in Punjab*. New York: Human Rights Watch, 1994.

Hunt, Lynn. *Inventing Human Rights: A History*. New York: W.W. Norton, 2007.

Hussain, Nasser. "Beyond Norm and Exception: Guantanamo." *Critical Inquiry* (Summer 2007): 734–53.

Hussain, Nasser. *The Jurisprudence of Emergency: Colonialism and the Rule of Law*. Ann Arbor: University of Michigan Press, 2019.

"India's Democracy at 70." *Journal of Democracy* 28, no. 3 (July 2017): 39–40.

Isaac, Jeffrey C. "The American Politics of Policing and Incarceration." *Perspectives on Politics* 13, no. 3 (2015): 609–16.

Jagadeesh, N. "Narco Analysis Leads to More Questions Than Answers." *Indian Journal of Medical Ethics* 4, no. 1 (November 2016): 9. https://ijme.in/articles/narco-analysis-leads-to-more-questions-than-answers/

Jauregui, Beatrice. "Beatings, Beacons, and Big Men: Police Disempowerment and Delegitimation in India." *Law and Social Inquiry* 38, no. 3 (2013): 643–69.

Jauregui, Beatrice. *Provisional Authority: Police, Order, and Security in India*. Chicago: University of Chicago Press, 2016.

Jesani, Amar. "Editorial." *Indian Journal of Medical Ethics* 7, no. 3 (July–September 2010).

Jesani, Amar. "Dr Ramanadham Memorial Lecture." In *Twenty Second Dr Ramanadham Memorial Lecture*. Delhi: People's Union for Democratic Rights, 2008.

Jha, Nishita. *Trial by Error: The Aarushi Files*. Podcast, 2016.

Jha, Vikrant. "NH Conversation: A case of doctored narco-analysis." National Herald India.com, May 12, 2017. https://www.nationalheraldindia.com/nh-conversation/2017/05/12/nh-conversation-a-case-of-doctored-narco-analysis-abdul-wahid-shaikh-mumbai-train-blast-case-begunah-qaidi

Kalhan, Anil, G. P. Conroy, M. Kaushal, and S. S. Miller. "Colonial Continuities: Human Rights, Terrorism, and Security Laws in India." *Columbia Journal of Asian Law* 20, no. 1 (2006): 93–234.

Kannabiran, K. G. *The Wages of Impunity: Power, Justice, and Human Rights*. New Delhi: Orient Longman, 2003.

Kannabiran, Kalpana, ed. *Violence Studies*. Delhi: Oxford University Press, 2016.

Kannabiran, Kalpana. *Tools of Justice: Non-discrimination and the Indian Constitution*. New Delhi: Routledge, 2012.

Katju, Justice Markandey. "Torture as a Challenge to Civil Society and the Administration to Justice." *Supreme Court Cases Journal* 2 (2000): 39–43.

Kaufman-Osborn, Timothy V. "Gender Trouble at Abu Ghraib?" *Politics and Gender* 1, no. 4 (2005): 597–619.

Kaufman-Osborn, Timothy V. *From Noose to Needle: Capital Punishment and the Late Liberal State*. Ann Arbor: University of Michigan Press, 2002.

Kaviraj, Sudipta. "On the Enchantment of the State: Indian Thought on the Role of the State in Narrative of Modernity." In *The Trajectories of the Indian State*, 40–77. Delhi: Orient Blackswan, 2010.

Kearns, Thomas R., and Austin Sarat, eds. *Law's Violence*. Ann Arbor: University of Michigan Press, 1995.

Keller, Linda. "Is Truth Serum Torture?" *American University International Law Review* 20, no. 3 (2005): 521–612.

Khalili, Laleh. *Time in the Shadows: Confinement in Counterinsurgencies*. Stanford, CA: Stanford University Press, 2012.

Khanikar, Santana. *State, Violence, and Legitimacy in India*. Delhi: Oxford University Press, 2018.

Kolsky, Elizabeth. "'The Body Evidencing the Crime': Rape on Trial in Colonial India, 1860–1947." *Gender & History* 22, no. 1 (2010): 109–30.

Kolsky, Elizabeth. *Colonial Justice in British India: White Violence and the Rule of Law*. Cambridge: Cambridge University Press, 2010.

Krishnan, Jayanth K. "India's 'Patriot Act': Pota and the Impact on Civil Liberties in the World's Largest Democracy." *Law & Inequality: A Journal of Theory and Practice* 22, no. 2 (2004): 265–300.

Langbein, John. *Torture and the Law of Proof: Europe and England in the Ancient Regime*. Chicago and London: University of Chicago Press, 1997.

Lasson, Kenneth. "Torture, Truth Serum, and Ticking Bombs: Toward a Pragmatic Perspective on Coercive Interrogation." *Loyola University Chicago Law Journal* 39 (2008): 329–60.

Law Commission of India. *One Hundred and Eighty Fifth Report on Review of the Indian Evidence Act, 1972*. New Delhi: Law Commission of India, 2003.

Law Commission of India. *One Hundred and Fifty Second Report on Custodial Crimes*. New Delhi: Law Commission of India, 1994.

Law Commission of India. *One Hundred and Thirteenth Report on Injuries in Police Custody*. New Delhi: Law Commission of India, 1985.

Leo, Richard A. *Police Interrogation and American Justice*. Cambridge, MA: Harvard University Press, 2008.

Littlefield, Melissa. *The Lying Brain: Lie Detection in Science and Science Fiction.* Ann Arbor: University of Michigan Press, 2011.

Lokaneeta, Jinee. "Debating the Indian Supreme Court: Equality, Liberty, and the Rule of Law." *Law, Culture, and the Humanities* (2015): 1–16. https://doi.org/https://doi.org/10.1177/1743872115596158

Lokaneeta, Jinee. "Defining an Absence: Torture 'Debate' in India." *Economic and Political Weekly* 49, nos. 26–27 (2014): 69–76.

Lokaneeta, Jinee. "Narco Videos, Forensic Psychologists and the Truth Telling Apparatus: Tracing Evidence, Law and Media Trials." In *The Act of Media: Workshop on Law, Media, and Technology in South Asia.* Sarai Programme, Centre for the Study of Developing Societies, Delhi, January 8–10, 2016.

Lokaneeta, Jinee. "Rule of Law, Violence, and Exception: Deciphering the Indian State in the Thangjam Manorama Inquiry Report." *Law, Culture and the Humanities* (2018): 1–21.

Lokaneeta, Jinee. *Transnational Torture: Law, Violence, and State Power in the United States and India.* New York: New York University Press, 2011.

Lokaneeta, Jinee. "Truth-Telling Techniques: The Aditi Sharma Case and the Implications for Human Rights in India." In *The State of Human Rights in Postcolonial India, 1947—2014*, edited by Om Dwivedi and V. G. Julie Rajan, 95–109. New York: Routledge 2016.

Lokaneeta, Jinee, and Amar Jesani. "India." In *Does Torture Prevention Work?*, edited by Richard Carver and Lisa Handley, 501–47. Liverpool: Liverpool University Press, 2016.

Lynch, Michael, Simon A. Cole, Ruth McNally, and Kathleen Jordan. *Truth Machine: The Contentious History of DNA Fingerprinting.* Chicago: University of Chicago Press, 2012.

Math, Suresh Bada. "Supreme Court Judgment on Polygraph, Narco-Analysis & Brain-Mapping: A Boom or a Bane." *Indian Journal of Medical Research*, no. 134 (July 2011): 4–7.

Mathur, Nayanika. *Paper Tiger: Law, Bureaucracy and the Developmental State in Himalayan India.* Cambridge: Cambridge University Press, 2015.

McBride, Keally. *Mr. Mothercountry: The Man Who Made the Rule of Law.* New York: Oxford University Press, 2016.

McBride, Keally. "Punitive Politics in the United States: The End of an Era?" *Perspectives on Politics* 13, no. 3 (2015): 749–53.

McCoy, Alfred. *A Question of Torture: CIA Interrogation, from the Cold War to the War on Terror.* New York: Metropolitan Books, 2006.

Mehta, P. B. "The Inner Conflict of Constitutionalism: Judicial Review and the Basic Structure." In *India's Living Constitution: Ideas, Practices, and Controversies*, edited by E. Sridharan Zoya Hasan and R. Sudarshan, 179–206. London: Anthem Press, 2005.

Mehta, Uday S. "Constitutionalism." In *The Oxford Companion to Politics in India*, edited by Niraja Gopal Jayal and Pratap Bhanu Mehta, 15–27. Oxford: Oxford University Press, 2010.

Menon, Nivedita. *Recovering Subversion: Feminist Politics Beyond the Law*. Chicago: University of Illinois Press, 2004.

Mertz, Elizabeth, and Jothie Rajah. "Language-and-Law Scholarship: An Interdisciplinary Conversation and a Post-9/11 Example." *Annual Review of Law and Social Sciences* 10 (2014): 169–83.

Ministry of Home Affairs. *Annual Report*. Government of India, 2013–14.

Mishra, Aruna, Devinder Singh, and Dr. Himakshi Bharadwaj. "Objectifying the Subjectivity in Polygraph Examination Procedure in Context of Personality Patterns." *Indian Police Journal* (October–December 2013): 236–42.

Mishra, Sangay. "Race, Religion, and Political Mobilization: South Asians in the Post-9/11 United States." *Studies in Ethnicity & Nationalism* 13, no. 2 (2013): 115–37. https://doi.org/10.1111/sena.12034

Misra, Gopal Ji, and C. Damodaran. *Perspective Plan for Indian Forensics: Final Report Presented to the Ministry of Home Affairs Government of India*. New Delhi: July 2010.

Mitchell, Timothy. "The Limits of the State: Beyond Statist Approaches and Their Critics." *American Political Science Review* 85, no. 1 (1991): 77–96.

Mitchell, Timothy. *Rule of Experts: Egypt, Techno-Politics, Modernity*. Berkeley: University of California Press, 2002.

Mitchell, Timothy. "Society, Economy, and the State Effect." In *Anthropology of the State*, edited by Sharma and Gupta, 169–86.

Mohan, Bannur Muthai. "Misconceptions about Narcoanalysis." *Indian Journal of Medical Ethics* 4, no. 1 (January–March 2007).

Mohanty, Manorajan. "Indian State: The Emerging Trends." *Social Action* 40 (July–September 1990): 219–31.

Mohanty, Manoranjan, Partha N. Mukherji, and Olle Törnquist. *People's Rights: Social Movements and the State in the Third World*. New Delhi: Sage, 1998.

Moriarty, Jane Campbell. "Visions of Deception: Neuroimaging and the Search for Evidential Truth." *Akron Law Review* (2009): 739–61.

Mukundan, C. R. "Scientific Methods of Extraction of Information from Suspects: An Analysis of Current Trends." *Indian Journal of Clinical Psychology* 38, no. 2 (2011): 129–40.

Mulla, Sameena. *The Violence of Care: Rape Victims, Forensic Nurses, and Sexual Assault Intervention*. New York: New York University Press, 2014.

National Human Rights Commission. *Annual Report*. New Delhi: NHRC, 2001–2002.

National Human Rights Commission. *Annual Report*. New Delhi: NHRC, 2003–2004.

National Research Council. *The Polygraph and Lie Detection*. Washington, DC: National Academies Press, 2003.

Navlakha, Gautam. "Pota: Freedom to Terrorise." *Economic and Political Weekly* 38, no. 29 (2002): 3038–40.

Neocleous, Mark. "Theoretical Foundations of the 'New Police Science.'" In *The New Police Science: The Police Power in Domestic and International Governance*, edited by Markus D. Dubber and Mariana Valverde, 17–41. Stanford, CA: Stanford University Press, 2006.

Noorani, A. G. "Torture; Human Rights." *Economic and Political Weekly* (1999): 3159–61.

Parry, John T. *Understanding Torture: Law, Violence, and Political Identity*. Ann Arbor: University of Michigan Press, 2010.

Peerenboom, Randall. "Varieties of Rule of Law." In *Asian Discourses of Rule of Law: Theories and Implementation of Rule of Law in Twelve Asian Countries, France and the U.S.*, edited by Randall Peerenboom, 1–55. London: Routledge, 2004.

Peers, Douglas M. "Torture, the Police, and the Colonial State in the Madras Presidency, 1816–55." *Criminal Justice History* (1991): 29–56.

People's Union for Democratic Rights. *Capital Crimes: Deaths in Police Custody, Delhi 1980–1997*. Delhi: People's Union for Democratic Rights, 1998.

People's Union for Democratic Rights. *Custodial Deaths in Delhi, 2003*. Delhi: People's Union for Democratic Rights, 2004.

People's Union for Democratic Rights. *Custodial Rape: A Report on the Aftermath*. Delhi: People's Union for Democratic Rights, 1994.

People's Union for Democratic Rights. *Dead Men's Tales: Deaths in Police Custody*. Delhi: People's Union for Democratic Rights, 2000.

People's Union for Democratic Rights. *In Custody: An Investigation into 5 Cases of Sexual Assault*. Delhi: People's Union for Democratic Rights, 2004.

People's Union for Democratic Rights. *Pudr Paper*. Delhi: People's Union for Democratic Rights, 2008.

People's Union for Democratic Rights. *Trial of Errors: A Critique of the POTA Court Judgement on the 13 December Case*. New Delhi: People's Union for Democratic Rights, 2003.

Peters, Edward. *Torture*. Expanded Edition. New York: B. Blackwell, 1996.

Physicians for Human Rights. *Broken Laws, Broken Lives*. 2008. http://brokenlives.info/?page_id=69

"Pota: Well-Founded Fears." *Economic and Political Weekly* 38, no. 14 (2003). http://www.epw.in/journal/2003/14/editorials/pota-well-founded-fears.html

Prakash, Gyan. *Emergency Chronicles: Indira Gandhi and Democracy's Turning Point*. Princeton, NJ: Princeton University Press, 2019.

"Project Mkultra, the CIA's Program of Research in Behavioral Modification, Joint Hearing before the Select Committee on Intelligence and the Subcommittee on Health and

Scientific Research of the Committee on Human Resources United States Senate." August 8, 1977.

Puranik, D. A., S. K. Joseph, B. B. Daundkar, and M. V. Garad. "Brain Signature Profiling in India. Its Status as an Aid in Investigation and as Corroborative Evidence—as Seen from Judgments." Paper presented at Proceedings of XX All India Forensic Science Conference, Jaipur, November 15–17, 2009.

Pustilnik, Amanda L. "Neurotechnologies at the Intersection of Criminal Procedure and Constitutional Law." In *The Constitution and the Future of Criminal Justice in America*, edited by John T. Parry and L. Song Richardson, 109–33. Cambridge University Press, 2013.

Rajah, Jothie. *Authoritarian Rule of Law: Legislation, Discourse, and Legitimacy in Singapore*. Cambridge: Cambridge University Press, 2012.

Ramakrishnan, Nitya. *In Custody: Law, Impunity and Prisoner Abuse in South Asia*. New Delhi: Sage, 2013.

Raman, Bhavani. *Document Raj: Writing and Scribes in Colonial India*. Chicago: University of Chicago Press, 2012.

Rao, Anupama. "Problems of Violence, States of Terror: Torture in Colonial India." *Economic and Political Weekly* 36, no. 43 (2001): 4125–33.

Rao, Anupama. "Torture, the Public Secret." *Economic and Political Weekly* 39, no. 23 (2004): 2347–50.

Ray, Bibha Rani, and S. R. Singh. "Polygraph Examination: Indian Experience." *CBI Bulletin* (June–December 2006): 29–39.

Ray, Shyamalkumar Sinha. "Introduction of Polygraph in Criminal Investigation in India: A New but Cautious Stride." *Criminal Law Journal* (1988): 117–19.

Rejali, Darius. *Torture and Democracy*. Princeton, NJ: Princeton University Press, 2007.

Rosenfeld, J. Peter. "'Brain Fingerprinting': A Critical Analysis." *Scientific Review of Mental Health Practice* 4, no. 1 (2005): 20–37.

Rosso, Jared Del. "The Toxicity of Torture: The Cultural Structure of US Political Discourse of Waterboarding." *Social Forces* 93, no. 1 (September 2014): 383–404.

Roy, Srirupa. *Beyond Belief: India and the Politics of Postcolonial Nationalism*. Durham, NC: Duke University Press, 2007.

Samaddar, Ranabir. "Crimes, Passion and Detachment: Colonial Foundations of Rule of Law." In *Challenging the Rules of Law: Colonialism, Criminology, and Human Rights in India*, edited by Kalpana Kannabiran and Ranbir Singh, 355–81. New Delhi: Sage, 2008.

Sarat, Austin. *Gruesome Spectacles: Botched Executions and America's Death Penalty*. Stanford, CA: Stanford University Press, 2014.

Sarat, Austin. *Pain, Death, and the Law*. Ann Arbor: University of Michigan Press, 2001.

Sarat, Austin. *When the State Kills: Capital Punishment and the American Condition*. Princeton, NJ: Princeton University Press, 2001.

Sarat, Austin, and Thomas R. Kearns. *A Journey through Forgetting: Towards a Jurisprudence of Violence*. In *The Fate of Law*, edited by Austin Sarat and Thomas Kearns, 209–73. Ann Arbor: University of Michigan Press, 1991.

Sathe, S. P. *Judicial Activism in India*. Delhi: Oxford University Press, 2002.

Satyogi, Pooja. "Law, police and domestic cruelty: Assembling written complaints from oral narratives."*Contributions to Indian Sociology*. February 25, 2019. https://doi.org/10.1177/0069966718812522

Scarry, Elaine. *The Body in Pain: The Making and Unmaking of the World*. New York: Oxford University Press, 1985.

Scheper-Hughes, Nancy, and Philippe Bourgois, eds. *Violence in War and Peace: An Anthology*. Malden, MA: Blackwell, 2003.

Scheppele, Kim Lane. "Law in a Time of Emergency: States of Exception and the Temptations of 9/11." *University of Pennsylvania Journal of Constitutional Law* 6, no. 5 (2004), 285–340.

Schultz, William F., ed. *The Phenomenon of Torture: Readings and Commentary*. Philadelphia: University of Pennsylvania Press, 2007.

Sen, Avirook. *Aarushi*. India: Penguin, 2015.

Sen, Sankar, P. S. V. Parsed, and A. K. Saksena. "Custodial Deaths in India: A Research Study." Hyderabad: S.V.P. National Police Academy, 1994.

Sengoopta, Chandak. *Imprint of the Raj: How Fingerprinting Was Born in Colonial India*. London: Macmillan, 2003.

Seri, Guillermina. *Seguridad: Crime, Police Power, and Democracy in Argentina*. New York: Bloomsbury, 2012.

Seri, Guillermina, and Jinee Lokaneeta. "Police as State: Governing Citizenship through Violence." In *Police Abuse in Contemporary Democracies*, edited by Michelle D. Bonner, Guillermina Seri, Mary Rose Kubal, and Michael Kempa, 55–80. New York: Palgrave Macmillan, 2017.

Sethi, Manisha. *Kafkaland: Prejudice, Law, and Counterterrorism in India*. Gurgaon: Three Essays Collective, 2014.

Shaikh, Abdul Wahid. *Begunah Qaidi (in Hindi)*. New Delhi: Pharos Media & Publishing, 2017.

Sharafi, Mitra. "The Imperial Serologist and Punitive Self-Harm: Bloodstains and Legal Pluralism in British India." In *Global Forensic Cultures: Making Fact and Justice in the Modern Era*, edited by Ian Burney and Christopher Hamlin, 60–85. Baltimore, MD: Johns Hopkins University Press, 2019.

Sharma, Aradhana. *Logics of Empowerment: Development, Gender, and Governance in Neoliberal India*. Minneapolis: University of Minnesota Press, 2008.

Sharma, Aradhana, and Akhil Gupta, eds. *The Anthropology of the State: A Reader*. Malden, MA: Blackwell, 2006.

Sharma, Aradhana, and Akhil Gupta. "Introduction: Rethinking Theories of the State in an Age of Globalization." In *Anthropology of the State*, edited by Sharma and Gupta, 1–41. Malden, MA: Blackwell, 2006.

Shue, Henry. "Torture." *Philosophy of Public Affairs* 7, no. 2 (1978): 124–43.

Shukla, Rakesh. "Police Torture: Prevention Is Better Than Compensation." *Lawyers Collective* 8, no. 5 (1993): 9–12.

Silverman, Lisa. *Tortured Subjects: Pain, Truth, and the Body in Early Modern France*. Chicago: University of Chicago Press, 2001.

Singh, Anuskha. *Sedition in Liberal Democracies*. Delhi: Oxford University Press, 2018.

Singh, Navsharan, and Patrick Hoenig, eds. *Landscapes of Fear: Understanding in India*. Delhi: Zubaan Books, 2014.

Singh, Nikhil Pal. "The Whiteness of Police." *American Quarterly* (2014): 1091–99.

Singh, Ujjwal Kumar. *The State, Democracy, and Anti-Terror Laws in India*. New Delhi: Sage, 2007.

Singh, Ujjwal Kumar. "State and Emerging Interlocking Legal Systems: 'Permanence of the Temporary.'" *Economic and Political Weekly* 39, no. 2 (2004): 149–54.

Singha, Radhika. *A Despotism of Law: Crime and Justice in Early Colonial India*. Delhi: Oxford University Press, 1998.

Squillacote, Rosa, and Leonard Feldman. "Police Abuse and Democratic Accountability." In *Police Abuse in Contemporary Democracies*, edited by Michelle D. Bonner, Guillermina Seri, Mary Rose Kubal, and Michael Kempa, 135–64. New York: Palgrave Macmillan, 2018.

Stenson, Kevin. "Crime, Control, Governmentality, and Sovereignty." In *Governable Places: Readings on Governmentality and Crime Control*, edited by Russell Smandych, 45–73. Dartmouth: Ashgate, 1999.

Subramanian, K. S. *Political Violence and the Police in India*. New Delhi: Sage, 2007.

Sundar, Nandini. "Interning Insurgent Populations: The Buried Histories of Indian Democracy." *Economic and Political Weekly* 46, no. 6 (2011): 47–57.

Sunder Rajan, Rajeshwari. *The Scandal of the State: Women, Law, and Citizenship in Postcolonial India*. Durham, NC: Duke University Press, 2003.

Suresh, Mayur. "The social life of technicalities: 'Terrorist' lives in Delhi's courts." *Contributions to Indian Sociology*, February 25, 2019. https://doi.org/10.1177/0069966718812523

Tamanaha, Brian Z. "The History and the Elements of the Rule of Law." *Singapore Journal of Legal Studies* (2012): 232–47.

Taussig, Michael T. *Defacement: Public Secrecy and the Labor of the Negative*. Stanford, CA: Stanford University Press, 1999.

Tilly, Charles. "War Making and State Making as Organized Crime." In *Bringing the State Back In*, edited by Dietrich Rueschemeyer, Peter Evans, and Theda Skocpol, 169–87. Cambridge: Cambridge University Press, 1985.

Torture: Indian State's Instrument of Control in Indian administered Jammu and Kashmir. Association of Parents of Disappeared Persons (APDP) and Jammu Kashmir Coalition of Civil Society (JKCCS), February 2019.

Valverde, Mariana. "Police, Sovereignty, and Law: Foucaultian Reflections." In *Police and the Liberal State*, edited by Markus D. Dubber and Mariana Valverde, 15–32. Stanford, CA: Stanford University Press, 2008.

Valverde, Mariana, and Markus D. Dubber. "Policing the Rechtsstaat." In *Police and the Liberal State*, edited by Markus D. Dubber and Mariana Valverde, 1–14. Stanford, CA: Stanford University Press, 2008.

Vaya, S. L. *National Resource Center for Forensic Psychology*. Gandhinagar, Gujarat: Directorate of Forensic Science, 2013.

Vaya, S. L. *Normative Data for Brain Electrical Activation Profiling*. Gujarat: Directorate of Forensic Science, March 2006–March 2008.

Vaya, S. L., and Vinod Goyal. "Narcoanalysis in Crime Investigation: A Human Approach." *CBI Bulletin* (September 2003): 35–37.

Vaya, S. L., and J. M. Vyas. "The Polygraph (Lie Detector) Technique." *CBI Bulletin* (December 1998): 23–25.

Volpp, Leti. "Citizens and Terrorists." *UCLA Law Review* 49 (2002): 1575–1600.

Wahl, Rachel. *Just Violence: Torture and Human Rights in the Eyes of the Police*. Stanford, CA: Stanford University Press, 2017.

Wahl, Rachel. "Justice, Context, and Violence: Law Enforcement Officers on Why They Torture." *Law & Society Review* 48, no. 4 (2014): 807–36.

Walker, Samuel. "An Introduction on the Wickersham Commission Report." 1997. http://www.lexisnexis.com/documents/academic/upa_cis/1965_WickershamCommPt1.pdf

Weaver, Vesla M. "Black Citizenship and Summary Punishment: A Brief History to the Present." *Theory and Event* 17, no. 3 (2014).

Weber, Max. "Bureaucracy." In *Economy and Society: An Outline of Interpretive Sociology*. Edited by G. Roth and C. Wittich. Reprinted in *Anthropology of the State*, edited by Sharma and Gupta, 211–42.

Weber, Max. "The Economic System and the Normative Orders." In *Law in Economy and Society*, edited by Max Rheinstein, 10–40. Cambridge, MA: Harvard University Press, 1966.

Weisman, Eyal. *Forensic Architecture: Violence at the Threshold of Detectability*. New York: Zone Books, 2017.

Wilde, J. F. "Narco-Analysis in the Treatment of War Neuroses." *British Medical Journal* (July 4, 1942): 4–7.

Winter, Alison. "The Making of 'Truth Serum.'" *Bulletin of the History of Medicine* 79, no. 3 (2005): 500–533.

Wolpe, Paul Root, Kenneth Foster, and Daniel D. Langleben. "Emerging Neurotechnologies for Lie-Detection: Promises and Perils." *Scholarly Commons*, Center for Neuroscience & Society, University of Pennsylvania, March 1, 2005. http://repository.upenn.edu/neuroethics_pubs/7

Yadav, Anjali, Dr. M. S. Dahiya, B. B. Daundkar, and Dr. M. V. Garad. "Differentiating between the Profiles of Participants vs Witness of an Event Using Beos Test." *Indian Police Journal* (July–September 2012): 115–29.

Yang, Anand A. "Disciplining 'Natives': Prisons and Prisoners in Early Nineteenth Century India." *South Asia: Journal of South Asian Studies* 10, no. 2 (1987): 29–46.

INDEX

Aamir, Mohammad, 160
Aarushi (Sen), 133, 167n3
Aarushi-Hemraj murder case, 1, 100, 167nn1–3, 210n155, 215n78
   limits of Supreme Court intervention in, 132–34
   Trial by Error podcast, 133–34
Abu Ghraib prison, 73, 154
accountability, police reform and, 41
ACHR (Asian Centre for Human Rights), 4
African Americans
   lie detectors and, 52
   narcoanalysis used against, 61
Agamben, Giorgio, 3, 16
alcohol, forensic psychiatrist administration of, 103
Alder, Ken, 57, 64, 70–71
Alter, Jonathan, 48, 73
American Polygraph Association, 82–83
Andhra Pradesh Preventive Detention Act, 1970, 114–15
Andhra Pradesh Suppression of Disturbances Act, 1967, 114
anthropometry, 108–9
Anti-Terrorism Squad (ATS), 148–49
Armed Forces Special Powers Act, 5, 135, 158
art of government
   custody in, 129–31
   elements of, 126
   medical professionals in, 127–30
   science in, 126–27
   Supreme Court on truth machines and, 125–31, 163–64
   torture and flawed, 130–31, 163–64
Asian Centre for Human Rights (ACHR), 4

ATS (Anti-Terrorism Squad), 148–49
Avery, Steven, 70–71, 195n151
Axxonet, 60, 66, 71, 100–101, 204n65

Balagopal, K., 12
Basu, D. K., 45, 142
Baxi, Pratiksha, 44, 51–52
Baxi, Upendra, 29, 36,140
   on institutional constraints of police, 45
   on torture, 41
Begunah Qaidi (*Innocent Prisoner*) (Shaikh), 136, 151
Belur, Jyoti, 28
BEOS. *See* brain electrical oscillation signature
BFP. *See* brain fingerprinting
Bharatiya Janata Party, 142
brain electrical oscillation signature (BEOS), 1
   convictions based on, 118
   costs of, 101
   criticism of, 68–69
   defense and promotion of, 71, 100–101
   DFS facilities for, 92
   Nagaraja Committee on, 91–93
   origins of, 59–60, 89–90, 168n5
   science and forensics clashing over, 89–94
   scientific validity of, 49
   Supreme Court on, 66–67
   Supreme Court on admissibility of, 93
   technique of, 59–60
   validation efforts for, 195n152
brain fingerprinting (BFP), 1, 194n142, 194n145
   accuracy of, 68–70
   cold cases and, 67–68, 207n115
   commercial interests in, 69–70

brain fingerprinting (*continued*)
  costs of, 101
  criticism of, 68–69
  in *Making a Murderer*, 49, 70–71, 195n151
  origins of, 58
  at Raksha Shakti University, 93–94
  science and forensics clashing over, 89–94
  scientific validity of, 49
  technique of, 58–59
  U.S. cases using, 65–66
brain scanning, 2
  costs of, 101
  cultural production of, 65–71
  defense of, 69–71
  environmental factors in, 117
  legitimacy of, 31
  lie detectors compared to, 69
  methods for, 1, 58–60
  Nagaraja Committee on, 91–93
  origins of, 58–60
  science and forensics clashing over, 89–94
Brainwave Science, 67–71, 93, 194n142, 195n147
Brennan, William J., 75
Brooks, Peter, 110
Brown, Wendy, 9
Brown v. Mississippi, 55
Bunn, Geoffrey, 52, 56–57, 64
  on spectacular science, 65
bureaucracies, Weber on, 16, 17, 21, 26, 32

case backlogs, in criminal justice system, 3–4
CBI (Central Bureau of Investigation), 1, 81, 83–84, 147
CCTV (closed-circuit television), 152
Central Bureau of Investigation (CBI), 1, 81, 83–84, 147
Central Forensic Science Laboratory (CFSL), 82, 95, 120
Central Intelligence Agency (CIA), 71–73, 197n174
CFSL (Central Forensic Science Laboratory), 82, 95, 120
Chakravarti, Uma, 176n80
Chander, Ravi, 142, 148
Chandrasekharan, P., 98, 117
Chatterjee, Partha, 11–12, 50–51
Chaudhury, Shoma, 132, 167n3
Chavez v. Martinez, 198n183

Cheesman, Nick, 138
Chevers, Norman, 51
Choudhurie, Inder P., 201n35
Church Committee, 71
CIA (Central Intelligence Agency), 71–73, 197n174
CIDT (cruel, inhuman, or degrading treatment), 73
closed-circuit television (CCTV), 152
Code of Criminal Procedure (CrPC), 23, 35, 39, 122, 129, 139, 183n117
cold cases, BFP and, 67–68, 207n115
Cold War, narcoanalysis in, 71–73
Cole, Simon, 105, 108–9
colonialism
  colonial rule of difference and, 50
  police and, 29–30
  rule of law and legacy of, 138–40
  science and, 126
  state violence origins in, 114–15, 135
  truth and, 50–51
compensation, for torture, 144
confessions
  Foucault on, 141
  inadmissible, 85
  police reform and, 43–44
  reliability of, 110
  resisting, 159–60, 162
  of terrorism suspects, 145, 147
  truth machines for, 107
  video cameras capturing, 151, 159–60, 162
Congress Party (India), 33, 34
consent
  in custody, 150
  in Indian Constitution, 121, 125
  legal discourses on, 121–25
  lie detectors and, 85–86
  narcoanalysis and, 95, 117, 121–22
  voluntary, 85, 99
Constitution, Indian
  consent in, 121, 125
  on police, 4
  self-incrimination in, 85, 118, 120–21, 150
contingent state, 3
  frameworks of, 162–63
  infrastructure of, 165
  police in, 163–64
  structural contingency and, 163
Counter Terrorism Center (CTC), 76

crime scene management, 68
criminal justice system, Indian
   analyze methods for studying, 6–8
   case backlogs in, 3–4
   Malimath Committee recommendations for, 35–37
   safeguards of, 140, 215n4
CrPC (Code of Criminal Procedure), 23, 35, 39, 122, 129, 139, 183n117
cruel, inhuman, or degrading treatment (CIDT), 73
CTC (Counter Terrorism Center), 76
cultural production, of truth machines, 49, 77, 215n78
   brain scanning and, 65–71
   lie detectors and, 64–65
   narcoanalysis in Cold War and, 71–73
   narcoanalysis in U.S., early use, 60–64
   narcoanalysis in War on Terror and, 73–76
custodial deaths, 4–6
   CCTV for reducing, 152
   medical professionals and, 128
   NCRB reports on, 38
   police concerns with, 45–47
   Supreme Court on, 129–31, 163
custodial violence, 5–6, 129, 148, 160, 182n94
custody
   in art of government, 129–31
   consent in, 150
   duration of, torture and, 39–40
   medical professionals supervising, 130
cyborgs, forensic psychologists as, 79, 81, 102, 110, 199n2

Das, Veena, 9, 10
Daubert v. Merrell, 192n108
democracy, in India, 6
Dershowitz, Alan, 48, 75
DFS (Directorate of Forensic Science), 88, 92, 95
DGP (director general of police), 170n19
Directorate of Forensic Science (DFS), 88, 92, 95
director general of police (DGP), 170n19
Discipline and Punish (Foucault), 50, 141, 161
discretion, police, 26–27, 163
distrust of police, torture motivated by, 41–42
Dix, Dorothy, 63

D. K. Basu case, 6, 45, 142
DNA fingerprinting, 52, 68, 107–8
DNA tests, 37, 52
   truth machine reliability compared to, 2
   documentation, for rule of law, 158–59
Dr. Malini vs The State of Karnataka, 207n111
Dubber, Markus D., 22, 28, 46
duBois, Page, 50
due process, 126–27, 146, 147
duration of custody, 39–40

Eckert, Julia, 28
economic offenses, narcoanalysis for, 146
Economy and Society (Weber), 16
EEG. *See* electroencephalogram
EK (experiential knowledge), 109–10
electroencephalogram (EEG), 1, 59, 60
empathy, forensic psychologists using, 104–5
empirical studies, on police, 14
Enloe, Cynthia, 155
exception, state violence and, 3
excess violence, 3, 22, 76, 115, 169n11
   See also torture
experiential knowledge (EK), 109–10
expertise
   of forensic psychologists, 80–102, 166
   of medical professionals in art of government, 127–28
   for police reform, 34, 38
   progress and, 80
extraordinary laws, 114–15, 134, 157–58

Farwell, Lawrence, 58–59, 66, 67, 69–70, 90, 195n147
federal torture statute (FTS), 76
Feitlowitz, Marguerite, 160
Feldman, Leonard, 29
feminism, 14, 176n80
feminization, of terrorism suspects, 154–57
Ferreira, Arun, 24, 160
fingerprinting, 52, 68, 108–9
first information report (FIR), 144, 170n22
fMRI (functional magnetic resonance imaging), 58
FOIA (Freedom of Information Act), 71, 185n3
forensic medicine, truth machines and, 99
forensic nurses, 81, 102, 199n9
forensic psychiatrists, 103–4, 107–8, 203n51

forensic psychologists, 18, 23, 68, 165
  brain scanning clash between science and, 89–94
  claims and visibility of, 87–89
  court recognition of, 83, 86
  as cyborgs, 79, 81, 102, 110, 199n2
  empathy used by, 104–5
  experience of, 107–8
  expertise of, 80–102, 166
  gender typing of, 81, 105–6
  importance of, 84
  legal status of, 78–79
  lie detectors and, emergence of, 81–87
  narcoanalysis administration by, 103–4
  on narcoanalysis in U.S., 48
  patience of, 106
  police compared to, 79, 103–7, 111–12
  repetition used by, 109
  rise, fall, and resurrection of, 96–102
  scientific status of, 79
  in state forensic architecture, 88, 102–10, 169n12
  subjectivity of, 102
  success of, 84
  training of, 84, 103
  truth machines' relationship to, 108–10
  truth obtained by, 110–11
  women as, 81, 105–6
forensic science laboratories (FSLs), 2, 7, 17–18, 78
  entering, 103
  Indian history with, 200n12
  number and organization of, in India, 202n43
  police reform and, 37
  understaffing at, 101
formal legality, rule of law and, 138
Foucault, Michel, 27, 140, 161
  on confessions, 141
  on juridico-medical complex, 128
  on pastoral power, 120
  on torture, 50
  on welfare, 28, 46, 120–23
Freedom of Information Act (FOIA), 71, 185n3
FSLs. *See* forensic science laboratories
FTS (federal torture statute), 76
functional magnetic resonance imaging (fMRI), 58

gamma amino butyric acid (GABA) inhibition, 117
Gandhi, Indira, 33, 34, 172n30, 181n73
Gandhi, Rajiv, 98
Ganguly, A. K., 82–83
Ganguly, Sumit, 6
Geelani, Syed Abdul Rahman, 158
gender typing, of forensic psychologists, 81, 105–6
GFSU (Gujarat Forensic Science University), 90
globalization, state decline with, 9
Goddard, Calvin, 62
Gogoi, Ranjan, 3–4
Gore Committee Report on Police Training, 31–33, 127
Guantánamo Bay prison, 73, 128
Gujarat Forensic Science University (GFSU), 90
Gujarat Police Manual, 83
Gupta, Akhil, 8–10, 16, 26

Haksar, Nandita, 158
Harrington, Terry, 66, 69
Hoenig, Patrick, 15
Homo Sacer, State of Exception (Agamben), 16
Horsley, J. S., 61
House, Robert E., 53–56, 60–61, 72, 73, 188n48
Howe, Cymene, 164–65
Hudson, George, 60–61
human rights
  custodial deaths and, 4–6
  groups for, 1970s and 1980s, 5
  Indian Supreme Court and, 6
  medical professionals violating, 128
  narcoanalysis violating, 24, 148, 150
  police and violations of, 4–6
  SVS and, 166
  truth machines as violative of, 116, 126
Human Rights Act, 1993, 5, 45
Hussain, Nasser, 139

Ika, Krishna, 194n142
Imprint on the Raj (Sengoopta), 213n51
impunity, 14–16
India. *See specific topics*
Indian Evidence Act, 1872, 35, 42, 82, 127, 139–40, 183n117

Indian Penal Code, 1860, 29, 35, 139
Innocent Prisoner (Begunah Qaidi) (Shaikh), 136, 151
involuntary use of truth machines, Supreme Court on, 2, 124–25
Isaac, Jeffrey C., 13
Islamophobia, 154

Jauregui, Beatrice, 15, 29, 44–45, 154
Jesani, Amar, 116–17, 124, 129
Jha, Nishita, 133–34, 215n80
juridico-medical complex, 128
jurisprudence, violence of, 140
Just Violence (Wahl), 15

Kannabiran, Kalpana, 30, 223n139
Kannabiran, K.G., 12, 114–15
Katju, Markandey, 127
Kaviraj, Sudipta, 11–12
Keeler, Leonarde, 57
Khalili, Laleh, 26, 154
Khan, Mohammad Aamir, 157
Khanikar, Santana, 15, 44, 175n69
Kolsky, Elizabeth, 51, 139
Kumar, Ashwani, 98, 214n66

Lahiri, S. K., 82–83
Langleben, Daniel, 58
Larkin, Brian, 165
Larson, John A., 57
Lasson, Kenneth, 75, 198n187
law
　definition of, 114
　due process and, 126–27
　extraordinary, 114–15, 134, 157–58
　state violence and, 113–16
　See also rule of law
"learned helplessness," 198n192
legal discourses
　on consent, 121–25
　on self-incrimination, 120–21
　Supreme Court on involuntary use of truth machines, 2, 124–25
　on truth machines for modernization, 119–20
legal violence, 169n11
　See also state violence
Lexicon of Terror (Feitlowitz), 160
lie detectors (polygraphs), 1–2
　African Americans and, 52
　brain scanning compared to, 69
　cases using, 49, 86
　CBI advocating for, 83–84
　consent and, 85–86
　costs of, 101
　cultural production of, 64–65
　early studies on, 64–65
　forensic psychologists and emergence of, 81–87
　mystique surrounding, 65
　NHRC concerns with, 85–86
　origins of, 56–58, 89, 168n5
　police reform and, 37
　in popular culture, 57–58
　process of, 56
　scientific validity of, 49
　in U.S., 56–58, 64, 186n7, 192n108
　uses of, 56
　women and, 52
Littlefield, Melissa, 53, 65, 69
LSD, 71–72

Madhava Menon Report, 203n48
Madras Commission report, 1855, 33
Madras Suppression of Disturbances Act of 1947, 114
Maharashtra Control of Organised Crime Act (MCOCA), 148, 159, 215n4, 219n67
Making a Murderer, 49, 70–71, 195n151
Malimath Committee, 35–37, 43–44, 127, 182n86, 203n48, 212n28
Malini, S., 67, 79, 90, 99–100
Maoists, 142–43, 146
Marston, William Moulton, 57
Marxism, state conception in, 11, 28, 174n66
Mathur, Nayanika, 10
McBride, Keally, 13, 139
MCOCA (Maharashtra Control of Organised Crime Act), 148, 159, 215n4, 219n67
Mecca Masjid case, 140–49
media. *See* cultural production, of truth machines
medical professionals, in art of government, 127–30
Ministry of Home Affairs (MHA), 81–82, 91, 94–96, 165
Misra, Dipak, 3–4
Mitchell, Timothy, 9–10, 80–81, 96, 120

Modi, Narendra, 142
Mohan, B. M., 87, 99–100, 124, 211n20
moral duty, of police, 29
Mukundan, Chetan, 60, 91
Mukundan, C. R., 59–60, 66, 79, 90–92, 204n65
Mulla, Sameena, 80–81, 102
Mumbai blasts, 2006, 136, 148–52
Munsterberg, Hugo, 53
Muslim youth, as terrorism suspects
    feminization of, 154–57
    Mecca Masjid case and, 140–48
    Mumbai blast case and, 136, 148–52
    racialization of, 154–57
Myanmar, 138

Nagaraja Committee, 91–93
narcoanalysis
    adverse reactions to, 122–23
    African Americans and, 61
    CIA experiments with, 71–73, 197n174
    in Cold War, 71–73
    consent and, 95, 117, 121–22
    costs of, 101
    cultural production of, 60–64, 71–76
    definition of, 1
    DFS manual for, 95
    dissemination of results from, 118
    early tests on, 62–63
    for economic offenses, 146
    extralegal techniques with, 103–4
    forensic psychiatrist administration of, 103–4
    as health hazard, 121–23
    as human rights violation, 24, 148, 150
    as instrumental, 23
    leaking videos of, 2
    legality of, 76–77
    legitimacy of, 23, 31
    MHA reports on, 95–96
    origin of, 53–56
    prison test cases for, 94–95
    prolonged damage from, 76
    for psychotherapy, 63
    rule of law violated by, 147–48
    scientific compared to unscientific, 25
    scientific reliability of, 117
    scientific validity of, 49
    self-incrimination and, 118, 150

skepticism with, 61–62
spectacular, 23
state forensic architecture and, 94–96
for terrorism suspects, 145–47, 149–52
as torture, 55, 116, 118, 145–46, 198n187
unofficial, 202n36
U.S. and, 48–49, 53–56, 60–64
National Crimes Research Bureau (NCRB) reports, 38
National Human Rights Commission (NHRC), 4–6, 45, 81, 163
    lie detector concerns of, 85–86
National Institute of Medical Health and Neuro-Sciences (NIMHANS), 87–89, 92–93
National Investigative Agency (NIA), 147
National Police Commission (NPC) reports, 33–35, 40, 43–44
National Research Council (NRC), 64
National Seminar on Forensic Science, 2002, 37
NCRB (National Crimes Research Bureau) reports, 38
Neocleous, Mark, 22
Neuro Signature System (NSS), 60, 71
NHRC. *See* National Human Rights Commission
NIA (National Investigative Agency), 147
NIMHANS (National Institute of Medical Health and Neuro-Sciences), 87–89, 92–93
NPC (National Police Commission) reports, 33–35, 40, 43–44
NRC (National Research Council), 64
NSS (Neuro Signature System), 60, 71
nurses, forensic, 81, 102, 199n9

Opposing the Rule of Law (Cheesman), 138

P-300 MERMER, 59, 89–92, 117
pastoral functions of police, 28, 45–47, 163
patience, of forensic psychologists, 106
Peoples Union for Democratic Rights (PUDR), 5, 118
physical force, police reform and, 34–35
physician-patient privacy, 129
police
    colonialism and, 29–30
    Constitution on, 4

contemporary studies on, 12–15
in contingent state, 163–64
custodial death concerns of, 45–47
discretion, 26–27, 163
distrust in, 4
distrust of, torture motivated by, 41–42
documentation of, 158–59
empirical studies on, 14
ethical agents, 23
everyday practices of, 22
forensic psychologists compared to, 79, 103–7, 111–12
gender typing of, 106
human rights violations and, 4–6
ideological framing of, 20–21
impunity and, 14–15
institutional constraints of, 45
legitimacy of, 44–45
moral duty of, 29
neutrality assumption with, 22
number of, 4
pastoral functions of, 28, 45–47, 163
patience lacking in, 106
pragmatic logic of, 39–44
repressive functions of, 28, 45–47, 163
rule of law and, 137
state and centrality of, 27–28
state power and, 2, 3, 12, 20–21
state violence and, 11–12, 21, 27–31, 46–47, 161, 177n4
structure of, Indian, 170n19
suspect communities and, 154–55
terrorism suspect patterns of, 153
testimonial narratives on, 14
torture concealed by, 24
torture justified by, 28–29, 44, 46
trials controlled by, 153–54
truth machine motivations of, 17, 22–23
U.S. studies on, 13–14
Police Act, 1861, 4, 29, 179n47
police reform
accountability and, 41
confessions and, 43–44
expertise for, 34, 38
FSLs and, 37
Gore Committee Report on Police Training and, 31–33, 127
lie detectors and, 37
Malimath Committee recommendations for, 35–37, 43–44, 127, 182n86, 203n48, 212n28
modernization in, 32
NPC reports and, 33–35, 40, 43–44
physical force and, 34–35
Ribeiro Committee and, 182n94
science-based, 32–33, 37–38
torture and, 34–35, 37, 43–44
training and, 31–32
truth and, 36–37
truth machines and, 30–31
Polygraph Protection Act, 1988, 192n108
polygraphs. *See* lie detectors
Poole, Deborah, 9, 10
Posner, Gerald, 74
power. *See* state power
Prakash Singh & Ors. vs. Union of India & Ors, 34, 37, 181n76, 182n94
pretest and posttest interviews, for truth machines, 84, 107, 209n140
Prevention of Terrorism Act, 2002, 115
prison test cases, for narcoanalysis, 94–95
progress, expertise and, 80
property recovery, torture motivated by, 42–43
Provisional Authority (Jauregui), 15, 44–45
psychiatrists, forensic, 103–4, 107–8, 203n51
psychotherapy, narcoanalysis for, 63
public secrecy, 39
PUDR (Peoples Union for Democratic Rights), 5, 118

racialization (criminal), of terrorism suspects, 154–57
Rahasya (film), 167n2
Rajah, Jothie, 138
Raksha Shakti University, 67, 93–94
Ramakrishnan, Nitya, 39
Ramchandra Ram Reddy v. The State of Maharashtra, 121
rational bureaucracy, 3
Ray, Bibha, 84
recovery, torture motivated by, 42–43
Rejali, Darius, 12, 63
repressive functions of police, 28, 45–47, 163
resistance, to confessions, 159–60, 162
Ribeiro Committee, 182n94
Rockefeller Commission reports, 71
Rogers, Will, 63–64

Rohtagi, Mukul, 5
Rosenfeld, J. Peter, 68–69, 117, 118
Roy, Srirupa, 32
Rule of Experts (Mitchell), 80
rule of law, 20, 115, 134
    colonial legacy of, 138–40
    definition of, 137
    documentation for, 158–59
    experience as element of analysis of, 157–61
    formal legality and, 138
    narcoanalysis violating, 147–48
    police and, 137
    rule by law compared to, 138
    scaffolding of, 140–41, 144, 154, 158–61
    state power limited by, 137–38

Samaddar, Ranabir, 139
Santokben Sharmanbhai Jadeja v. State of Gujarat, 123
Sarat, Austin, 26
scaffolding, of rule of law, 140–41, 144, 154, 158–61
SCDL (Scientific Crime Detection Laboratory), 62
Scheffer v. United States, 192n108
Schmerber v. California, 198n184
Scientific Crime Detection Laboratory (SCDL), 62
scientific techniques. *See* brain scanning; lie detectors; narcoanalysis; truth machines
scopolamine, 53–56
Scrivenor, William, 54
secrecy, public, 39
self-incrimination, in Indian Constitution, 85, 118, 120–21, 150
Selvi & Others v. State of Karnataka, 96–97, 121–22, 129
Sen, Avirook, 133–34, 167n3
Sengoopta, Chandak, 213n51
Seri, Guillermina, 21–22
Sethi, Manisha, 158, 159
sexual violence, 176n80
Shah Commission, 33–34, 181n73
Shaikh, Abdul Wahid, 136, 151, 153–57, 159–60, 162
Sharma, Aditi, 118, 131–32, 134
Sharma, Aradhana, 8–9
SIMI (Students Islamic Movement of India), 148

Singapore, 138
Singh, Navasharan, 15
Singh, Ujjwal K., 12, 114–15, 140
Singha, Radhika, 139
Slaughter v. Oklahoma, 66
slavery, truth and, 50
Sodium Pentothal, 1, 117, 202n36
state
    art of government, truth machines and, 125–31
    cultural framing of, 8–9
    everyday formation of, 10
    globalization and decline of, 9
    historical conceptualizations of, 9–10
    Indian scholarship on, 11–12
    Marxist conception of, 11, 28, 174n66
    police centrality to, 27–28
    truth machines defended by, 119–20
    violence limitation desires of, 134–35
State, Violence, and Legitimacy in India (Khanikar), 15
state forensic architecture, 78–80, 199n1
    consolidation challenges with, 96
    forensic psychologists in, 88, 102–10, 169n12
    narcoanalysis and, 94–96
    Supreme Court mediating development of, 96–97
    truth machines embraced by, 110–11
    types of, 164–65
State of Andhra Pradesh v. Smt. Inapuri Padma and Ors., 119
state power
    police and, 2, 3, 12, 20–21
    rule of law limitations on, 137–38
    truth machines and, 3, 15–19
state terror, 125, 130–31
    See also custodial deaths; torture
state violence
    colonial origins of, 114–15, 135
    exception and, 3
    frameworks for, 2–3
    impunity and, 16
    law and, 113–16
    police and, 11–12, 21, 27–31, 46–47, 161, 177n4
    sexual, 176n80
    state desire to limit, 134–35
    truth machines and, 15–17, 113–14

Weber on, 21
women and, 14
state violence studies (SVS), 15, 166, 223n6
Stephen, James Fitzjames, 139
stripping, torture and, 155–57
Students Islamic Movement of India (SIMI), 148
Structural effect (Mitchell), 9-10, 23
Subramanian, K. S., 29–30
Supreme Court, Indian, 19
   on BEOS, 66–67, 93
   on custodial deaths, 129–31, 163
   on due process, 126–27
   extraordinary laws upheld by, 157–58
   faith in science of, 127
   human rights and, 6
   on involuntary use of truth machines, 2, 124–25
   on medical professionals in art of government, 129
   state forensic architecture development mediated by, 96–97
   on truth machines, limits of, 131–34
   on truth machines and art of government, 125–31, 163–64
suspect communities, 154–55
SVS (state violence studies), 15, 166, 223n6
Syed, Adnan, 49, 167n3

Talvar (film), 167nn2–3
Talwar, Aarushi, 1, 132–34, 167n1
Tamanaha, Brian Z., 137–38
Taussig, Michael, 39
Terrorism and Disruptive Activities (Prevention) Act, 1985, 115, 219n67
terrorism suspects
   communities for, 154–55
   compensation for torture of, 144
   confessions of, 145, 147
   feminization of, 154–57
   Mecca Masjid case and Muslim youth as, 140–48
   Mumbai blast case and Muslim youth as, 136, 148–52
   narcoanalysis for, 145–47, 149–52
   police patterns with, 153
   racialization of, 154–57
   torture of, 142–43, 146–47, 149–52, 155–57
   truth machines for, 87–88, 136

testimonial narratives, on police, 14
third-degree interrogations. *See* torture
Tilly, Charles, 16
Tokyo Declaration, World Medical Association, 1975, 117
torture (third-degree interrogations)
   Baxi, U., on, 41
   compensation for, 144
   custodial deaths and, 4–6
   custody duration reason for, 39–40
   flawed art of government and, 130–31, 163–64
   Foucault on, 50
   legitimacy problems with, 39
   medical professionals contributing to, 128
   narcoanalysis as, 55, 116, 118, 145–46, 198n187
   NCRB reports on, 38
   NPC reports on, 34
   police concealing, 24
   police distrust motivating, 41–42
   police justifying, 28–29, 44, 46
   police reform and, 34–35, 37, 43–44
   pragmatic logic of, 39–44
   rationale for, 1–2, 50
   recovery motivations for, 42–43
   stripping and, 155–57
   terminology of, 168n6
   of terrorism suspects, 142–43, 146–47, 149–52, 155–57
   training issues with, 43
   truth and, 50
   truth machines as, 26, 52–53, 97–98, 116
   War on Terror and, 73
   women threatened with, 156–57
Townsend v. Sain, Sheriff, et al., 71, 74–75
trauma, 105
Trial by Error podcast, 133–34
trials, police control of, 153–54
Troubling Confessions (Brooks), 110
trust, torture motivated by lack of, 41–42
truth
   colonialism and, 50–51
   forensic psychologists obtaining, 110–11
   police reform and, 36–37
   slavery and, 50
   torture and, 50
   two-finger test and, 51–52
   women and, 51–52

truth machines
    adverse reactions to, 122–23
    for confessions, 107
    costs of, 101
    critics of, 116–19
    DNA test reliability compared to, 2
    expansion of, 78–79, 97
    forensic medicine and, 99
    forensic psychologists' relationship to, 108–10
    as health hazard, 121–23
    as human rights violations, 116, 126
    legal discourses on, 119–20
    legitimacy of, 31, 97, 100
    modernization and, 18, 119–20
    origins of, 53–60, 80
    police motivations for using, 17, 22–23
    police reform and, 30–31
    pretest and posttest interviews for, 84, 107, 209n140
    self-incrimination in Indian Constitution and, 118, 120–21
    state defense of, 119–20
    state forensic architecture embracing, 110–11
    state power and, 3, 15–19
    state violence and, 15–17, 113–14
    Supreme Court on, limits of, 131–34
    Supreme Court on art of government and, 125–31, 163–64
    Supreme Court on involuntary use of, 2, 124–25
    for terrorism suspects, 87–88, 136
    as torture, 26, 52–53, 97–98, 116
    types of, 1, 20
    validity of, 107
    for welfare of accused, 120
    See also brain scanning; cultural production, of truth machines; lie detectors; narcoanalysis
truth serum. See narcoanalysis

United States (U.S.)
    BFP used in cases in, 65–66
    DNA fingerprinting in, 52
    lie detectors in, 56–58, 64, 186n7, 192n108
    narcoanalysis and, 48–49, 53–56, 60–64
    police studies in, 13–14
    suspect communities in, 154–55
Unlawful Activities Prevention Act, 1967, 148, 215n4
Unlawful Activities Prevention Act, 2008, 140

Valverde, Mariana, 22, 28
Vaya, S. L., 68, 79, 83–84, 86–87, 102, 105–6, 209n140
video cameras, confessions captured on, 151, 159–60, 162
The Violence of Care (Mulla), 80–81
violence of jurisprudence, 140
voice analyzer, 7, 172n34
Vollmer, August, 57
voluntary consent, 85, 99
Vyas, J. M., 84, 209n140

The Wages of Impunity (K. G. Kannabiran), 114
Wahl, Rachel, 15, 28–29
War on Terror, narcoanalysis in, 73–76
Warren, Earl, 74
waterboarding, 151
Weber, Max, 3, 10
    on bureaucracies, 16, 17, 21, 26, 32
    on state violence, 21
Wickersham Commission, 55, 57, 168n6, 188n44
Wilde, J. F., 62
Winter, Alison, 54, 62, 71
Wolpe, Paul, 70
women
    as forensic psychologists, 81, 105–6
    lie detectors and, 52
    state violence and, 14
    torture threats towards, 156–57
    truth and, 51–52
World Medical Association, Tokyo Declaration, 1975, 117

Zubaydah, Abu, 74, 197n174